UNIT 20

_Marcos Cruz

_Salvador Pérez Arroyo

The Bartlett School of Architecure
University College London
22 Gordon street, London WC1H 0QB
www.bartlett.ucl.ac.uk

Editors
Marcos Cruz and Salvador Pérez Arroyo

Collated,   designed   and   prepared   by:
K a r e n   W i l c o x
with the help of Annika Schollin

**Published by the Universidad
Politécnica de Valencia
Camino de vera s/n
46021 Valencia, Spain
www.upv.es**

Distributed by: ACTAR
Roca i Batlle. 2
08023 Barcelona
Tel +34 93 418 77 59
info@actar-mail.com

ISBN 84-9705-275-7

Incentrix. cluster city

Incentrix.ciudad en racimos

Glean-ville, a tale of sedimentary survival

Glean-ville, una historia de supervivencia

CMYK choreography

CMYK coreografía

Helsinki ice suburb

Helsinki suburbio de hielo

Decycle. dirty rotten architecture

Decycle. arquitectura en descomposición

Alquetecture

s[c]i [O]rbita

Acoustic wind membrane
Granja eólica

Urban farming
Granja urbana

Contaminant
Contaminante

Hydroponic farm
Granja hidropónica

Undefined boundaries
Límites indefinidos

Inhabitable growthscape
Crecimiento sobre paisaje

A viscous pulse
un ritmo viscoso

Human power plant
Planta de energía humana

Laminar flow
Fluido laminar

Living propagation
Vida multiplicada

Vertigo exposure
Plataforma hacia el vértigo

The human resource centre
Centro de recursos humanos

Reconstruction lounge
Centro de reconstrucción

Kevin Chu

Lisa Silver

Karen Willcox

Tom Foster

Annika Schollin

Steven Pike

Zoran Orescanin

Mark Mueckenheim

James Foster

Jens Ritter

Robert Marinus Grindley

Stephen Clements

Natalia Traverso Caruana

Daniel Schwaag

Jia Lu

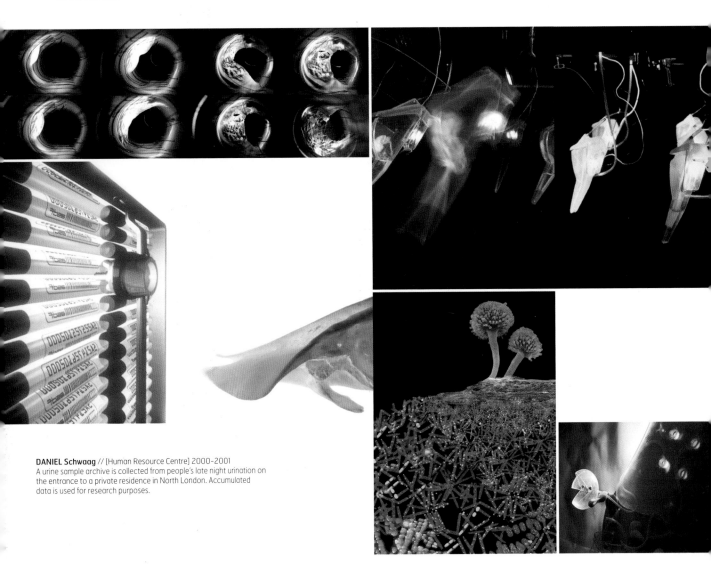

JENS Ritter // [Underground Air Filter] 2000-2001
A perspex model exploring the notion of a malleable, air-sensitive membrane, which filters the polluted air flows of the London Underground system.

JAMES Foster // [Inhabitable Growthscape] 2000-2001
A series of incubators with controlled light, heat and medium supply were built in order to intensify the growth process of beans. Construction: vacuum formed perspex, electronic circuitry,

DANIEL Schwaag // [Human Resource Centre] 2000-2001
A urine sample archive is collected from people's late night urination on the entrance to a private residence in North London. Accumulated data is used for research purposes.

ANDY Shaw // [Chicago Urban Farm] 2001-2002
Studies of fungal growth were carried out with mushrooms, creating the basis for an urban farm on the Chicago lake shore.

GABRIEL Tang // [Lobstamata] 2000-2001
A mechanical chimera, in which the behavioural patterns of lobsters act as a trigger for a 'smart surface'.

STEVE Pike // [Sarriko Microbiological Factory] 1999-2000
The design of vessels for bacteriological growth was undertaken in collaboration with the microbiology department at UCL.

STEVE Pike // [Sarriko Microbiological Factory] 1999-2000
The design of vessels for bacteriological growth was undertaken in collaboration with the microbiology department at UCL.

JIA Lu // [Bone-tissue Transformation] 2001-2002
Installation, which tests a physical transformation from liquid to solid states, suggesting the process of calcification in human bone growth.

TOM Foster // [Helsinki Ice Suburb] 2000-2001
Reconfigurable techno-plasma module. Visual representation with glue and electronic circuitry

MARTYN Weaver // [Urban Light Dance] 2001-2002
Light-sensitive plankton model with projected animation.

KEVIN Chu // [Incentrix – Cluster City] 2000-2001
Studies of insect movement

peter cook _vicente vidal _josé mariá lozano _unit text salvador pérez arroyo and marcos
architecture _james foster//the humanpower architectural transformation_exhibitio

6

DONDE LOS ESTUDIANTES MARCAN EL CAMINO QUE SEGUIRÁN LOS CONSTRUCTORES.

Ni miopía ni arrogancia subyace en esta declaración, sino el agradable convencimiento de que los sueños y las divagaciones
- que nosotros alentamos, desactivamos y volvemos a lanzar, que protegemos ocasionalmente (y luego vuelven y nos
protegen), que nosotros rumiamos en exámenes y sesiones críticas—son el material de la arquitectura. Ellos son el espíritu de la
arquitectura antes de que haya sido borrado por la niebla de las distorsiones y sútiles excusas.
Sin la sofisticación de un diseño maduro y a menudo sin mucho repertorio de estrategias o experiencia de causa-efecto, el
estudiante entusiasta se encontrá con una gran idea. Un complejo juego de referencias. Un collage de influencias. Mejor aún
él o ella pueden convertirse en el más raro de todos los híbridos creativos: el relajado y obsesivo.
Tomemos el extraño, onírico mundo, del Gleanville de Lisa Silver por ejemplo. Imaginémonos dentro, ¿Pensemos en los
objetos—son muy reales no es cierto? Imaginémonos encontrando a Billy-Bob, Mary-Lou y Jimmy-Ray—bastante posible, por
supuesto. Pensemos estar en los espacios, todavía posibles, pero empujando los límites de nuestra experiencia, reforzando un
sentido de extrañeza (aún no devorado) por el pánico. ¿Qué tipo de mente, qué tipo de sensibilidad puede haber llevado a este
escenario? ¿qué tipo de composición es esta en la que se esparcen semejante combinación de lo familiar y lo improbable en un
espacio extrañamente orquestado?
Entonces hagamos la pregunta: ¿en qué tipo de mundo vive ella? ¿Es este trabajo la culminación de una aislada, mística vida en
una isla remota rodeada por las llovizas y la compañía de águilas? ¡Pero Lisa no vive en absoluto así :una brillante muchacha
de Londres con una mente rápida y "anillos para emparejar", ¿ Probemos otra pregunta ¿Qué tipo de paisaje la rodea? ¿Qué
es la Bartlett? Un lugar donde al tiempo la exótica y tecnológicamente sofisticada Natalia Traverso teje estructuras de acero
y petróleo tan sistemáticamente o tan ensoñadoramente como una araña teje su tejido. Donde el ostensiblemente práctico
Tom Foster empieza a deslizarse y burbujear con sus objetos inventados en un Norte helado, hasta un momento en el que
empezamos a creer en todas esas viejas sagas sobre la Atlántida perdida. Donde los bosques de animales de Kevin Chu
empiezan a seducirte, invitarte, rodearte, siempre agradablemente. Su talento realista se ha animado de algún modo a seguir
adelante en un entorno de obsesión amigable. La elasticidad desarrollada poco a poco como para resistir (implícitamente) y
no saltar fuera del trineo.
¿Qué clase de magos están dando lugar a que todo esto ocurra? ¿Qué juegos están construyendo con sus estudiantes?
Seguramente (puedo casi oír a sus compañeros, los que enseñan en las Universidades de Europa diciendo), "Arroyo y Cruz
deben ser un par de raros!."
Pero echémosles un vistazo: Salvador el hombre del Renacimiento: con más de dos décadas de edificios sofisticados,
agradables, detrás de él: un experto en política, automóviles, filosofía, artefactos, idiomas, cámaras, jardinería, estructuras,. No
es un candidato probable.Entonces Cruz ¿Qué decir sobre sus románticos y elásticos experimentos con un nuevo urbanismo
de látex?. ¿Quizá? Pero echemos una mirada más próxima a su modo metódico de enseñar y la precisión de su habilidad crítica.
No es tampoco un candidato inevitable. ¡Por toda la Bartlett hay ejemplos similares de trabajos extraños y ciertamente
inventivos que emana de espíritus aparentemente sanos y normales.
Entonces¿ que ocurre?
Hay sólo una conclusión razonable—y ciertamente debe ser mi deseo de ser razonable al intentar explicar lo incómodo. Un
trabajo como éste ha salido de una cierta alquimia que se ha desarrollando durante varios años. En donde los protagonistas se
envían entre ellos incesantes señales hacia delante y hacia atrás: como los cerdos alimentándose gruñen con deleite, resoplan

Professor Peter Cook Bartlett School of Architecture, London

WHERE THE STUDENTS LEAD THE BUILDERS WILL FOLLOW.

Neither myopia nor arrogance lie behind that statement, more a delighted realisation that the dreams and constructs - that we egg-on, that we dis-arm and re-arm, that we out-flank occasionally (and then they fly back in to out-flank us), that we chew over in reviews and critiques – they are the stuff of architecture. They are the spirit of architecture before it has become obliterated by the fog of distortions and their attendant excuses.

Without the sophistry of mature design and often without much repertoire of gambits or experience of causes-and-effects, the enthusiastic student will jump in on a hunch. A scrambled set of references. A collage of influences. Best of all, he or she can become that weirdest of all creative hybrids: the loose-limbed obsessive.

Take the strange, dreamy world of Lisa Silver's Gleanville for instance. Imagine yourself into it. Take hold of the objects – they're very real aren't they? Imagine yourself meeting Billy-Bob, Mary-Lou and Jimmy-Ray – quite possible, of course. Think yourself into the spaces – still possible, but pushing to the limits of one's experience, building up a sense of strangeness close (but not yet devoured by) bewilderment. What kind of mind, what kind of sensibility can have led to this scenario? What kind of composition is this which scatters such a combination of the familiar and the unlikely into an exotically orchestrated space?

Then ask the question: what kind of world does she live in? Is this work the corollary of a lonely, mystic life on a remote island surrounded by mists and the company of eagles? But Lisa doesn't come across like that at all: a chirpy London girl with a quick mind and ringlets to match! So let's try another question? What kind of scenery does she hang around? What is this Bartlett? Where the simultaneously exotic and technologically sophisticated Natalia Traverso weaves structures of steel and oil as systematically or as dreamily as a spider weaves its web? Where the ostensibly practical Tom Foster starts to glide and fizzle with his invented objects in the frozen North, until such moment that we begin to believe in all those old sagas about the lost Atlantis. Where Kevin Chu's animalistic forests begin to charm you, invite you, engulf you, but remain benign. His very real talent has somehow been encouraged to 'run with it' in an environment of fellow obsessives. The looseness-of-limb developing month by month as each one (implicitly) dares the other not to jump off the sledge.

What manner of wizards are standing by whilst all this is happening? What games are they playing with their students? "Surely (I can almost hear their fellow teaching architects from the Universities of Europe saying this), Arroyo and Cruz must be a couple of weirdos!".

But come on, take a look at them: Salvador the Renaissance man: with more than two decades of sophisticated, commodious buildings behind him: an expert on politics, cars, philosophy, engines, language, cameras, gardening, engineering structures. Not a likely candidate. What about Cruz then? What about his own romantic and elastic experiments with the new latex urbanism ? Maybe? But take a closer look at his very methodical approach to teaching and the precision of his critical ability.

Not an inevitable candidate either. Down the corridor of the Bartlett there are similar casers of exotic, or certainly inventive work emanating from apparently sane and homely souls!

So what is it all about?

There is only one reasonable conclusion – and surely it must always be my wish to be reasonable when trying to explain the uncomfortable. Such work as this has come out of a certain alchemy that has been developing for several years. Wherein the protagonists send continual signals back and forth to each other: like pigs at feeding time with little grunts of delight and snorts of frustration, wiggles of investigation and trots of pursuit. There are smells and sounds from across the farmyard and a glance across to the cows and hens who have their own signals to make.

con frustración, investigan inquietos o se persiguen con trotes. Hay olores y sonidos en el corral y una mirada hacia las vacas y las gallinas que tienen sus propios sonidos.

Hasta qué punto la Bartlett es una granja aislada no estoy tan seguro: casi todos venimos y vamos a las llamadas oficinas reales y Londres es una ciudad activa y competitiva. Pero hay una cierta y colectiva forma escénica que se intensifica cuando nos acercamos a una Unidad caliente. En este caso, un consecuente y favorable desarrollo de magia técnica apoyada por la destreza gráfica que es pura exuberancia (más allá de la competencia y deleite). Caracterizado por la jugosidad de Mark Munckenheim, los remolinos de Jens Ritter (Dios mío aún lo recuerdo cuando era un buen y aseado racionalista cerca de la frontera Suiza. ......¡qué hemos hecho de él!), por las perturbación atmosféricas de Jia Lu y el mundo exuberante, colorista, de Karen Willcox.

Explicación simplista :

Lo que ha pasado aquí es la combinación de estudiantes de talento y maestros sabios. Una institución liberal y una ciudad viva. La computadora y una intensidad basada en la competencia y el trabajo duro.

Pero hay más que esto:

 Los estudiantes de talento disfrutan ellos mismos. No solo como la munición para construir una serie de trabajos doctrinarios. Ni la bonita e independiente poesía de los días de la Cooper Union de John Hejduk, ni la insistencia rigurosa pero firme del ETH de Zurich. Ni la posición socialmente consciente pero estéticamente flácida de las escuelas inglesas que son demasiado inglesas. Las Lisas, Natalias o Kevins son personas inequívocas. Personalidades incluso nutters *. Animados a ser más y más como ellos son y para hacerlo realidad a través de su propio trabajo y animados a verter ese trabajo en el guiso de las ideas. Los dos maestros indudablemente obtienen algo elevado en esto y arrancan de lo más profundo, los mejores recursos de respuestas. Hay una pequeña reserva ibérica aquí—Salvador es sin embargo el más cosmopolita y rico de los intelectuales, muy lejos de la línea de Rafael Moneo de la escuela de Madrid. Marcos se ha aventurado lejos de su raíces Oporto-Alemania y disfruta racionalizando lo exótico y reventando lo racional.

El grupo de profesores está lejos de ser inglés, pero de algún modo influido por ciertas características de las que nosotros los ingleses estamos orgullosos : la locura creativa, un bajo umbral para el aburrimiento, la invención por su propio placer y la creación de escenarios.

Enojosamente, la escena de Londres está en este momento caracterizada por muchos ingleses que intentan ser más fríos que los suizos, tan reservados como los holandeses y tan sinceros como los americanos. Significa que estamos en una apreciable fase de provincianismo y educado modernismo.

Irónico, ¿no es cierto? que un grupo de (predominantemente) maestros y estudiantes europeos están marcando los modos a la próxima arquitectura británica: un espacio mágico, bien diseñado sembrado de objetos extraños pero familiares.

*nutter: un término familiar inglés describe (afectuosamente) una persona en la calle mentalmente loca.

Peter Cook
Chairman of the Bartlett School of Architecture

Professor Peter Cook_Bartlett School of Architecture, London

To what extent the Bartlett is an isolated farm I am not so sure: nearly everyone comes and goes to so-called 'real' offices and London is a busy, competitive city. But there surely is a form of collective séance that intensifies when you get close to a 'hot' Unit. In this case, a consistent and highly developed level of technical wizardry supported by graphic dexterity that is sheer exuberance (it is beyond mere competence and delight). Characterised by Mark Munckenheim's juiciness, Jens Ritter's swirls (my goodness I do remember him when he was a good clean-living Rationalist from near to the Swiss border......now what did we all do to him!), by Jia Lu's atmospherics and celebrated in Karen Willcox's exuberant, coloured world.

Simplified explanation:

What has happened here is the combination of talented students and wise teachers. A liberal institution and a lively city. The computer and an intensity based upon competition and hard work.

But there is more to it:

The talented students are enjoyed as themselves. Not just as ammunition for a thrusting, doctrinaire statemental series of work. Neither the beautiful but selfconscious poetry of John Hejduk's Cooper Union days, nor the rigorous but tight-lipped insistence of Zurich's ETH. Nor the socially conscious but aesthetically limp position of English schools that are too English. The Lisas, Natalias and Kevins are unmistakable people. Personalities. nutters* even. Encouraged to be more and more like they're like and to live it out through the work itself and then encouraged to cast that work into the pot of ideas. The two teachers undoubtedly get a kind of 'high' from this and pull out from the depths all of their own resources of response. There is little Iberian reserve here – Salvador is anyway that most cosmopolitan and resourceful of intellects and strays far from the Madrid line of the Rafael Moneo school. Marcos has ventured far from his Oporto-German strictures and takes delight in rationalising the exotic whilst exploding the rational.

The gang is far from being English, but somehow affected by certain characteristics of which we English are proud: creative silliness, a low threshold of boredom, invention for its own sake and the making up of scenarios.

Irritatingly, the London scene is at the moment characterised by many Englishmen trying to be as cool as the Swiss, as coy as the Dutch and as straightforward as the Americans. It means that we are going through a rather provincial 'polite modernist' phase.

Ironic, isn't it, that a bunch of (predominantly) mainland European teachers and students are pointing the way to the next British architecture: one of magical, well-engineered space scattered with evolved (but nearly familiar) strange objects.

*nutter : an English colloquial term often used to describe (affectionately) a mentally deranged person seen in the street.

Peter Cook
Chairman of the Bartlett School of Architecture

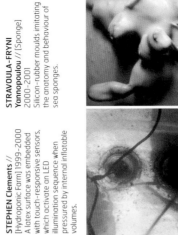

STRAVOULA-FRYNI Yannopoulou // [Sponge]
2000-2001
Silicon-rubber moulds imitating the anatomy and behaviour of sea sponges.

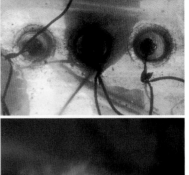

STEPHEN Clements //
[Hydroponic Farm] 1999-2000
A latex surface was embedded with touch-responsive sensors, which activate an LED illumination sequence when pressured by internal inflatable volumes.

KAREN Willcox // [Sensorial Mattress] 2000-2001
A plastic model integrates a series of layered liquids. According to body pressures the surface creates a choreography of colours and textures.

HUI HUI Teoh // [Moving Boundaries] 2001-2002
The observation of a hydra inspired the proposal of an infinitely reconfiguring living entity.

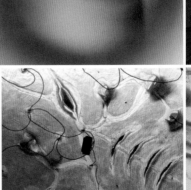

KAREN Willcox // [Photographic Laboratory]
2001-2002
Colour studies were carried out through the filtering of projected light on to photo-sensitive paper.

JAMES Henman // [Wind sensitive membrane]
2000-2001
Pores, sphincter openings and various protrusions were used for atmosphere and light manipulation on the roof membrane of a clinic for seasonal affective disorder in Helsinki.

KEVIN Chu // [Soft textures] 1999-2000
Abstract studies mixing diverse liquids.

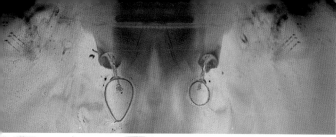

GALIT Tandet // [Pouring Wax] 2001-2002
Wax model representing apertures on the earth
surface in Missouri, USA.

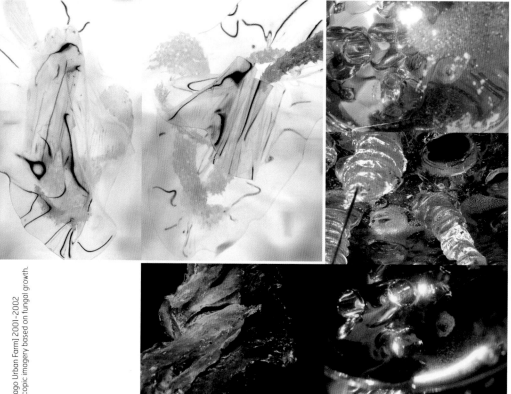

ANDY Shaw // [Chicago Urban Farm] 2001-2002
Aesthetics of microscopic imagery based on fungal growth.

GWEN Shao Jun Lee // [AlgaEnergy] 2001-2002
Apparatus illustrating the cyclical growth of crystals in a controlled
environment (purpose-blown glass with electronic circuits).

GWEN Shao Jun Lee // [AlgaEnergy] 2001-2002
Glass-wax model of a bio-energy factory generating hydrogen gas through the
cultivation of algae.

Contents

SOBRE EL CURSO DE SALVADOR PEREZ ARROYO Y MARCOS CRUZ EN LA BARTLETT SCHOOL OF ARCHITECTURE EN EL 2002

Enmarcar un curso de arquitectura tan peculiar como el UNIT 20, desde la contemporaneidad, necesita en mi caso asumir, que por un principio autobiográfico la obra que se presenta resulta lateral a mi experiencia personal. Pero esta particularidad conlleva desde un punto de vista crítico, cierta neutralidad que nos brinda la ocasión de aprovechar una oportunidad para hacer conjeturas sobre un futuro que se intuye incierto en su continuidad histórica, pues al perder la tensión que la clasicidad aporta, puede acabar fabricándose tanto la impostura de la tradición inventada como del devenir inventado, sin que las grandes bases evolutivas de la sociedad como son la estructura social reproductora y la que se forma alrededor de los medios cambiantes de producción, ofrezcan una verdadera sustitución en sus modos de operar.

Ambos principios están cuestionados desde los distintos tribunos teóricos que rigen la sociedad y su cultura; no obstante si queremos encontrar diferencias apreciables en la estructura celular de la familia, tenemos que admitir que las condiciones reales de la norma que regula su control, cambia tan despacio como para tener que referirnos al tiempo de Noé. No ocurre lo mismo si nos queremos referir a los cambios que los medios de producción material han experimentado en un breve periodo que abarca desde la revolución industrial a nuestros días.

La tradición oral que se reconoce bajo la fórmula "en un principio era el verbo" nos lleva a pensar que la tradición de la escritura bien podría desplazarse a la remota grafía donde si en un principio se reconocía trazo y signo como el fundamento del dibujo que necesita de la experiencia de la mano, sigue siendo el dibujo el punto de partida de la reflexión sobre los trabajos que nos ofrece la edición del libro que nos ocupa, pero los dibujos han cambiado, se han mutado como otras veces, de medio en fines, han pasado desde una actitud de creciente duda sobre el mito del funcionalismo a una puesta al día del organicismo dentro del cual todavía se reconoce el principio de subordinación. El alumno de la UNIT 20 propone un marco de referencia con cierto grado de verosimilitud dentro del cual el proyecto se inicia apoyándose sobre una hipótesis argumentada con el rigor de lo científico, y al mismo tiempo desincrustada de los otros argumentos no menos científicos como la gravedad, lo cristalográfico, lo geométrico, lo escalar, la tensión de la historia.........

Una pregunta pertinente seria; ¿que ocurriría cuando una civilización propusiera "en un principio fue la pantalla"?. En ese momento tenemos que asumir como una característica del tiempo, que el mensaje está directamente afectado por el medio, pero esa transcripción directa del proyecto como adiestramiento en las herramientas de la construcción del espacio físico, necesariamente se muta en el adiestramiento de la producción única de un soporte virtual.
Ocurre que cuando miramos dibujos que no han sido codificados como nexo entre pensamiento y materialidad, observamos la atracción de la forma visiva pero no incorporamos la traducción de su forma a una experiencia espacial, porque seguramente nuestros recuerdos de los cuales se nutren los sueños son de origen distinto.

Otra pregunta es ¿"quien coloniza a quien"?. Si la base formal del expresionismo abstracto que procede del mundo de la pintura es tomada como principio expresivo en una escuela de arquitectura, una semantización continua hará que tengan una influencia recíproca en el campo de la pintura, no obstante la potencia de las máquinas empleadas y su compleja manipulación reduce el campo de experimentación a personas dotadas e instituciones preparadas especialmente para este fin; ambas condiciones se dan en la UNIT 20 de la Bartlett School of Architecture.

Vice Dean Vicente Vidal_ Universidad Politécnica de Valencia

A COMMENTRY ON THE COURSE OF SALVADOR PÉREZ ARROYO AND MARCOS CRUZ IN THE BARTLETT SCHOOL OF ARCHITECTURE IN THE 2002

To place an architecture course as unusual as that of UNIT 20 within its contemporary context needs, in my case at least, to accept that the work presented is not familiar to my personal experience. This particularity results from a critical approach: certain neutrality that allows us the advantage of making speculations on a future that appears uncertain in its historical continuity. By surrendering the tension that the classical culture contributes, one is able to invent and create without the hindrance of the past. One is able to re-examine complex architectural issues, such as the generators of social structure and changing means of production and materials from a fresh angle. Both issues are questioned from the diverse theoretical outlooks that govern society and culture; however, if we want to instigate and control significant differences in the fundamental structure of our environment, we must accept the reality that change requires time. The same does not apply to the vast and rapid changes that have occurred in production methods and material sciences since the industrial revolution.

The communication of an architectural idea is first expressed as a drawing and over time a specific and universal architectural language has evolved of lines and signs unveiled through the analytical skill of the authors hand.
The drawing remains the starting point for contemplating the works that are presented in this publication, but the drawings have changed, mutated from the established dialect into a new one that embraces and reflects new media and form.

While speculative in nature, the proposals of unit 20 provide us with a certain degree of plausibility by grounding the brief and response on a hypothesis that is argued with the rigor of a scientific experiment. At the same time the proposals liberally detach themselves from other established arguments such as 'seriousness', crystallography, geometry, scale and the tension of the history.

In examining the projects and their expression, we have to assume that their message is directly affected by their means.

By designing the architectural solution directly in three-dimensional virtual space rather than in two-dimensions as line on paper, the proposals become defined by their unique method of production. The virtual format of the computer becomes an active mediator between thought and communication. When we look at drawings that have not been expressed as a union between thought and materiality, we observe the attraction of the visual form but we don't understand the spatial experience they provide.

If the spatial experience is not fully expressed its interpretation is left inconclusively open to the viewer. However, If the formal base of abstract expressionism is borrowed from the world of the painting and adopted as an expressive principle in an architecture school, the power of the computer and more specifically the skillful manipulation by its user, reduce the level of interpretation left to the viewer. Consequently, greater control is achieved over the creation and communication of the spatial experience, especially to gifted people and institutions aware of this notion. Both conditions are applicable to Unit 20 of the Bartlett School of Architecture.

When a graphical production is not reliant on established 'codes', it travels different cultural circuits; its literacy relies on the individual and unique interpretation of the viewer. Teaching in architecture schools is based on instructing students in the disciplines that will allow them to communicate and support an idea from its plausible gestation to its material realisation.

These new modes of communication revitalize and renovate this old profession but by designing in a virtual world devoid of materiality, they also create confusion. This contradiction that presupposes to detach the architectural object from

16

peter cook _vicente vidal _josé mariá lozano _unit text salvador pérez arroyo and marcos
architecture _james foster//the humanpower architectural transformation_exhibitio

Cuando una grafía supuestamente no codificada recorre circuitos culturales distintos, es leída en función de los códigos que maneja su intérprete. La enseñanza en las escuelas de arquitectura se basa en la instrucción de los alumnos en aquellas disciplinas que servirán de soporte a una ideación y una práxis que garantice cierto nivel de verosimilitud en la concreción material de la idea germinal. Sus líneas docentes acusan crisis periódicas que revitaliza y renueva esta antigua profesión pero también se observa con perplejidad cómo es frecuente que los alumnos se desplacen desorientados hacia territorios estériles para cultivar una forma de proyecto empeñado en su concreción física desvinculada de su producción material. La contradicción que supone desvincular el objeto arquitectónico de su materialización no ha podido ser superada, pues el proyecto se inscribe dentro de un proceso colectivo largo y modesto que acepta como lugar de trabajo esta frágil corteza terrestre que nos ha sido legada, donde el esfuerzo anónimo de generaciones ha depositado con talento aciertos y ha producido con ignorancia desaciertos.

El medio en que se realiza la producción material de los dibujos dista bastante del determinado por el marco productivo dentro del cual se inscribe la ideación y planificación de la obra, pero sin embargo está dentro del marco de referencia de los productos que los mass-media ofertan como material del mundo visivo no necesariamente traducible a un código con grado de interpersonalidad amplio, y este punto de búsqueda visual introduce campos abiertos a los alumnos que cultivan su aprendizaje y les facilita su incorporación a otros campos profesionales donde su experiencia es generadora de nuevas y crecientes demandas.

La técnica de programación de ordenadores ha sido dirigida en el campo de la arquitectura hacia la simulación del dibujo geométrico. El dibujo de gran tradición icográfica, se realiza sobre la mesa. En él se refleja el pensamiento sobre objetos cuya estabilidad de la forma está ligada a la concentración. En los dibujos se piensa y representa en dos dimensiones espacios configurados por tres dimensiones. Disciplina de tradición Euclidea de formulaciones precisas que son traducidas a espacios cuya búsqueda de cuotas de verdad está comprometida por su construcción.

Pero la misma técnica que se expresa en ese mundo geométrico de funciones continuas con una gramática referida al punto, la línea y el plano, reúne en el ordenador una tradición mestiza que proviene del campo de la representación de funciones discontinuas, cuyas fracciones son fácilmente expresable con las potentes máquinas de simulación y producción de formas que provienen de un campo transdisciplinar, cuyo potencial está en la forma, desvinculando objeto y materialidad de su peso histórico y aceptando el peso visivo como fin final. Su búsqueda del "vellocino de oro", es cada vez más intensa, su imagen entre mito y realidad arrastra a nuestros jóvenes a aventurarse "como pilluelos consentidos que nadan sobre vejigas en un mar de gloria".........pero ellos pueden hacerlo.

Vicente Manuel Vidal Vidal
Catedrático de Proyectos Arquitectónicos

Vice Dean Vicente Vidal_ Universidad Politécnica de Valencia

its physical materialisation has not yet been overcome.

The technique of computer programming has been applied in the field of architecture to the simulation of the geo-metric drawing. The great iconographic tradition of drawing is carried out on the table. In it is reflected the thought of the objects whose stability is bound to their mode of production. Drawings are the representation of three-dimensional space in a two dimensional format, which only come to fruition once built.

In the drawing the limited geometric language and grammar of the point, the line and the plane determine and define the architectural product. In the computer the representation of discontinuous functions and fractions are easily explained by the powerful simulation power and consequently the resulting architectural product has its potential is in the shape, detaching the object from materiality and the weight of history and accepting the visual presence as the end result. The search for the "golden fleece", becomes more and more intense and its position between myth and reality drags our young successors to ven-ture "Like little wanton boys that swim on bladders, in a sea of glory" ... ..but they can make it.

Vicente Manuel Vidal Vidal
Professor of Architectural Design

18

peter cook _vicente vidal _josé mariá lozano _unit text salvador pérez arroyo and marcos
architecture _james foster//the humanpower architectural transformation_exhibitio

QUÉ MANERA DE ENTENDER LA ENSEÑANZA DE PROYECTOS!

Conozco a Salvador Pérez Arroyo desde hace más de década y media (su arquitectura rigurosa y sus escritos profundos, desde antes) cuando lo encontré hablando de rascacielos en la Escuela de Arquitectura de La Coruña acompañado del que entonces era uno de sus jóvenes ayudantes, Juan Herreros. Mi entusiasmo por la tecnología y por la industrialización de la arquitectura me allanaron un camino —no tan sencillo de recorrer habitualmente- hacia lo que es hoy una consistente amistad de la que me enorgullezco. El inicio de ésta me llevó a reconocer su obra construida y a entender la proyectada, para hacer de toda ella en su conjunto un magnífico campo de reflexión acerca de aquellas cuestiones que más me preocupaban por entonces (las mismas, por cierto, que me ocupan ahora): modernidad, rigor constructivo, estricta utilidad, duración razonable, ... o si se quiere: "espacio-forma-belleza", esencia última de la arquitectura (o, remedando a Mies, su resultado inevitable).

Mis encuentros con Salvador empezaron a ser frecuentes; los provocaba yo con buenas excusas y así obtuve sustanciosas charlas, conversaciones íntimas, y su participación en conferencias en la Escuela de Valencia, en reuniones, seminarios y cursos cortos, en "jurys" y tribunales de proyecto fin de carrera o de tesis doctorales; allá donde encontraba necesario afianzar mis planteamientos sobre razón y forma en la arquitectura con el sólido prestigio, y la manera elegante de evidenciarlo, de mi invitado.

Cuando tuve la ocasión espléndida de prologar el libro acerca de su arquitectura —compartiendo letra impresa con Gregotti — las iguanas habían entrado y salido sucesivas veces de las casas de Neutra y también de la estancia de la casa Valverde que Pérez Arroyo construyó en la Sierra de Madrid. También Salvador había demostrado su inequívoca vocación de profesor de proyectos y su sobrada capacidad para serlo (por mucho que hubieran disentido algunos de mis colegas), mientras llenaba las aulas de Construcción de la Escuela de Madrid.

Unos cuantos años más tarde me encuentro añadiendo este breve comentario a la publicación de trabajos de sus estudiantes de la Unit 20 de la Bartlett School of Architecture, en la que imparte docencia de proyectos junto a Marcos Cruz, con motivo de la exposición de los mismos en la Universidad Politécnica de Valencia a la que yo pertenezco. Y lo hago en primer lugar desde la lealtad al amigo, pero también desde el compromiso ineludible que con la docencia de la arquitectura tengo contraído y desde el justo reconocimiento de la experiencia que este libro muestra al lector.

Tal vez resulte innecesario —por conocido- abundar en las características de la Bartlett, en su sistema de selección del alumnado (y del profesorado), en la estrategia pedagógica de su plan de estudios, en sus recursos y medios materiales, pero se me admitirá que resulta un referente imprescindible para comprender —compártase o no- lo que aquí digo y por qué lo digo; los dibujos de proyectos que comento y por qué los comento; las reflexiones abiertas que pretendo trasladar al estudiante y al estudioso de proyectos con la esperanza de recobrarlas completadas, enriquecidas, en cualquier lugar del mundo en el que todavía se preste atención a este viejo oficio que es la arquitectura y a su enseñanza institucionalizada o a su aprendizaje personalizado. Porque, se quiera o no se quiera, la crisis en que disciplina y transmisión de la misma se encuentran sumidas es tan evidente y global como enfermiza. Mientras que desde mi condición de Profesor Especial Invitado permanente de la Facultad de Arquitectura de La Habana, sin dejar de serlo en Valencia, he dictado cursos cortos o he dirigido talleres monográficos sobre vivienda social, por ejemplo, en Torreón (México), Porto Alegre (Brasil) o Managua, el profesor Pérez Arroyo ha concentrado parte de su energía en este prestigioso centro de estudios londinense, atendiendo a la vez tantas o más nacionalidades de

rens holm _briefs _fieldtrips _technical studies_natalia traverso caruana//ferrofluidic
ure _ *Professor José María Lozano_ Universidad Politécnica de Valencia* ndex

19

HOW DOES ONE KNOW HOW TO TEACH ARCHITECTURE?

I first met Salvador Pérez Arroyo more than 15 years ago at the Coruña School of Architecture (though I knew of his rigorous architectural and written work already) when I attended a lecture he gave with his young assistant Juan Herreros on skyscrapers. My enthusiasm for the technology and industrialisation of architecture of which they spoke launched me down a twisting road towards what is today a consistent friendship of which I am very proud. At the start of this road I learned through projects and built works, the strength of those architectural cornerstones that have informed and occupied me since: modernity, honest construction, functionalism, reasonable duration… or if one wants: " space-form-beauty ", the essence of architecture (or, to borrow from Mies, their unavoidable result).

My encounters with Salvador began to be more frequent; I often arranged them with excuses such as his participation in conferences, meetings, seminars, short courses and the juries of final projects or doctoral theses at the Valencia School. Through these and substantial chats and intimate conversations I found it necessary to secure my position with regard to meaning and form in architecture with the solid dignity, and elegant knowledge, of my guest.

When I had the honour of writing the foreword to a book about their architecture -sharing the printed page with Gregotti – the "iguanas" had visited the Valverde house that Pérez Arroyo built in the Madrid Sierra many times. Salvador had also unequivocally demonstrated his worth as teacher (no matter how much some of my colleagues disagreed) by continually replenishing the classrooms at the Construction School of Madrid.

Now, some years later, I am writing this brief comment on the publication of the work of Unit 20 at the Bartlett School of Architecture, (which Salvador runs with Marcos Cruz) to accompany the exhibition at the Polytechnic University of Valencia. I am doing this first from loyalty to my friend, but also from the unavoidable commitment that I have to the teaching of architecture and in deserved recognition of the experience that this book presents to the reader.

Perhaps it is unnecessary to comment on the well renowned favourable characteristics of the Bartlett - their selection system of pupils and staff, the pedagogic strategy of their studies, their resources and material means - but I consider that it is essential in order to understand the context of (whether one agrees or not) what I say here and why I am saying it; the drawings of projects that I comment on and why I do so. I seek to convey my open reflections, unfettered and enriched to 'students' anywhere whose attention is still lent to this old occupation and to its institutionalized teaching or its personalised learning. It is apparent that the issues and dilemmas in architecture, its communication and teaching are of a global nature. As the head of architecture at the Polytechnic University of Valencia and as Permanent Guest Professor of the Havana school, I have dictated short courses and have directed workshops about, for example, social housing in places as far afield as, Mexico, Brazil

20

peter cook _vicente vidal _josé mariá lozano _unit text salvador pérez arroyo and marco:
architecture _james foster//the humanpower architectural transformation_exhibitio

origen y ha "desparramado", con inusual generosidad y medida sabiduría, su vivo conocimiento de la historia de la arquitectura sobre temáticas tan diversas como autobiográficas sugeridas o directamente elegidas por sus propios estudiantes. Y así encuentro yo una suerte de paralelismo vital –en mi modestia- que me autoriza, y me presta autoridad, para escribir aquí. ¡Qué manera de entender la enseñanza de proyectos! ...y qué manera de ponerla en práctica. Voy a obviar intencionadamente cuestiones colaterales que aunque no exentas de importancia no vienen al caso para detenerme directamente en las que entiendo resultan de fondo y así intentar dilucidar cuanto hay de arquitectura en una operación a primera vista mucho más amplia que sondea en el espacio y en el tiempo de nuestra época como si de un territorio único y espléndido se tratara. Porque seguramente es ésta la primera circunstancia de interés que los dibujos de los estudiantes de la Bartlett están mostrando, coincida o no (a ellos corresponde manifestarlo) con las intenciones de sus autores y los objetivos de sus propulsores. Por mi parte no encuentro sino una sutil diferencia –a favor, claro está, de la ambición territorial de estas propuestas- entre los más habituales enunciados de ejercicios arquitectónicos de nuestras escuelas que suelen limitar entornos más o menos reducidos y aislar necesidades humanas concretas y la abstracción universal de dimensión y uso que habita en estos otros. Y dónde si encuentro un abismo diferencial es en el talante de profesores y estudiantes, en un compromiso efectivo con la realidad circundante evadido –como si de un ladrón de guante blanco de las mejores películas del género se tratara- de otros códigos previamente establecidos que no sean los de honor. De manera que cada ejercicio, en su complejidad de origen, necesita de la fundamentación argumental y de la "esencialización" procedimental como mecanismos de resolución de incertidumbres y de motivación de una creatividad ordenada.

Y tanto es así que precisamente en esa complejidad reside la oportunidad de la puesta en marcha de una estrategia proyectual que se sustenta a la vez en la experiencia y en el riesgo científico de adentrarse en las sendas de la investigación de lo inexistente, y cuya materialidad resultara en la práctica más difícilmente explorable cuanto más aparentemente acotada. No me cabe duda alguna acerca de la abundancia de conocimiento previo que el estudiante de la Unit 20 de la Bartlett necesita en cuanto a métodos de expresión, desde los manuales tan artesanales como sofisticados que permiten la construcción de magníficas maquetas mecánicas, hasta los gráficos o fotográficos que con el soporte informatizado de menor o mayor cantidad de gigaoctets facultan la definición de espléndidos documentos planos. Ni de la necesidad de que los oportunos recursos materiales de una u otra clase amueblen aulas y talleres de proyectos en la escuela o, más modestamente, formen parte de las herramientas de uso personal de los estudiantes. Tampoco ignoro que un bagaje cultural profundo, que incluye filosofía e historia, unido al más específico de la experiencia arquitectónica que deviene de la lectura y visita de espacios construidos, es condición imprescindible para recorrer itinerarios de nuevo trazado. Ni dejo de apreciar el esfuerzo de dedicación –en horas/día y en atención exclusiva- que corresponde al estudiante en justo reconocimiento del que manifiesta la actitud del profesor. No es mi intención que este escrito devenga en panegírico de la labor docente de Salvador Pérez Arroyo y Marcos Cruz en su taller de proyectos de la Bartlett, ni mucho menos en detrimento de las más convencionales situaciones en las que yo mismo me veo inmerso. Pero sí de comparación lícita que como objetivo tiene la puesta en valor de la primera y de revisión al alza, que siempre cabe, de las segundas. He sabido –pues no se ocultan- de críticas aceradas de algún colega, que sin embargo no aciertan a explicar con precisión (tal vez no desean explicitarlo) si lo son al método, a los resultados, o sencillamente a la operación en sí y a la ideología que subyace. También son manifiestas posiciones más comprensivas y esperanzadoras, como la de Vicente Vidal junto a estas mismas páginas, no sólo fruto de la cortesía. En cualquier caso unas y otras vienen a constatar la importancia de la experiencia y la debida atención que suscita en este confuso –y en ocasiones confundido- mundo académico de la enseñanza de los proyectos de arquitectura.

Professor José María Lozano_ Universidad Politécnica de Valencia

and Nicaragua. Likewise, Pérez Arroyo, the teacher, has concentrated part of his energy on this noted London centre of studies assisting students from all over the world, with unusual generosity, with his measured wisdom and deep knowledge of the subject. It is my fortune in being able to draw such a comparison that, in my modesty, lends me the authority to write here.

How does one know how to teach architecture? ...And how does one put it into practice? In the interests of clarity and due to the confines of space and time in the face of such a large and complex question, I will deliberately side step certain issues that I consider of secondary concern to those that I wish to deal with in respect to the works of this publication.

It is the drawings rather than the ideas that are inevitably the first impression of this book and exhibition. However, for my part I don't find much space between the two, as the territorial ambition of these proposals is equally apparent especially when compared with the more familiar school proposals - that usually limit themselves to reduced environments, to isolated and concrete human necessities, and to the universal abstraction of these dimensions and uses. Where I find the greatest contrast is in the mood of the teachers and students, in their energetic commitment and ability to not be hindered by the surrounding reality. The brief of each project, in its origin and complexity, needs its own rules and essential procedures to be carefully set out as both mechanisms and generators of its resolution. So much so that the complexities and opportunities of the program define the strategy and sustain its development by necessitating the scientific risk of researching unfamiliar fields and materials. I do not doubt the abundance of presentation experience the students of Unit 20 require in the production of these projects, from the handmade manuals that allow the sophisticated construction of magnificent mechanical scale models, to the graphics and photography that allow their documentation. Nor do I doubt the material resources available to the students. Also I do not dispute the depth of cultural experience available to the students that includes philosophy and history, together with the more specific indispensable architectural experience that comes from travelling and visiting built spaces. Neither do I neglect to appreciate the dedication and effort -in hours and days that the students work as a result of their teacher's attitude.

It is by no means my intention that this text becomes merely a flattery of the educational work of Salvador Pérez Arroyo and Marcos Cruz, at the detriment of the more conventional establishments that I myself am part of. It is however my intention to draw a justifiable comparison between the two methods - with the former as a possible objective in the revision of the latter.

I am aware of the open criticisms of the Bartlett of some colleague's, although it is never explained accurately (perhapsthey don't want find out) if they are opposed to the method, the results, or simply to the operation and to the ideology that underlies it.

22

peter cook _vicente vidal _josé mariá lozano _unit text salvador pérez arroyo and marcos
architecture _james foster//the humanpower architectural transformation_exhibitic

Escribí hace unos años ya "acerca de la enseñanza de proyectos en España" desde el conocimiento suficientemente infor-
mado de los Proyectos Docentes de los profesores más reconocidos y de la organización pedagógica de los Departamentos
de Proyectos de nuestras Escuelas, más que sobre los resultados más o menos aleatorios que los trabajos –de fin de carrera, por ejemplo- de los estudiantes parecían anunciar. Valoraba entonces método, disciplina e indicadores de modernidad,
inevitablemente desde la óptica de mis propias opciones y seguramente –ahora puedo afirmarlo con mayor claridad- desde
mis propias dudas e incertidumbres razonables al respecto. El tiempo no ha pasado en vano y salvo contadas (que no voy a
recontar yo aquí) excepciones, hoy tenemos "más de lo mismo". Por mucho que resulten loables los empeños personalísimos
de una minoría que se esfuerza en lograr un intento de transmisión oral del oficio basada en el modelo maestro-aprendiz (y que
no siempre queda justificada desde la calidad de la producción del supuesto maestro); por mucho que un vertiginoso deseo de
actualidad de otros (y no precisamente coincidentes con los más jóvenes) los convierta en comunicadores instantáneos de lo
más reciente para consumo inmediato –y normalmente indigesto- del estudiante; y por mucho que un reducido grupo (del que
me siento más próximo) siga haciendo de los viejos principios más disciplinares y de una reformulación de la "tríada vitruviana"
que la asimila definitivamente a la idea de "confort", en el sentido más complejo del término (debo confesar que es idea propia
y no estoy seguro de que resulte muy compartida), la más sólida estructura de pensamiento y por ende de creación del hecho
arquitectónico; son más "los viejos maestros que, con memoria de ayer, pretenden explicar con métodos de hoy, lo que va a
ocurrir mañana" (y esta vez cito de oído al profesor Justo Nieto).

Así las cosas, los minuciosos trabajos de los estudiantes de la Unit 20 de la Bartlett School of Architecture que componen el
grueso de esta publicación, acaecen –quiérase o no- un fresco vendaval que remueve los cimientos de la enseñanza univer-
sitaria de proyectos. Por mi parte declararé que al desconcierto inicial que su contemplación me produjo, complementada por
las entusiastas y precisas explicaciones del profesor Pérez Arroyo, y a la inevitable seducción que la aceptación confiada de
una y otras me hizo admitir, ha seguido una posición reflexiva no exenta de un lógico escepticismo, que es la que me gustaría
estar ahora transmitiendo al lector desprejuiciado y dispuesto a hacer lo propio.

No encuentro necesario hacer patentes las reservas –por otro lado evidentes- que se deducen de las diferencias sustanciales
de contexto entre la Universidad estatal española y la Bartlett, ni las relativas a sus respectivos currícula disciplinares o a las no
menos significativas notas biográficas de los estudiantes de una y otra. Por tanto nada más lejos de mi interés que establecer
como objetivo una ramplona adaptación y mucho menos aceptar una suerte de copia fácil que terminaría en un daño mayor
que el remedio pretendido: la banalización del modelo. Hago pública aquí mi advertencia a mis propios estudiantes acerca
del riesgo residual que el consumo precipitado de las ilustraciones que componen el grueso de este libro puede producir en
musculaturas intelectualmente poco desarrolladas. De manera que las lecturas superficiales –a las que el joven estudiante de
arquitectura es especialmente proclive- resultarán el más perverso de los procedimientos, a menudo consentido cuando no
estimulado por los profesores más frívolos y más presuntuosamente "a la page".

Por el contrario, el interés profesional que estos dibujos me suscitan, habita en sus estructuras más profundas y en su capacidad indiscutible de hacer aguzar el instinto y proclamar definitivamente la cultura del esfuerzo. La inevitable condición
verdaderamente interdisciplinar que subyace en sus planteamientos de origen, tan alejada de la farsa del mestizaje cultural que
reside en los vendedores de humo que hacen de "la idea" motor a la vez que objetivo, no es sino el más sincero reconocimiento

Professor José María Lozano_ Universidad Politécnica de Valencia

Alongside these, more understanding and optimistic views also exist, such as that of Vicente Vidal in this very book - which are not only the product of courtesy. Anyway this conflict of views only verifies the experience of this book by highlighting the intricacies and confusion that surrounds the academic teaching of the architecture.

As I have already mentioned, I wrote some years ago (from a sufficiently informed knowledge of the educational processes of our schools) that the built works of the students we seemed to produce were more or less random from the teaching of architecture in Spain. Now I can assert this notion with more clarity from my own doubts and reasonable uncertainties. Generally and with the exception of a minority (that I won't recount here) time has not resulted in a change to this. Despite the praiseworthy personal zeal and vertiginous desires of the few that make an effort to pass on knowledge and experience through the time honoured master-apprentice relationship our system transforms students into instantaneous communicators of the most recent style for immediate, and usually indigestible consumption. Despite the resistance of a minority (to which I belong) our processes continue to build on old principles by merely reshaping the "Vitruviana" triad (that, by its very definition, assimilates itself to the idea of "comfort" in the most complex sense of the term): teachers that, with yesterdays memory, seek to explain with today methods, what will happen tomorrow.

It is in this context that the meticulous works of Unit 20 - regardless of their viable reality - represent a fresh wind that erodes at the foundations of the university teaching of architecture. For my part, I will admit to my initial bewilderment at the work. Nevertheless, following my logical scepticism the unavoidable seduction of the proposals supplemented by the enthusiastic explanations of Pérez Arroyo has led me to confidently accept their merit. I urge the readers to not be prejudiced by my experience but to come to their own conclusions.

I do not find it necessary to make concessions for the substantial differences of context that exist between the Spanish State University and the Bartlett, or even the relative differences between their enviable resources of academic staff and students. My interests lie far away from imitating, or even adapting, an educational system in order to disrupt our pattern of banality, as this would cause greater harm than remedy. I make public here a warning to my own students about the residual risk of wilfully consuming the illustrations displayed here without taking into account their resolute intellectual development. Any such superficial reading —of which the young architectural mind is especially inclined - will lack the necessary wisdom to be successful when not stimulated by the teacher and the experience of the process. On the contrary, the professional interest that these drawings raise in me exists in their deeper structures and in their unquestionable capacity to sharpen the instinct and to proclaim the culture of their effort conclusively.

24

peter cook _vicente vidal _josé mariá lozano _unit text salvador pérez arroyo and marco
architecture _james foster//the humanpower architectural transformation_exhibitio

de la arquitectura como manifestación formal y material de la vida misma. Procesos, morfosis y metamorfosis; crecimiento, evolución y equilibrio; muerte, involución e inestabilidad permanente; pueden ser –entre otras variables cuya relación no pretendo agotar- referentes existenciales de los proyectos que los estudiantes de la Bartlett han desarrollado bajo la atenta mirada de sus profesores. Elaboradas geometrías, retículas bidimensionales o redes tridimensionales, espesores propios del cuidadoso conocimiento de la materia o membranas de inapreciable calibre, ajustadas sintaxis constructivas en ocasiones más platónicas que aristotélicas, subyacen en el atractivo resultado formal que garantiza su rotunda pertenencia al universo de la arquitectura.

Poco importa que finalmente parte de esta sinergia educativa vaya a parar al mundo del cine, de la publicidad avanzada, del diseño industrial de sofisticados componentes o -iqué sé yo!- del teatro, de la música, o de la magia. Cuanto hay de investigación espacial y de búsqueda tecnológica que la sustenta, deviene inmediatamente patrimonio expreso de la disciplina arquitectónica.

Y así, no se me tachará de iluso o de visionario por atreverme a trasladarles cómo he querido encontrar en estos proyectos la modernidad permanente de las megalíticas Taulas menorquinas, la elegancia del Templo griego, los avanzados mecanismos de las máquinas de Leonardo, el sereno clasicismo de Schinkel, la fuerza de la razón de Le Corbusier o la capacidad creativa de Buckminster Füller, por citar episodios que me resultan, a mí, particularmente relevantes. Ni de ingenuo por manifestarlo aquí sin gana de provocación alguna. Sí desearía, sin embargo, contrastar esta lectura tan mía con la de sus propios autores, con la de sus valedores y con la de sus detractores también. En una futura reedición del libro prometo añadir -si lo tengo- el resultado.

Como casi siempre ocurre, las imágenes que ilustran los proyectos son más explícitas que los breves textos que las acompañan, y mucho más que éstas mías que a modo de prólogo de innecesaria atención pongo en sus manos movido más por una buscada y consentida complicidad que por la pretensión de utilidad aclaratoria. De manera que renuncio a glosar siquiera las que más me han inquietado, a distinguirlas por tendencias o más aún a valorarlas o jerarquizarlas. Elijo, no sin alguna premeditación subconsciente, los atractivos dibujos de la Piscifactoría en Helsinki cuya autora es Natalia Traverso para, sin pretender equivalencias, elaborar un juicio sintético llevado de mi condición docente y del compromiso que supongo lícito exigirme. En ellos la visión territorial no sólo alcanza la corteza terrestre sino que, traspasando el espejo de agua, se introduce en el ambiente marino creando una suerte de transparencias, continuidades y discontinuidades que no persiguen sino la siempre oportuna unidad del hecho arquitectónico, al tiempo que una forma de equilibrio armónico entre lo "superficial" y lo "profundo" –que transmite con claridad la sección- es testimonio del cuidado por la dimensión y la proporción que normalmente conviene a la obra de arte y a la arquitectura también. Hasta donde mi análisis puede llegar, los aspectos funcionales resultan tan estrictos como eficaces y denotan el debido conocimiento, y la correspondiente "manipulación arquitectónica" del programa, sin cuya anuencia el proyecto de arquitectura se vacía hasta quedar en no mucho más de un dibujo, en el mejor de los casos hermoso. Finalmente las soluciones de detalle indican el amor por las cosas bien hechas, la pulcritud tecnológica y "los pies sobre la tierra" del estudiante que intuye –si es que no lo sabe ya casi con la certidumbre del profesional- que la construcción fina de la arquitectura es condición imprescindible, hasta el punto de que (desechado el viejo tópico que distingue entre una y otra, y substituido por la constatación de la diferencia entre buena arquitectura y arquitectura mala, o mejor todavía, entre

Professor José María Lozano_ Universidad Politécnica de Valencia

The unquestionably scholarly approach that underlies each project also manifests itself in the concepts that drive its maturation into sincere architectural and material products. The proposals investigate existential conceptual processes of morphology and metamorphosis; growth, evolution and balance; death, complexity and permanent uncertainty; under the attentive look of their professors. The representation and configuration of these processes as elaborated geometries, two-dimensional grids and three-dimensional nets, membranes of inestimable calibre resolve the attractiveness of the formal result and guaranty their membership to the architectural landscape.

The eventual outcomes of this educational synergy borrow heavily from the fields of cinema, advertising, industrial design, theatre, music and magic. All of which in their own way can be seen to belong to the architectural environment, as they are spatial investigations sustained by technical understanding. Without visionaries who dare to challenge the norm we would be without the permanent modernity of the megalithic "Taulas menorquinas", the elegance of the Greek Temples, the advanced mechanisms of Leonardo's machines, the classicism of Schinkel, the force of the reason of Le Corbusier or the creative ingenuity of Buckminster Füller. I am not being as presumptuous as to make any direct comparisons when I say this, but merely to highlight the importance of dreaming.

As it usually happens, the images that illustrate the projects are more explicit than the brief texts that accompany them, and far more so than any words, I can add in this brief foreword. I will therefore let them talk for themselves rather than distinguish between them. I will however mention the attractive drawings of the Helsinki Fish Farm by Natalia Traverso with the aim of elaborating on the points I have already made.

In them the territorial vision reaches beyond the surface of the earth, sinking beneath the mirrored water into the marine atmosphere below – to a world of transparencies, infinities and distortions. A foreign environment into which architectural realities are introduced as a harmonic balance between the surface and the deep. As far as my analysis can reveal, the functional aspects are as strict and effective as the knowledge they impart and the corresponding architectural program and spatial manipulation is as beautiful as the drawings that communicate it. Finally the detail of the solutions testify to her love for well made things and the technological neatness shows she has kept her feet on the ground. She demonstrates with almost the certainty of a veteran- that the fine construction of architecture lies in embracing he detail without becoming fastidious.

The beauty of the group is evident, it transcends the usual rules to take us to an alternative plane of aesthetic enjoyment, and of cultured roots, that has avoided the long path of history. So, I finish, celebrating the occasion that the teachers and students of Unit 20 of the Bartlett School of Architecture has presented to us, and return once more to the routine of our

26

peter cook_vicente vidal_josé mariá lozano_unit text salvador pérez arroyo and marco
architecture_james foster//the humanpower architectural transformation_exhibiti

arquitectura y lo que no lo es) pudieran llegar a identificarse sin más remilgos. La belleza del conjunto es evidente y trasciende los códigos usuales para situarnos en otro plano de goce estético de raíces ilustradas, que recorrido el largo itinerario de la historia –con eventuales pausas para repostar en Marinetti o en Prouvé- llega incluso hasta el "elogio de la fealdad" que en su momento escribiera el codirector de la Unidad en la que Natalia Traverso ha cursado sus estudios.

Y, termino, celebrando estrictamente la ocasión que profesores y estudiantes de la Unit 20 de la Bartlett School of Architecture nos han dado, para enfrentarnos una vez más a la rutina en nuestras viejas aulas de arquitectura, para la revisión de nuestros no menos viejos Proyectos docentes, para la discrepancia tolerante y para el permanente entusiasmo del profesor de proyectos en su relación con sus estudiantes. Primero con la cuidadosa y prolija exposición de sus trabajos en la Universidad Politécnica de Valencia y después con la publicación de este libro-catálogo que da cuenta de ésta y de aquéllos.

París, septiembre de 2002.

José María Lozano Velasco.
Catedrático de Proyectos Arquitectónicos de la Universidad Politécnica de Valencia.

rens holm _briefs _fieldtrips _technical studies_natalia traverso caruana// ferrofluidic
Professor José María Lozano_ Universidad Politécnica de Valencia index

27

old architecture classrooms, by calling for the revision of our own educational Projects and in praise of the role of the teacher and its relationship with its students. First with the careful and meticulous exhibition of their works in the Polytechnic University of Valencia and later with the publication of this book-catalogue.

Paris, September 2002.

José María Lozano Velasco.
Professor of Architectural Design, Polytechnic University of Valencia.

>Natalia Traverso Caruano // Flocking Boids [2001-2002] p_222

30

peter cook _vicente vidal _josé mariá lozano _unit text salvador pérez arroyo and marco
architecture _james foster//the humanpower architectural transformation_exhibitic

UNIT 20 GROUND CERO: BUSCANDO UN NUEVO TERRITORIO.

" *Me atrae pensar en todo como potencialmente posible. Es posible que no podamos hoy realizar estructuras tan ligeras como el aire, pero es interesante pensar en ello. Algún día es posible que lo consigamos. Estoy seguro que mucho antes de que la gente sepa como volar habrá mucha personas que habrán pensado en ello. Exigiría una gran cantidad de tecnología y trabajo conseguirlo, ¿no es cierto?. Pienso que será necesaria una gran cantidad de tecnología y trabajo para conseguir algunas de los objetivos que somos capaces de concebir como ideas, pero no aún capaces de poner en práctica.*
¿Dónde está el beneficio de pensar cosas que no podemos hacer?. Pienso que en primer lugar nos hace pensar en el estado en el que nos movemos hoy. No es un actitud muy sana si interpretamos esta situación como un "handicap". Si podemos pensar en ello como un signo de que somos jóvenes y estamos creciendo, no al final de una época sino al principio de otra, entonces es excitante. Si nos vemos a nosotros mismos como el final de una época entonces es deprimente.

The New and Different in Architecture (charla dada por Bruce Goff en Octobre 28, 1953 en la Escuela de arquitectura de Norman, Oklahoma) in Goff on Goff - Conversations and Lectures (ed. Philip B. Welch), University of Oklahoma Press, 1996 (p.88/89)

Creemos que la enseñanza de la arquitectura hoy debería ser más que nunca sensible a los cambios sociales, las transformaciones culturales y del entorno que están generando nuevos campos de actuación, nuevas realidades sobre las que trabajar. Estamos convencidos, que el idealismo de los arquitectos del Movimiento Moderno, nuestros abuelos, es imposible. Las nuevas condiciones de diseño, las que nos unen con nuestro entorno contemporáneo, nos obligan a abandonar el pasado y los mitos con los que se ha construido la historia del siglo XX. Dejar el pasado es nuestro punto de partida, olvidar la idea del arquitecto como agente de un cambio social, desmontar el mito del arquitecto al servicio de una visión funcional o monumental de la ciudad.

Enseñamos desde un nivel cero, sin conocer el resultado final y sin pensar en encontrar ideas predeterminadas con las que oscurecer nuestros errores. Cada proyecto es una aventura, una lucha por resolver con la experimentación, un sistema en el que ideas e información pueden ser integradas en una solución creíble. Es difícil saber si este sistema vale para todos. El estudiante debe ser consciente del hecho de que cada proyecto es una aventura y que los tutores, con frecuencia, están envueltos en los mismos riesgos y errores.

Nuestro trabajo en la Bartlett puede servir a múltiples objetivos y nosotros no estamos preocupados con definir estos límites. Muchos de nuestros estudiantes no trabajarán como arquitectos, su futuro se dirigirá hacia el diseño gráfico o el cine, o la investigación aplicada: la construcción la ingeniería o la biología. Nos preocupa más reproducir las condiciones contemporáneas de diseño. Es posible que se nos acuse de seguir un nuevo idealismo que ignora las contradicciones sociales o la necesidad de integrar al arquitecto en un movimiento de conciencia social determinado. Creemos más en la acción directa próxima a los objetos y en el optimismo creativo que en un método general. Nosotros no pensamos y después actuamos, pensamos a través del trabajo.

El sistema pedagógico de la Bartlett, exige mucho tiempo y dedicación. Esto significa al contrario de lo que ocurre en otras escuelas de arquitectura que el tiempo dedicado a la teoría es mínimo. Hoy la información llega rápida y continuamente

brens holm _briefs _fieldtrips _technical studies_natalia traverso caruana/ /ferrofluidic
ure _srit _ c bnu feu r studentc curri urr u ith c ackn ments _index

31

Professor Salvador Pérez Arroyo and Marcos Cruz *Unit 20 text*

UNIT 20 – GROUND ZERO: LOOKING FOR NEW TERRITORY

" It is interesting for me to think of everything as potentially possible. Maybe we won't be able to realise structures lighter than air in our lifetime, but it is interesting to think about it. Someday, maybe we will accomplish it. I am sure that long before people knew how to fly there were plenty of people who felt the need to fly. It took a great deal of technology, and work, to accomplish the feat, didn't it? I think it is going to take a lot of technology and work to accomplish some of the feats we are able to think of as ideas, and still not able to put into practice today.
What is the good of thinking of things you can't do? I think for one thing it makes you realise that what you are doing is in a very primitive stage. This is not a healthy feeling if we think of it as a handicap. If we can think of it as a sign that we are young and growing, not at the end of an epoch, but at the beginning of one, then I think it is exciting. If we think of ourselves as ending an epoch then it is dismal."
The New and Different in Architecture (lecture given by Bruce Goff on October 28, 1953 to the School of Architecture in Norman, Oklahoma) in Goff on Goff - Conversations and Lectures (ed. Philip B. Welch), University of Oklahoma Press, 1996 (p.88/89)

We think that the teaching of architecture today should, more than ever, be sensitive to the social, environmental and cultural transformations which are generating new fields of work and new realities upon which we must act. With hindsight, we know that the idealism of the architects of the modern movement, our grandfathers, was impractical. The new conditions of design, those that unify us with our contemporary condition, force us to overlook the past and to abandon the myth with which the history of twentieth century architecture has been built: to abandon the past as a starting point for design; to abandon the notion of the architect as agent for social change and to discard the myth of the architect in service of a functionalistic or monumental vision of the city.

We teach from ground zero, without knowing the final result and without trying to meet pre-determined intentions that may conceal the inadequacies of the solution. In this respect each project is an adventure; a fight to discover, through experimenta-tion, a method in which ideas and information can be integrated into a final credible outcome. It is difficult to know if this mode of teaching works for everyone. The student must be conscious of the fact that each project is a risky venture and that the tutors can be, and often are, involved in the same oversights and errors.

Our work at the Bartlett can serve multiple purposes and we are not concerned with defining these within precise boundar-ies. Many of our students will not become architects, their futures may head towards graphic design or cinematography, or to applied research: construction, engineering or biology. We are more concerned that the creative analysis of the contemporary environment leads us to produce inventive and open solutions that reflect these conditions. It is possible that we will be accused of following a new type of idealism that ignores the social contradictions or the needs of integrating the architect in a move-ment of mass consciousness. We believe in direct action and in creativity that is optimistic and close to the 'object' rather than relying on a general method. We do not think and then work, we think through the work.

The pedagogical approach of the Bartlett demands both time and dedication to design. This means that in contrary to what happens in other architectural schools the value and the time devoted to established theory is minimal. Today information arrives rapidly and continually through many different media and consequently the teacher at certain levels has a reduced

32

peter cook _vicente vidal _josé mariá lozano _unit text salvador pérez arroyo and marcos
architecture _james foster//the humanpower architectural transformation_exhibitio

por muchos medios lo que ha replanteado el papel del profesor a ciertos niveles. Es necesario contrastar los métodos de investigación y entender el proyecto como el punto de encuentro entre teoría y conocimiento práctico.

Algunas de las propuestas de la unidad han sido desarrolladas en colaboración con otros departamentos de la universidad con el fin de obtener asesoría desde sus conocimientos prácticos. Cuanto más radical es la propuesta es más necesaria la colaboración interdisciplinar fuera de los límites tradicionales de la arquitectura. Nos preguntamos si esto no significa una anticipación del mundo híbrido que la arquitectura experimentará en el futuro.

Nos preguntamos con frecuencia como ser innovadores. Seguimos el Zeitgeist y buscamos vías para mejorar el entorno, mientras nos interesamos profundamente sobre lo que está pasando en otros campos de investigación y como seremos capaces de aplicar estos avances tecnológicos a nuestros propios experimentos de arquitectura.

Al organizar estos 20 proyectos de esta publicación en un orden coherente, nos dimos cuenta de la influencia de nuestras propias convicciones, creencias y coincidencias con las obsesiones e interés de nuestros estudiantes. Fue necesario agrupar los proyectos en familias de ideas. Pero muchos de ellos son tan amplios en sus implicaciones que se podrían ubicar simultáneamente en distintos grupos.
Diferencias de escala, metodología, programa y trabajo interdisciplinar han creado una entidad en la unidad que se puede dividir en seis familias de pensamiento básicas dirigidas a la innovación tecnológica.

1-Objetos, gadgets y aplicaciones técnicas: este grupo explora la riqueza de nuestra parafernalia doméstica y la vía en la que esta puede influir y determinar la estructura espacial de nuestro entorno. Aplicando diversas técnicas y uniéndolas con toda clase de objetos cotidianos se crea el esquema de una arquitectura diseñada desde el objeto.
2-Dinámica de fluidos: Estes proyectos investigan la influencia de la dinámica de fluidos en arquitectura. Comparte la creencia de que el espacio contemporáneo está fuertemente determinado por el fenómeno de la movilidad, datos , gente, viento o agua. Precisas observaciones del comportamiento de los fluidos se reflejan en las propuestas de diseño basadas en el control de superficies en relación activa con estos fluidos.
3-Transformación del material, nuevas superfícies: Históricamente los cambios en arquitectura han venido acompañados de revoluciones en las ciencias de los materiales y en las técnicas de construcción. Este grupo de proyectos explora los efectos de los más nuevos materiales en uso y de la percepción del espacio, en particular explorando la arquitectura desde un punto de vista fenomenológico.
4-Entorno inteligente y consumo de energía: superficies sensibles y activas es hoy un objetivo frecuente en muchos entornos académicos aunque en general aplicados a una menor escala y con un carácter más efímero. La integración de este saber en los edificios como una entidad nueva y viva es el objetivo del grupo. La escala y cantidad de componentes nos proponen la pregunta de cómo seremos capaces de integrar estos mecanismos funcional y formalmente en nuestro entorno construido y como seremos capaces de conservar el control y el mantenimiento de estos complejos aparatos. Algunas propuestas miran al mismo tiempo hacia sistemas alternativos de uso de la energía y la producción.
5-Cuerpo humano y arquitectura de prótesis: la creciente influencia de la medicina en nuestra vida diaria establece las premisas básicas de estas propuestas en las que un cuerpo actual busca una identidad nueva en términos de significado y apariencia externa. "Extropianismo" describe una generación que desea utilizar los avances tecnológicos para transformar las condiciones de vida internas y externas del cuerpo. La tecnología es contemplada como la prolongación natural de nuestro

orensholm _briefs _fieldtrips _technical studies _natalia traverso caruana/ /ferrofluidic
ure _critics _banfeld _students _curriculum vitae _acknowledgements _index

33

Professor Salvador Pérez Arroyo and Marcos Cruz Unit 20 text

role to play. It is necessary to contrast methods of investigation and understand design as the point of confluence between theory and applied knowledge. Several design proposals in the unit were developed in direct collaboration with other university research departments in order to benefit from their indispensable technological experience. The more radical the proposal the greater the need for interdisciplinary work outside of the traditional limits of architecture. We ask ourselves if this might not be anticipating a professional hybridisation of architecture with other fields?

We persistently ask ourselves how we can be innovative in architecture? We follow the 'Zeitgeist' and question ways of improving our environment, while at the same being acutely curious about what is happening in other research fields, and how we may be able to apply their technological advances to our own architectural experiments.

While organising the 20 projects of this publication into a coherent order, we became conscious of the influence of our own convictions, beliefs and juxtapositions with the evolving obsessions and interests of our students. Grouping the projects in 'families' of thought and recognising their similarities and differences was a necessary and interesting step. However, many of the design proposals are so broad in their implications that they can be allocated to different groups simultaneously. Differences of scale, methodology, programme or interdisciplinary work created a unit constellation divided into six basic families of thought geared towards architectural innovation.

1 - Objects, gadgets and technical appliances: this group explores the richness of our domestic paraphernalia and the way in which these might influence and determine the spatial structure of our environment. Exposing technical appliances and juxtaposing them with all sorts of mundane objects creates the layout of an architecture designed through the object.

2 - Dynamic flows: these projects look into the influence of fluid dynamics on architecture. They share the belief that contemporary space is strongly determined by mobile phenomena, such as data, people, wind or water. Careful observations of fluid behaviour triggered design proposals based on the control of reactive surfaces to these flows.

3- Material transformation, new surfaces: Historically, changes in architecture have been accompanied by revolutions in material sciences and construction techniques. This group of projects explores the affects of newly invented materials on the use and perception of space, in particular exploring architecture from a phenomenological viewpoint

4 - Intelligent environments and energy consumption: responsive and reactive surface making is becoming common ground in more sophisticated academic environments, although usually applied to small-scaled installations with ephemeral character. The integration of this technological know-how into buildings as new 'living' entities is the fundamental aim of this group. Scale and quantity of components raises questions of how we are going to integrate these mechanisms functionally and formally into our built environment and how we are able to keep the control and maintenance of this increasingly complex apparatus? Some proposals are simultaneously searching for alternative systems of energy use and production.

5 - Human body and architectural prosthesis: the increasing 'medicalisation'of our daily life establishes the basic premise for these proposals, inwhich the contemporary body seeks a new individual identity in terms ofmind and physical appearance. 'Extropianism' describes a generation that desires to use advances in technology in order to radically transform both the body's internal and external conditions of existence. Technology is regarded as a natural extension and expression of our human

34

peter cook _vicente vidal _josé mariá lozano _unit text salvador pérez arroyo and marco
architecture _james foster//the humanpower architectural transformation_exhibitic

intelecto y el cuerpo como un objeto manipulable.

6-Espacialidad estructural: Complejidad geométrica y estructuras extremadamente ligeras son el objetivo principal hacia la innovación de este grupo. Como ha ocurrido en el pasado, las estructuras siguen tomando prestadas muchas ideas de la biología. El fenómeno de colgar partes y piezas se convierte en una obsesión que establece un compromiso entre las exigencias de la gravedad y la libertad de la ligereza antigravitatoria.

Cada época de arquitectura expresa sus necesidades probando y experimentando conceptos para programas específicos. El Gótico se expresó con la construcción de catedrales. El Renacimiento con el diseño de plazas públicas y edificios. El Barroco construyendo palacios reales. El Neoclasicismo construyendo edificios para nuevas instituciones públicas. La Revolución industrial con la construcción de puentes y fábricas. El Movimiento Moderno se concentró en el tema del alojamiento. Pero ¿en qué campo entendemos que están las necesidades de nuestro tiempo?. La Unidad 20 está investigando continuamente sobre cinco campos específicos. Vivienda, ocio y cultura, intervenciones urbanas, colonias urbanas, granjas, procesos de manufactura y técnicas clínicas y de laboratorio. La mayoría de los proyectos y quizás algunas de las propuestas más radicales pertenecen a los últimos grupos, indicándonos a nosotros que estos temas son hoy de máximo interés.

Los estudiantes de la unidad 20 deben pensar hoy en escalas extremadamente diminutas. Desde la ingeniería química y molecular hasta la "nano" y "micro" robótica o en el crecimiento celular. Muchos de los proyectos sugieren un nuevo tipo de arquitectura ecológica, agrupando, vibrando, y lanzando esporas en racimos como una norma de esta interactiva y dinámica arquitectura.

La intensa dedicación al proyecto permite que el oficio de representar e investigar madure con gran rapidez. En muchos de estos proyectos es difícil entender la escala. En algunos casos la investigación geométrica se manifiesta como un experimento topológico abstracto. En otros los complejos modelos marcan el camino de investigación. Con frecuencia los proyectos intentan descifrar una realidad que ni los libros ni la historia pueden hacer. Buscamos explorar nuevas posibilidades de un mundo tecnológico y anti-vitruviano.

Otro mito caído es el de la obsesión por una visión global de la realidad. Con frecuencia trabajamos sobre fragmentos intentando agotar los límites de la idea en un territorio reducido. En otras ocasiones, intentamos relacionar campos distantes sin tener miedo a jugar con conceptos que desde su carácter utópico pueden parecer sueños simplistas. A veces imitamos las máquinas y seguimos la psicología ficción de ciertos seres. En muchos de nuestros proyectos, impulsamos la narrativa, intentando relacionarla con un profundo conocimiento científico. Muchas de nuestras historias poseen un valor poético al tiempo que son un manifiesto tecnológico.

Professor Salvador Pérez Arroyo and Marcos Cruz

rens holm _briefs _fieldtrips _technical studies_natalia traverso caruana/ /ferrofluidic
ure ries critics barn fo students curriculum vitae ackn we ents _index

35

Professor Salvador Pérez Arroyo and Marcos Cruz Unit 20 text

intellect and the body as manipulable object.

6 - Structural spatiality: geometrical complex and extremely light structures were the main pursuit towards innovation in this group. As it often happened in the past, structural ideas continued to be borrow from biological conditions. The 'hanging phenomenon' of bits and pieces in space becomes an obsession that establishes a compromise between the constrains of gravital heaviness and the freedom for non-gravital lightness.

Each architectural epoch expresses the 'needs' of its time by inventing and testing experimental concepts for specific briefs. If the Gothic era expressed itself best in the construction of cathedrals; the Renaissance with the design of public squares and buildings; the Baroque raising royal palaces; the Neo-classicism constructing buildings for new public institutions; the industrial revolution with the construction of bridges and factories; and the modern movement with the theme of housing; then in which programmatic territory are we closest to the needs of our own time? The unit is continuously investigating appropriate solutions for five programmatic research themes: housing, leisure / cultural facilities, urban interventions /urban colonies, farming / manufacturing processes, and clinical /laboratory facilities. The majority of the projects and perhaps some of the more radical propositions belong to the two latter groups, suggesting to us that these themes are of particular relevance today.

The students of Unit 20 are challenged by recent developments in extremely small-scale environments. From engineered molecular chemistry to nano and micro robotics or cellular growth many of the projects suggest a new kind of architectural ecology. Flocking, swarming and sporing clusters are becoming the norm in this increasingly responsive and dynamic architecture.

This intense dedication to the design allows the skills of representationand investigation to mature very quickly. In many of the presented projects it is difficult to understand the scale. In some cases, the geometric investigation is manifested as an abstract topological experiment. In others, the skills and intricacies of model making define the projects path. Often the projects attempt to decipher a reality, which neither books nor history can describe. We look to explore new possibilities of a technological and anti-vitruvian world.

Another discarded myth is the obsession for a global vision of reality. Frequently we work on fragments trying to exhaust the limits of the ideas in an apparently constrained territory. On other occasions, we try to relate distant fields without being afraid of playing with concepts, which through their utopian character seem to be simplistic dreams. Sometimes we imitate machines or follow the psychology of fictional characters. In many of our projects, we push the narrative, endeavoring to merge it with a deep scientific understanding. Many of our stories gain a poetic value as well as becoming a technological manifesto.

Professor Salvador Pérez Arroyo and Marcos Cruz

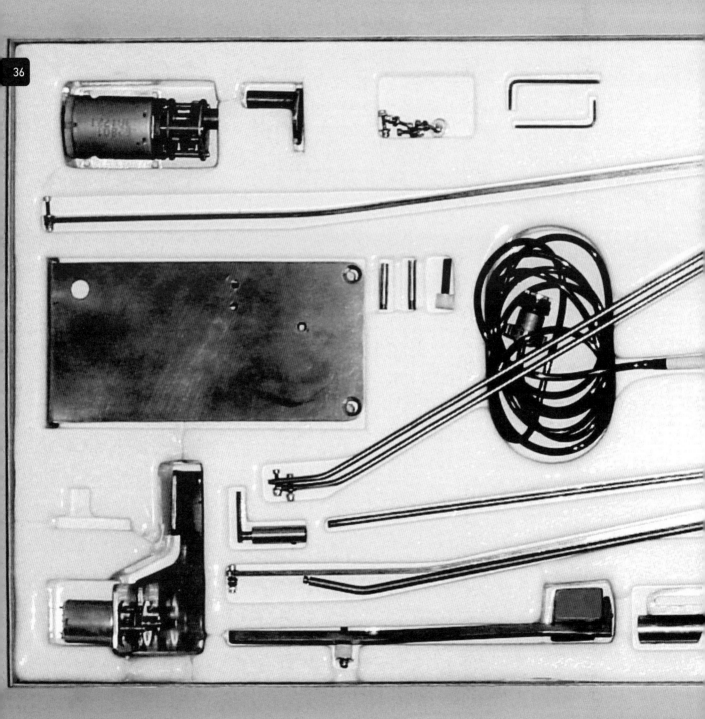

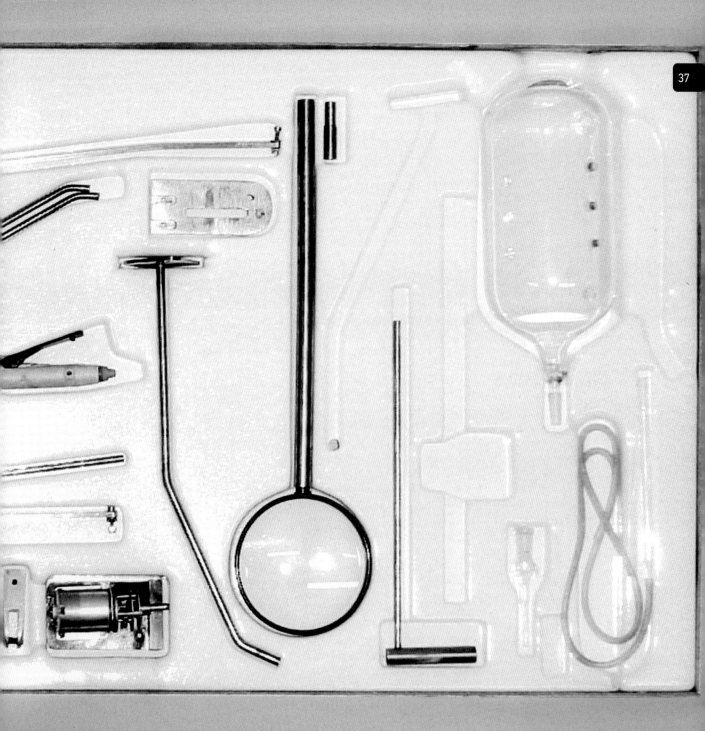

nika Schollin // Decay machine: Decycle Dirty Rotten Architecture [2001-2002] p_96

38

peter cook _vicente vidal _josé mariá lozano _unit text salvador pérez arroyo and marco
architecture _james foster//the humanpower architectural transformation_exhibitic

EL SUPERSTRUCTURADO EXSPEACIO DE LA IUNIDAD 20

Es siempre interesante ver cómo los objetivos de los tutores de proyectos de la Bartlett se amplifican y se distribuyen en la producción de sus estudiantes. Salvador se interesa por las estructuras y los espacios que crecen fuera de ellas. Construye y enseña tecnología en Madrid. Marcos está completando su tesis doctoral sobre pieles arquitectónicas, desollando arquitectura. Está interesado en las posibilidades generadoras de la piel como metáfora biológica, forma y función. (Juntos, pensaríamos, podrían diseñar un edificio bastante interesante, Salvador haría los interiores, Marcos los pedazos visibles, su presencia en la ciudad.) Los dos son optimistas sobre las posibilidades de la arquitectura como el arte de construir. Hay algo aquí sobre lo que hablar.

En estos proyectos vemos el cuerpo por todas partes, pero no dónde y del modo que nos han enseñado: recordemos la idea de Oscar Schlemmer, o la máquina (para vivir) qué une necesidad corporal y espíritu. En la U20 el cuerpo se explora en su inmensidad microscópica. El cuerpo es millones de células, billones de moléculas, un algoritmo de eternas y repetitivas transacciones de información y energía. Algunos de los proyectos de la U20 son notables. Estoy pensando en el suburbio de hielo de Helsinki que se forma todos los inviernos aglomerando cristales de hielo; el mercado urbano en el que la producción de comida cae desde las torres urbanas y se despliega debajo en los puestos del mercado callejero; la línea de unión como celdas automodificables; su entorno cercano, la identificación de la memoria y el diagnóstico de la enfermedad explorando unidades verticales (estas dos últimas sugieren que la arquitectura todavía esté aún dentro de sus poderes de ironía); la planta de teñido de tejidos cuyos componentes parecen multiplicarse por el paisaje - el color aparece totalmente extraño de nuevo, como si nosotros viviéramos en un mundo dirigido hacia el color CMYK. El cuerpo se ve como proceso y ese proceso se proyecta por todas partes en las formas y programas de arquitectura.

La imagen de esta arquitectura de componentes repetidos, distribuidos en el espacio, tiene su origen en el desarrollo de la tecnología. Aproximadamente al mismo tiempo que se desarrollaba la locomotora de vapor, Charles Babbage estaba trabajando en un tipo completamente diferente de máquina—la computadora mecánica - que, como un efecto colateral, dio forma y imagen a la naturaleza de la información iterativa (ver su artefacto diferencial y el artefacto analítico en el Museo de la Ciencia).

Quizá el interés de la arquitectura en el cuerpo siempre ha sido tecnológico; y quizá la tecnología siempre ha sondeado el cuerpo. Es justo que cuando la tecnología evoluciona y analiza más profundamente y más minuciosamente se revela un cuerpo diferente. En lugar del cuerpo mecánico de partes móviles, el cuerpo de lo biotecnológico (yo no diré nano -) continua. Creo que esto es semejante a la tecnología instantánea de lo digital, la tecnología que reestructura el espacio, lo construye, lo

Lorens Holm_Bartlett School of Architecture, London

THE SUPERSUATURATED SPACE OF UNIT 20

It is always interesting to see how the interests of the Bartlett design tutors are amplified and scattered by the work of their students. Salvador is interested in structure and the spaces that grow out of structure. He builds constantly and teaches technology in Madrid. Marcos is completing his PhD (PhD by design) on architectural skins, skinning architecture. He is interested in the generative possibilities of skin as biologic metaphor, form, and function. Both are bullish about architecture as a building art. There is little talk about architecture here.

In these projects, we see the body everywhere, but not where and in the ways we are taught to expect it: think Oscar Schlemmer diagrams, or the machine (for living) which accommodates bodily need and spirit. In U20 the body is explored in its microscopic vastness. The body is millions of cells, billions of molecules, an algorithm of endlessly repeatable transactions of information and energy. A number of the 20 projects stand out. I am thinking of the suburb on Helsinki ice which forms like agglomerating ice crystals every winter; the urban market in which food production delaminates down from urban towers and unfolds into the street market stalls below; the assembly line-like body self-modification pods; its near neighbour, the memory identification and disease diagnosis self-scan vertical units (these last two suggest that architecture is still within its powers of irony); the fabric dye plant whose components seem to multiply all over the landscape - colour becomes completely strange again, as if we lived in a 'tipped-in' CMYK colour world. The body is viewed as process, and that process is projected everywhere in the forms and programs of architecture.

The image of this architecture of repeating components, distributed in space, has a provenance in the development of technology. At about the same time that the steam locomotive was being developed, Charles Babbage was working on an entirely different kind of machine — the mechanical computer - which, as a side effect, gave form and image to the iterative nature of information (see his difference engine and analytic engine in the Science Museum).

Maybe architecture's interest in the body has always been technological; and maybe technology has always probed the body. It's just that as technology evolves, probing deeper and more minutely, it reveals a different body. Instead of the mechanical body of moving parts, the body of biotechnological (I won't say nano-) processes. This is akin to the instantaneous technology of the digital, the technology which rearranges space, montages it, folds it back on itself, bringing disparate bits together, so that, as Victor Burgin wrote (ten years ago, at least) 'live pictures from Voyager II, as it passes through the rings of Saturn, may appear on television sandwiched between equally "live" pictures of internal organs, transmitted by surgical probes, and footage from Soweto.'[1]

40

peter cook _vicente vidal _josé mariá lozano _unit text salvador pérez arroyo and marco
architecture _james foster//the humanpower architectural transformation_exhibitic

pliega hacia atrás sobre sí mismo, reuniendo pedazos dispares, para que, como escribió Víctor Burgin (hace diez años, por lo menos) "imágenes reales del Voyager II, cuando atraviesa los anillos de Saturno puedan aparecer en televisión intercaladas igualmente entre imágenes reales de órganos interiores, transmitidos por sondas quirúrgicas, y grabadas desde Soweto. "

El trabajo de U20 se nos presenta con la fantasía de la tecnología. No sólo la tecnología (puede ser o no , este autor nunca lo sabrá), sino algo más potente y de mayor alcance. Ésta es la fachada gloriosa de la tecnología. La posibilidad del cuerpo y el espacio, el cuerpo en el espacio, el cuerpo como espacio, el cuerpo no localizado pero distribuido en un proceso iterativo por la aterradora superficie clara de una fantasía tecnológica. Y es interesante ver cómo ha vuelto la imagen de la perspectiva. Esa malla abstracta que se extiende desde lo infinitamente pequeño, a lo infinitamente lejano. Ya no es la perspectiva el monumento conmemorativo a un cierto tipo de cerramiento al que estamos familiarizados desde que los romanos inventaron la bóveda (piel, entonces vestidos, entonces las paredes, finalmente las esferas celestiales). Ha vuelto ahora como heraldo del espacio que es el lugar infinito para las tecnologías de la información instantánea que le atraviesan.

¿Cómo toma forma este pensamiento? ¿Cómo hace usted algo cuándo usted está arañando la piel del conocimiento? ¿Dónde en un espacio infinito y en el proceso interminable encuentra usted el sitio para un proyecto? ¿Cómo se detiene usted simplemente aquí, no allí, y qué tipo de 'aquí ' es este? Incluso la perturbación más ligera en una solución supersaturada lo hace precipitar; lo que había sido de cristal claro y súper frío, empieza a cristalizar. Lo que había sido viscoso, inmóvil, transparente, ilimitado, se pliega, materializa, cruzado por líneas de energía y deseo (en otro registro lo que había sido pulido se raya). Con estos proyectos observamos una perturbación tecnológica en el supersaturado espacio del cuerpo.

Lorens Holm
Arquitecto y estudiante de PhD en teoría arquitectónica en el Programa Doctoral del Consorcio de Londres .
Vive, trabaja y enseña en Londres.

Lorens Holm_Bartlett School of Architecture, London

The work of U20 presents us with the fantasy of technology. Not technology itself (it may or may not be, this author will never know), but something much more potent and far reaching. This is technology's glorious façade. The possibility of the body and space, the body in space, the body as space, the body not localised but distributed in an iterative process across the terrifyingly clear surface of a technological fantasy. And it is interesting how the image of perspective has returned. That abstract grid extending to the infinitely small, the infinitely far. No longer is perspective the memorial to a certain kind of enclosure we are familiar with since the Romans invented the vault (skin, then clothing, then walls, finally heavenly spheres). It has now returned as herald of the space that is the infinite site for the technologies of instantaneous information transfer that traverse it.

How does thought take shape? How do you make something when you are clawing at the envelope of the knowable? Where in an infinite space and endless process do you find the site for a project? How do you stop just here, not there, and what kind of 'here' is it? Even the slightest disturbance in a supersaturated solution causes it to precipitate; what had been crystal clear and super-cool, begins to crystallise. What had been viscous, still, transparent, limitless, becomes folded, material, crossed by lines of energy and desire (in another register altogether, what had been smooth becomes striated). With these projects we witness a technological disturbance in the supersaturated space of the body.

Lorens Holm
Architect and PhD student in architectural theory in the London Consortium Doctoral Program.
He lives, works and teaches in London.

[1] Victor Burgin, 'Geometry and Abjection', in In/Different Spaces: place and memory in visual culture, p. 44, (U. of California Press, Berkeley, 1996).

Expandable Structure
1999 – 2000

BILBAO informs the concerns of the year: it offers the site of the major project, and drives the experiments preliminary to it. The platform for the proposed urban incisions is the polluted industrial area along the river, which leaves behind open surfaces of wasteland. It divides the conurbation of BILBAO into two riversides with its margins extended for more than 12 km until the ocean. The unit's task is to work against the increasing residual character of the river by (re) defining its presence.

The first term is spent on a project of an EXPANDABLE STRUCTURE. It is explored through models, which taken to Bilbao will trigged an interpretation of the site. Each student has to carry out specific technologic investigations about expandable conditions and built up a personal portfolio of images and ideas.

While the program for the year project is determined individually, aesthetic and constructive implications have to be carried out with 'witty', solutions on a big scale building. Students are encouraged to give importance to urban contextualisation and to focus on the confrontation between 'soft', and 'hard', matter.

The unit has a special taste for complex geometric constructions, as well as choreographic qualities of repetitive imagery that borrows aspects from natural life conditions. This relies on a wide range of references from biology to medical sciences. Curvilinear formations combined with tectonic qualities of linear form define a pursuit of lightness, movement and Œintelligent, materiality.

Smart Surface 2000 – 2001

Innovations in technology are transforming both our immediate physical surrounding and the tools of its perception. In response to surreptitious changes in our environment, the boundaries of conventional architectural practice are now stretching to encompass new disciplines of science and art. It,s the unit,s challenge to speculate alternative applications for these immerging 'new' ecologies, in architectural realms of space, program, and site.

"I,d like to look at what might perhaps be the technologies that will affect the aesthetics of buildings in the future. The obvious one is information technology, which clearly affects the way in which people wish to use buildings, the mode of transit between them, and the use and operation within. The second aspect is the use of wire-less facilities. The idea one can communicate and control remotely without connections between two elements is emerging everywhere and this is influencing events inside the building. In 10 to 20 years, we can expect all control and communication within a building to be without wires, which one a great deal of flexibility and eliminates many internal design problems. In the past we,ve been able to make things on a human scale. The watch, so small and detailed, was a miracle of ingenuity. We've also been able to make things that are larger than human scale, to amplify our muscle: cranes, diggers and so forth. But we've had little skill in creating structures that are significantly smaller than human scale. What semi-conductive technology has shown is that we will be able to create techniques that can fabricate things a thousand times smaller than anything we might reasonably envisage today. We will make motors, mechanical devices, cooling devices, moving devices that are one hundred of a millimeter across ˆ dust size. This will significantly affect the way in which we design in the future." In A Real High-Technologist, ed. Iann Barron, architectural Design (Sci-Fi Architecture), vol. 69 No 3/4 March-April 1999

The first term will be spent on a project of a SMART SURFACE, in which topologic and morphologic qualities are explored through creative workshop – and/or computer modeling. Intense observation of our visible or non-visible surrounding is a decisive stimulus to create new ideas of surface. By registering innumerous design-hypothesis the aim is to build-up a large spectrum of imageries that create the outline of each architectural experience throughout the year. Besides that, it will be our task to interpret and define in each case the concept of smartness applied to architecture. According to its scale, surface behavior implies a definition of the 'generating' entity, and its influence on the architectural whole. Smart materials, interactive devices, complex structural forms and biological phenomena will be part of technological investigations/speculations that will support the development of each proposal.

An excursion to the extreme scenarios of TENERIFE and the urban context of HELSINKI will inform the concerns of the second and third term. The first offers the site of a short project, which will drive the experiments preliminary to it. Confronted with the 'radical' vocabulary, of its landscape imagery, project prepositions of a small-scaled proposal have

s cruz_lorens holm _briefs_technical studies_natalia traverso caruana//ferrofluidic
ure series _ critics_bartfolio__students _curriculum vitae_acknowledgements _index

43

Briefs

to be equally radical, immersing in preoccupations of architectural utopia. The latter site offers the context for the main project of the year. Each program is determined individually, while aesthetic and constructive implications will be carried out on a big scale intervention in the city. The projects will be pushed to confront their urban presence within the existing seafront scenery.

Growth 2001/02

Unit 20 is interested in G R O W T H. In times of an increasing 'medicalisation', of art and architecture, growth is an extremely complex phenomenon that raises especial interest, when applied to the architectural building practice. It make us think of principles of how to build, control, maintain and supply structures (with variable sources of energy), which in human scale might have unexpected consequences on the way, we perceive and use space. Our challenge this year is to open ways for new programmes and conditions of inhabitable growing form. Recent technologic advances, such as bio-mimetic structures, histo-compatible materials, artificial skin growth, or organ design are gradually overcoming thethreshold between living and dead form. They are evolving into a new materiality, which is result of the hybridization between growing systems and an increasingly sophisticated clinical apparatus.

In a first stage, many projects will be simultaneously developed in a very small and a very big scale. There might be formations of infinitely small behaviour and invisible presence that through their dynamic and time dependent conditions will occupy surfaces, flock into clusters or colonise territory of unprecedented existence.

The year's programme is divided into three proposals, which at the end should establish a clear and coherent progress of ideas and intentions. The first proposal is an experimental study that will drive many of the investigations for the two following projects. It is during the first term that the brief is interpreted individually, while the field trip will inform the choice of programme and context for the final building project. In many cases the two last proposals will merged into one single proposition.

We arrive as sediments In memory. Through acquisition.
> Lisa Silver

Our viscous pulse, our fluctuating heartbeat
> Natalia Traverso

Powering ourselves with our insomniac motions
> James Foster

Then we crack
> Robert Marinus Grindley

Then we decay

Buried in the earth. Living underground.
> Annika Schollin

Duality is the game we play
> Galit Tondet

Feeding off darkness living off light.
> Jason Park Fung Kur

Soon the hydra reconfigures itself.
> Andy Shaw

Paths of movement captured on film.
> Hui Hui Teoh

So on and off the shadows dance.
> Karen willcox

Growing. Aged. Transfection.
> Martyn Weaver

Thus occurs a self aesthetic. A body 'self-transformed'
> Gwen Shao Jun Lee
> Jia Lu

>poem by Gwen Shao Jun Lee for the Bartfest exhibition 2002

44

peter cook _vicente vidal _j.maria lozano _unit text salvador perez arroyo and marcos
Architecture _James Foster//The Humanpower Architectural Transformation_exhibiti

Design of a Plant (6 weeks)   Mon.Oct1 – Mon.Nov12 The first term will be spent on the Design of a Plant*. It will focus on the development of a series of probes of growing structures, adequate to build-up a large spectrum of imageries and a clear technologic proposition. This short project should be developed through models and 2D/3D computer drawings. Students not familiar with computer modelling programmes are invited to use this time to acquire basic skills in rendering and animation techniques. * According to its definition the word plant can have several meanings, such a s: (as a noun) a living thing that has leaves and roots, and grows: a factory: machinery: a person who is placed in a group of people thought to be criminals in order to discover facts about them (as a verb) to put in the ground: to put in the mind: to form (a centre of living) in an empty area of land by bringing in people; to settle (people) in a place; to hide on a person so that he will seem guilty

Bibliographic references:

Thomson, D.arcy Wentworth (ed. By John Tyler Bonner): On Growth and Form, Cambridge University Press, 1969
Hale, W.G.; Margham, J.P.: Saunders, V.A.: Collins Dictionary of Biology (second edition). Harper Collins Publishers 1995
Frazer, John: An Evolutionary Architecture, Architectural Press 1995
Oxtrod Concise Medical Dictionary, Oxford University Press 1998
Spiller, Neil: Digitaldreams ^ Architecture and the new alchemic technologies, Ellipsis, 1998
Angier, Natalie: The Beauty of the Beastly ^ New Views on the Nature of Life, Abacus 1995
Duncan, Jody: Borrowed Flesh in Cinefex num.49
Martin, Kevin H.: Jacking into the Matrix in Cinefex num. 79 (October 1999)
Sieburth, John Mcneill: Microbial Seascapes ^ A pictorial Essay on Marine Microorganisms and their Environments, University Park Press, 1975
Todd, C. D., Laverack, M. s., Boxshall, G. A.: Coastal Marine
Zooplankton ^ A practical manual for students (second edition), Cambridge Unuversity Press
Corner, James, Mclean, Alex F.: Taking Measures Across the American Landscape, Yale University Press, 1996
Berman, Irwin: Color Atlas of Basic histology (2nd edition), Appleton ξ Langer, 1998
Phillips, G.O.; Strong, D.M.; Von Versen, R.; Nather, A.: Advances in Tissue Banking, Vol. 3, world Scientific 1999
Hayward Gallery: Force Fields ^ The Phases of the Kinetic, (catalogue) Hayward Gallery, 2000

Intermediate PIN-UP   Thu.Oct11

C R I T   Thu.Nov1

Final PIN-UP   Mon.Nov12

Field Trip
From CHICAGO to DALLAS/FORT WORTH (Tracking down the architecture of Wright, Goff and Greene) (10 days field trip)
Wed.Nov14 – Sat.Nov24

Some of the Buildings to be visited:

Chicago, Illinois: Illinois Institute of Technology, 1964 (M.v.d.Rohe)
Oak Park, Illinois: House and Studio, (F.L.Wright)
Aurora, Illinois: Ruth Ford House, 1947 (Bruce Goff)
Bartlesville, Oklahoma: Redeemer Lutheron Education Centre, 1959 (Bruce Goff)
Bartlesville, Oklahoma: Joe Price House (Uni. Conf.), 1956 (Bruce Goff)
Bartlesville, Oklahoma: Price Tower, 1954 (F.L.Wright)
Norman, Oklahoma: Bavinger House, 1950 (Bruce Goff)
Norman, Oklahoma: Prairie House, 1962 (Herb Greene)
Oklahoma City, Oklahoma: Cunningham House, 1956 (Herb Greene)
Oklahoma city, Oklahoma: Mummers Theatre, 1971 (John Johansen)
Fort Worth, Texas: Kimbell Art Museum, 1964 (Louis Kahn)

Plant Infiltration
(7 weeks, including Christmas Vacation)   Mon.Nov26 – Thu.Jan10An excursion throughout the American Mid-West informs the concerns of the second project. The natural and rural landscape around DALLAS/FORT WORTH will offer the site for a second short project, focusing on the mediation between the concrete nature of architectural buildings and the abstractness of former conceptual work. The preliminary experiments are confronted with site-specific analysis and the development of a programme for a small-scaled (growing?) device. It should be worked out through models, installations (as necessary) and increasingly through 3D

rens holm _briefs _fieldtrips _technical dissertations_Natalia Traverso//FerroFluidic
ure series _ critics_bartfolio__students _curriculum vitae_acknowledgements _index

45

Briefs

Bibliographic references:

Forty, Adrian: Objects of Desire – Desig and Society since 1750, Routledge 2000
Foucault, Michel: The Birth of the Clinic – An Archaeology of Medical Perception, Vintage Books 1963
Gilman, Sander L.: Making the Body Beautiful – A Cultural History of Aesthetic Surgery, Princeton University Press 1999
Braddock, S. E.; O.Mahony, M.: Techno Textiles – Revolutionary fabrics for Fashion and Design, Thames & Hudson 1998
Chadwick,Helen: Effluvia, (catalogue) Museum Folkwang, Serpentine Gallery, Fundació "La Caixa" 1994 Edited by Nan Ellin:
Architecture of Fear, Princeton Architectural Press 1997
Ed. by Carl Haenlein: Rebecca Horn – The Glance of Infinity, (catalogue) Kestner Gesellschaft, Scalo Verlag 1997
Hesse, Eva: Eva Hesse, (catalogue) Galerie Nationale du Jeu de Paume 1993
Monchaux, Cathy de: Cathy de Monchaux, Whitechapel Art Gallery 1997
Hoptman, Laura; Tatehata, Akira; Kultermann, Udo: Yayoi Kusama, Phaidon 2000
Ennadre, Touhami: Touhami Ennadre – Black Light, Prestel 1996
Oxford Art Journal: Louise Bourgeois – Volume 22, Number 2, Oxford University Press 1999
Aguilera–Hellweg, Max: The Sacred Heart – An Atlas of the Body Seen Through Invasive Surgery, Bulfinch Press 1997
Oke, T. R.: Boundary, Layer, Climate (2nd edition). Routledge 2000
Banham, Reyner: Design by Choice, Academy Editions 1981
Ratner, Buddy D., Hoffman, Allan S., Schoen, Frederick J., Lemons, Jack E.: Biomaterials Science – An introduction to Materials in
Medicine, Academic Press 1996
Ed. Janine Marchessault: Wildscience – Redoing Feminism, Medicine and the Media, Routledge 2000

o

Intermediate PIN-UP   Thu.Dec20

C R I T   Thu.Jan10

Intermediate Portfolio Review Mon.Feb4

Urban Incisions

14.01.02 until 16.05.02 (18 weeks, including Intermediate PortfolioReview + Easter Vacations)

The urban centre of FORT WORTH offers the context for the mainproject of the year. Programmatic requirements will be
determinate individually and combined with spatial, structural and aesthetic preoccupations on the site.

Bibliographic references:

Miralles, Benedetta Tagliabue: Enric Miralles – Works and Porjects, 1975-1995, Monacelli Press, 1996
Zabalbeascoa, Anatxu: Igualada Cemetry: Enric Miralles and Carmen Pinos, Phaidon, 1998
Vieira da Silva, Marie Helena: Vieira da Silva nas Colecções
Portuguesas: Museu de Arte de Sao Paulo Assis Chateaubriand, Fundacao Calouste Gulbenkian, Centro de Arte Moderna, 1987
Mcdonald, Chris, Salter, Peter: Salter and Mcdonald, The Fish Restaurant, Tokyo in AA files, num.7, Sept. 84
Jencks, Charles: Le Corbusier and the Continual Revolution in Architecture, The Monacelli Press2000
Forty, Adrian: Words and Buildings – A Vocabulary of Modern Architecture, Thames and Hudson 2000
Nicholson, Ben: Appliance House, The Chicago Institute for Architecture and Urbanism 1990
Greene, Herb: Mind and Image – An essay on Art and Architecture, University Press of Kentucky1962
Goff, Bruce: Bruce Goff – Towards a Future Architecture, Oklahoma University Press1982
Rucker+Co, Haus: Haus Rucker + Co - 1967 bis 1983, Friedr. Vieweg & Sohn1984
DeLong, David G.: Bruce Goff – Toward absolute Architecture, MIT Press1988
Le Corbusier: L'Oeuvre Complete, Fondation Le corbusier 1988

C R I T   Thu.Mar3

C R I T   Thu.Apr4

F I N A L C R I T Thu.May16

FINAL PORTFOLIO REVIEW Mon.Jun3

TECHNICAL STUDIES

HOUSING

FARMING MANUFACTURING

LABORATORIES CLINICS

LEISURE cultural facilities

URBAN INTERVENTIONS

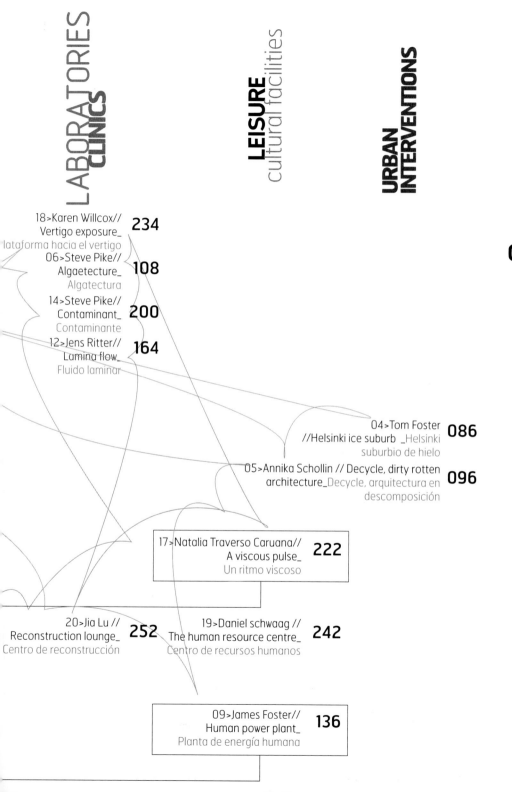

OBJECTS Gadgets
TechnicalAppliances

DYNAMIC
FLOWS

NEW SURFACES
Material
Transformation

ENERGY CONSUMPTION
intelligent
environments

Human body
architectural
prosthesis

Structural
Spatiality

clustering of robots forming a silicon mining factory in Tenerife.

mining robots breeding on a lake in Helsinki

Experimentation with insects activating a digital neural network computer model.

Incentrix cluster
Incentrix, ciudad en racimos
city

Kevin Chu

Helsinki
Finland
2000-2001

The insects are the protagonist in controlling the performance of the model, which mimics the activity of the sensory neurons in our body.

Cluster Architecture – a food processing industry located in Helsinki's old port consists of **small-scaled insect-like robots** which form a **tactile** and **transformable surface**.

A globally networked mainframe computer guides the clustering mechanisms according to the specificity of each site. Each robot peforms a pre-conceived purpose such as structure, cladding or foundation and the overall form alters according to the relocation of individual entities, in turn creating a nomadic architecture free from limitations.

These components embody dispersing qualities and trigger **infinite transformations of space** depending upon functional and programmatic requirements. Entomological studies of bees and locusts initiated the design and inspired the proposition of architecture.

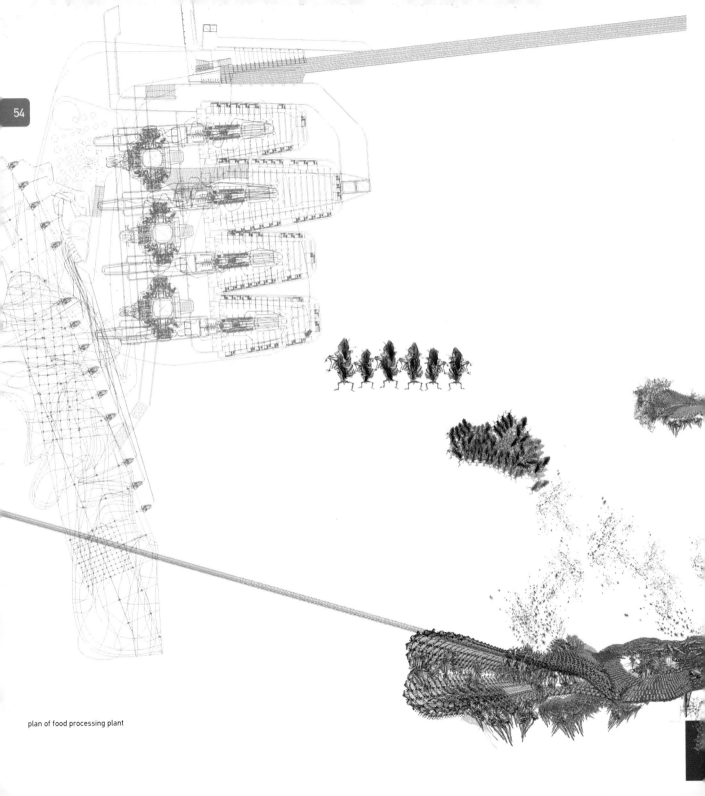

plan of food processing plant

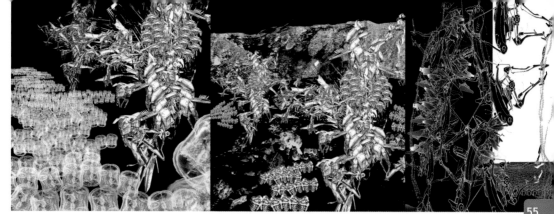

robots combined in a tactile surface creating enclosed spaces

process of clusteration in self-constructive architecture

zoom into robot clusters

57

site location of food processing plant
in the port of Helsinki

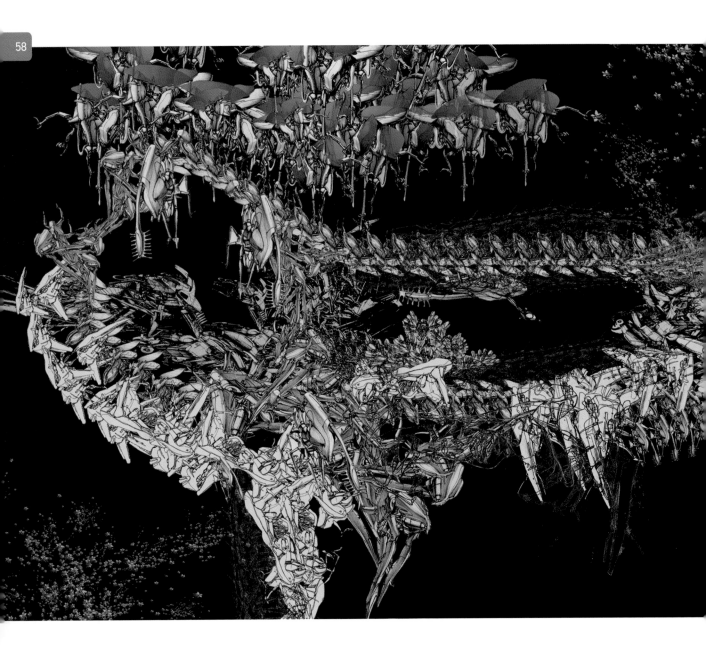

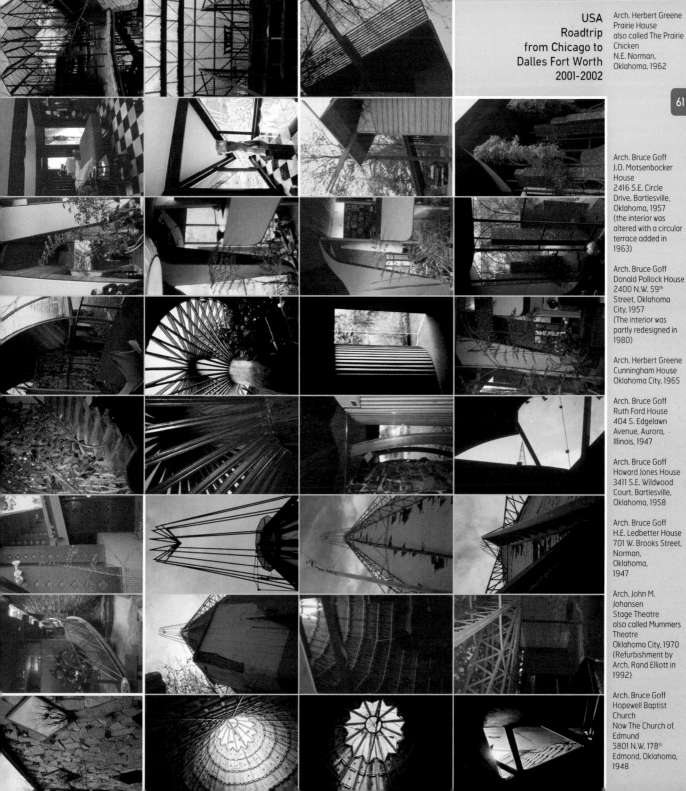

USA
Roadtrip
from Chicago to
Dalles Fort Worth
2001-2002

Arch. Herbert Greene
Prairie House
also called The Prairie
Chicken
N.E. Norman, Oklahoma, 1962

Arch. Bruce Goff
J.O. Motsenbocker
House
2416 S.E. Circle
Drive, Bartlesville,
Oklahoma, 1957
(the interior was
altered with a circular
terrace added in
1963)

Arch. Bruce Goff
Donald Pollock House
2400 N.W. 59th
Street, Oklahoma
City, 1957
(The interior was
partly redesigned in
1980)

Arch. Herbert Greene
Cunningham House
Oklahoma City, 1965

Arch. Bruce Goff
Ruth Ford House
404 S. Edgelawn
Avenue, Aurora,
Illinois, 1947

Arch. Bruce Goff
Howard Jones House
3411 S.E. Wildwood
Court, Bartlesville,
Oklahoma, 1958

Arch. Bruce Goff
H.E. Ledbetter House
701 W. Brooks Street,
Norman,
Oklahoma,
1947

Arch. John M.
Johansen
Stage Theatre
also called Mummers
Theatre
Oklahoma City, 1970
(Refurbishment by
Arch. Rand Elliott in
1992)

Arch. Bruce Goff
Hopewell Baptist
Church
Now The Church of
Edmund
5801 N.W. 178th
Edmond, Oklahoma,
1948

Billy-Bob's garage transforms into a 3d-art workshop, car dismantling platform and mechanics yard that form direct links via a bridge to the community of Greenville.

Lisa Silver

Architecture of Objects – In the heart of Mississippi County on a meander cut-off near the small town of Greenville, three characters are confined to three rooms within a house. The project narrates a psychological response to imprisonment within a single room, whereby in order to survive, the characters utilise mundane objects to create a more stimulating living space. A **transfiguring environment** begins as the bathroom, garage and study room of a traditional farmhouse shed their enclosure over time and **generate form through recomposed and subverted objects**. The house therefore transforms from the inside out and colonises the site in the form of **an enclave that combines living with object based enterprises**.

The Garage, where Billy-Bob's impaired vision encouraged an enjoyment of texture, smell and sound through 3D art, becomes a combined car mechanics workshop, dismantling platform and 3D artist's studio.

Glean-ville
a tale of sedimentary survival
una historia de supervivencia

Mississippi County, USA
2001-2002

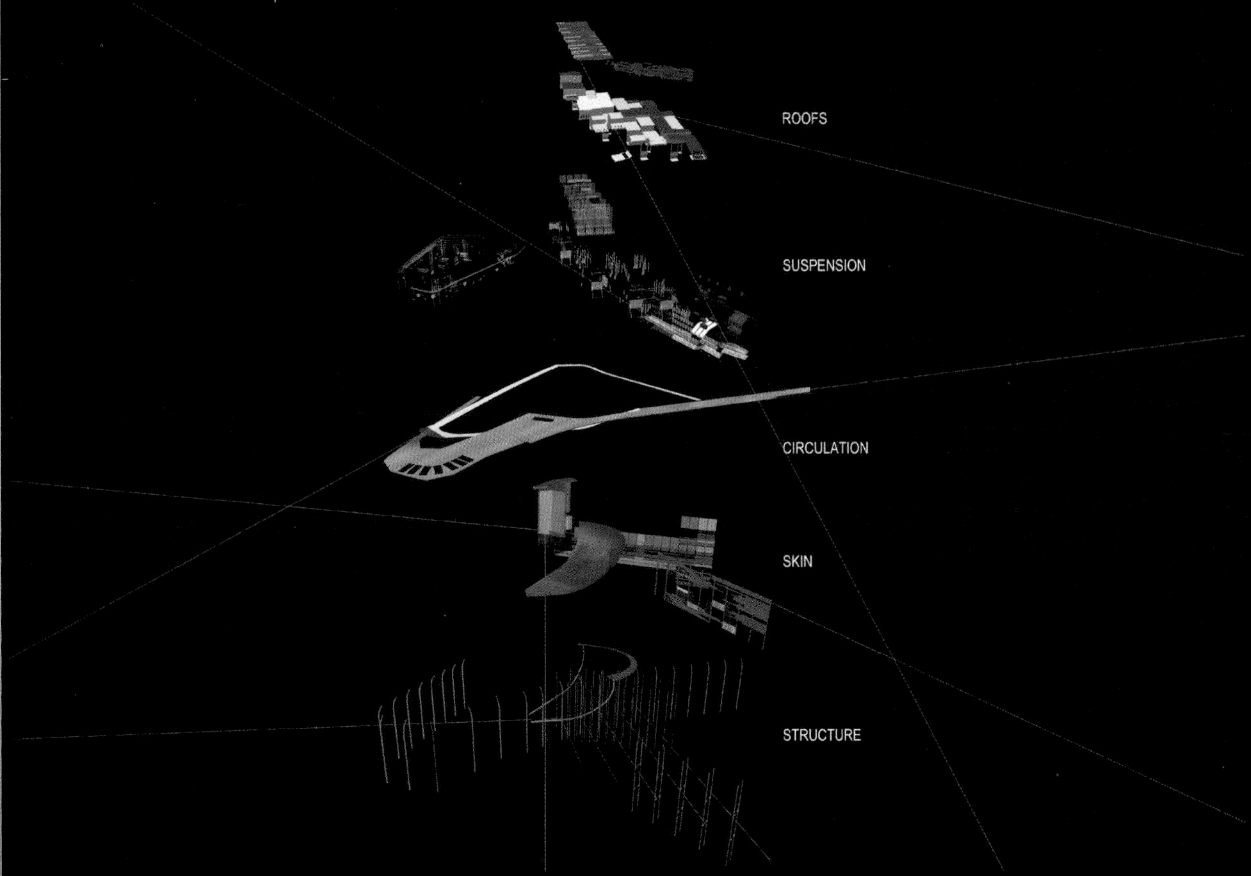

ROOFS

SUSPENSION

CIRCULATION

SKIN

STRUCTURE

Cross section: Though alien objects are fused, subverted and juxtaposed to form a unified whole, they are still expressed and recognised for their original meaning.

Site view

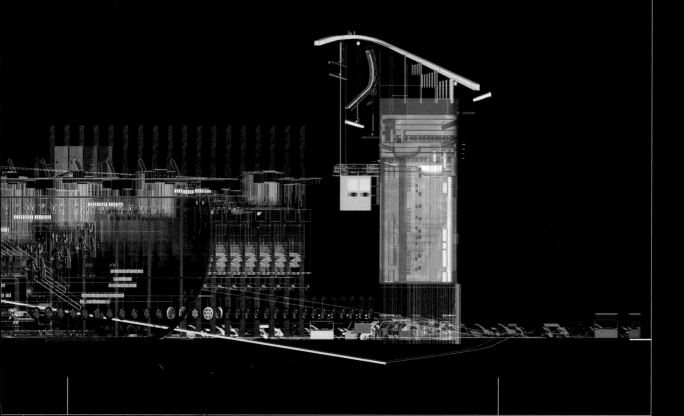

Mary - Lou Rest room

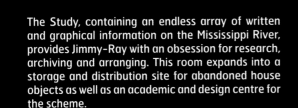

The Study, containing an endless array of written and graphical information on the Mississippi River, provides Jimmy-Ray with an obsession for research, archiving and arranging. This room expands into a storage and distribution site for abandoned house objects as well as an academic and design centre for the scheme.

The Bathroom, where Mary-Lou became claustrophobic and fascinated with river wildlife, transforms into a multifunctional tower containing a voyeur point disguised as a nature hide, as well as the public aspects of the scheme.

Mary-Lou's personal objects are contained within surfaces and meshes of varied transparency that slide and pivot to various levels of light, reflection and opacity within the tower.

Mary-Lou's bathroom objects reassemble and weave upward into a narrow tower that houses a panoramic look out point for nature enthusiasts and voyeurs.

The car-dismantling platform, partly comprised of a car-door-ventilation-wall-system, deconstructs vehicles for reuse in cars, as art medium and as a key building material.

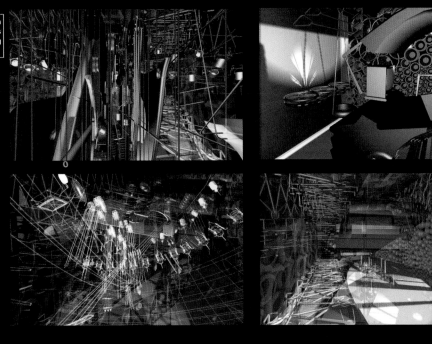

Billy-Bob's Garage

The continual movement of objects and people from one space to the next defines the zones as wholly interdependent and brings rhythms of balance and equilibrium to the site.

Therefore over time, the site builds up from a **primitive scattering of objects** to a **complex weaving of meticulously composed forms and systems.**

Billy-Bob's artwork requires the physical movements of skaters and cyclists to spread art material poured from a roof suspension system onto a ramp. Thus people and the processes of painting become the art form.

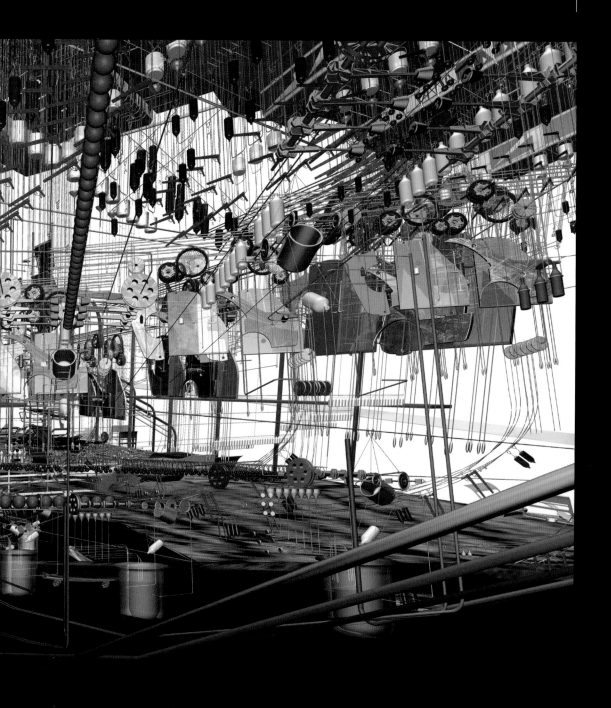

Alien objects fuse and juxtapose to form a unified whole while their original meanings are still expressed and recognised. The enclave physically illustrates the idiosyncrasies and practices of the individuals that constructed it, by the inventive composition of their personal and found objects, which transcend function and become ornament.

Jimmy - Ray´s Study Roo

detail of longitudinal section

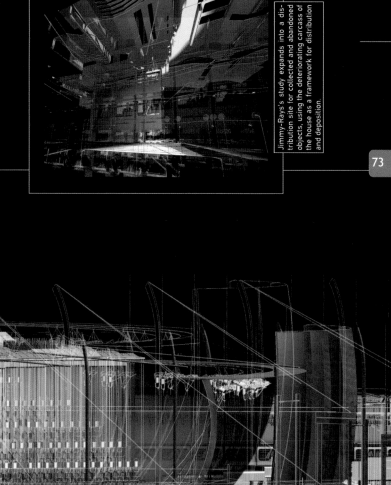

Jimmy-Rays's study expands into a distribution site for collected and abandoned objects, using the deteriorating carcass of the house as a framework for distribution and deposition.

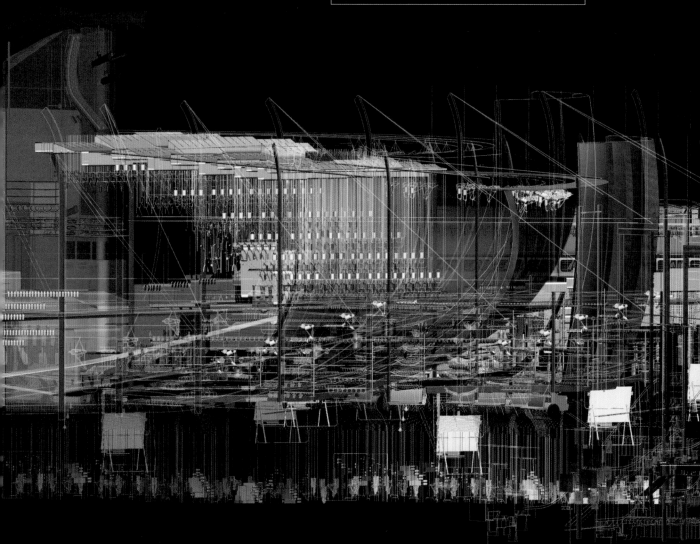

**BARTLETT
SCHOOL
OF
ARCHITECTURE**

GRADUATE
PROGRAMMES

**UNIVERSITY
COLLEGE
LONDON**

Core Graduate Staff
Peter Cook
Christine Hawley
Iain Borden
Dennis Crompton
Adrian Forty
Colin Fournier
Stephen Gage
Jonathan Hill
CJ Lim
Barbara Penner
Yael Reisner
Jane Rendell
Neil Spiller
Soo Ware

Recent Visitors
Will Alsop
Ron Arad
Rachel Armstrong
Ben van Berkel
Jennifer Bloomer
Neil Cummings
Barry Curtis
Neil Denari
James Donald
Paul Finch
Massimiliano Fuksas
Diana Ghirado
Zvi Hecker
Andrea Kahn
Nadim Karam
Patrick Keiller
Sharon Kivland
Marysia Lewandowska
Bruce Mau
Thom Mayne
Ben Nicholson
Marcos Novak
Kas Oosterhaus
Eric Owen Moss
Kyong Park
Steve Pile
Alessandra Ponte
Cedric Price
Wolf Prix
Hani Rashid
Helmut Richter
Joel Sanders
Patrick Schumacher
Lars Spuybroek
Stalker
Nigel Thrift
Mike Webb
Mark Wigley
Lebbeus Woods
Ken Yeang
Elia Zenghelis

Diploma in Architecture
Certificate in Professional Practice (Part 3)
MArch Architectural Design
MSc Architectural History
MSc Urban Design
MPhil/PhD Architecture by Design
MPhil/PhD Architectural History and Theory

www.bartlett.ucl.ac.uk/architecture

The book entitled Unit 20 was composed over the past 3 years, 1095 days and 26280 hours.

Bart-lett- phe·nom·e·na. 1. Architecture that moves and talks, de-materialized and simultaneously becomes elaborated to the point of clarity comprised of a singular and eloquent condition. 2. An occurrence, a circumstance, or a fact that is perceptible by the senses. 3. pl., phe·nom·e·nons. a. An unusual, significant, or unaccountable fact or occurrence; a marvel. b. A remarkable or outstanding person; a paragon. See Synonyms at wonder. 4. Philosophy. a. That which appears real to the mind, regardless of whether its underlying existence is proved or its nature understood.

Such a condition is viable due to the presence of the Bartlett, a place where a phenomenal amount of force and vitality, encompass a 24hour activity. The studios, computer rooms and shop are consistently being re-vitalized a sense of energy beyond the abilities of any machine, in a sense it is an anti-machine, laconically it is an incubator of thought and critical criteria whose energies and thoughts provoke a profound consideration of existing values and ideals, pushing architecture to the limit of social responsibility.

Chadi Chamoun

Architect and Mphil/PhD student at the Bartlett School of Architecture. He is an instructor at the Notre Dame University, Lebanon

Bartlett poster 2002 desioned by Laura Allen with image of Lisa Silver

Textile production in full process

A line of public buildings can be traced from the Olympic Stadium down to the city. The site lies between the opera house and the Finlandia concert hall. The building, a textile factory and theatre multiplex, *weaves* its spaces across the landscape, appearing and disintegrating within the body of the land. Like graduated threads of colour in a tapestryscape, the dyeing process and public route begin as monochromatic experiences

before **knitting** themselves into a **spectrum of colours.** The grey of the machinery contrasts with the white of the cotton,

creating a *cinematic façade* for the building. Visually stimulated, the users become active participants in the intricate choreography of machinery, nature and colour.

Karen Willcox CMYK choreography

Helsinki, Finland CMYK coreografia
2000-2001

view into the entrance area

the site view from street level

the site view from lake

View of the park when factory is in full production

external view of the façade facing the waterside

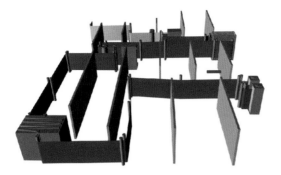

the textile weaves through the various levels

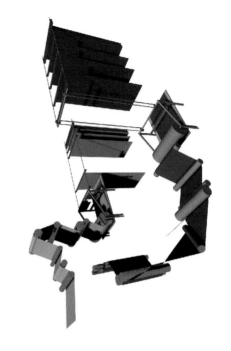

cutting process after the textiles has dried

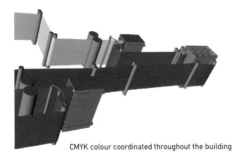

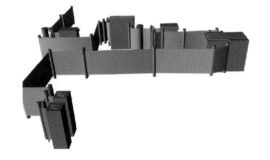

CMYK colour coordinated throughout the building

process choreography of the building

colour choreography created by different rythmns of process

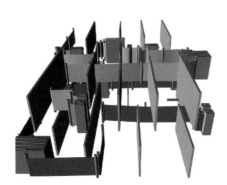

weaving of the CMYK

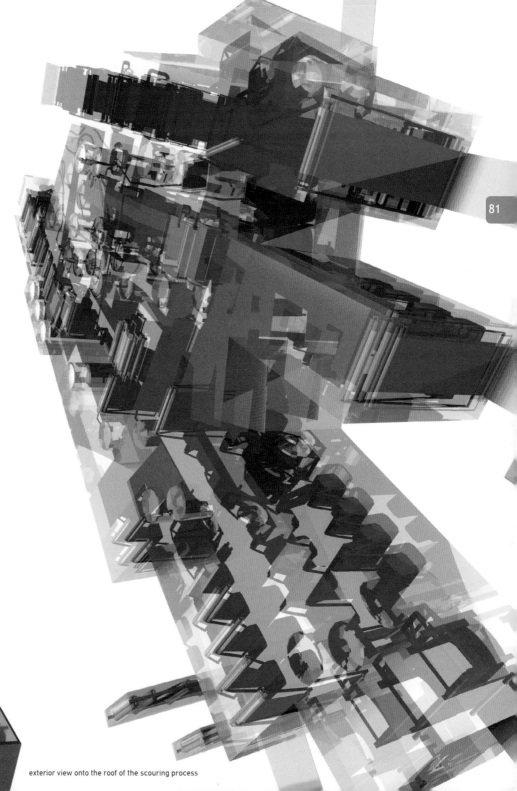

diagram showing the interaction of the process and the building

scouring and bleeching process

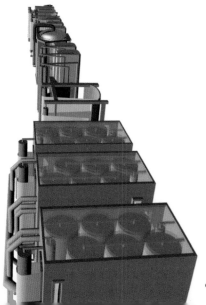

exterior view onto the roof of the scouring process

entering the waeving park: view from street level facing the lake

interior views of the theatres within the factory: The backdrop is created by the process

top view into bleach and scouring building: the start of the treatment of the textile before it gets transforms into C,M,Y or K

view from the dry room, the C,M,Y or K hanging to dry after the process of the dyeing is completed

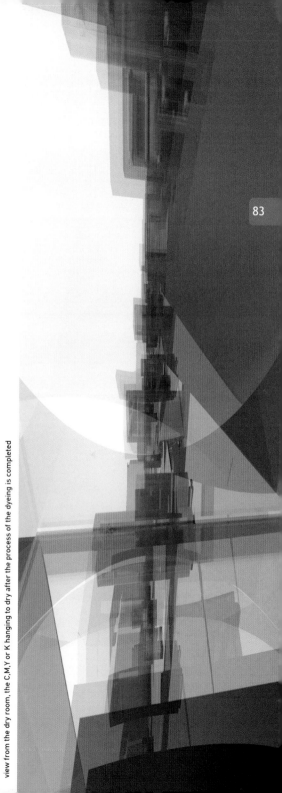

Field Trip to Helsinki + Tampere in January 2001

FINLAND

Manufactured ice harbours provide an arrival point for the fishing, research and icebreaker fleets

Helsinki ice suburb

Helsinki suburbio de hielo

Helsinki, Finland
2000-2001

Tom Foster

"There is no finality
in architecture, only
continuous change"
Walter Gropius

Distributed intelligence swarm of hyper crystallisation submersible robots (HSR's) artificially enhancing the ice sheet from underneath.

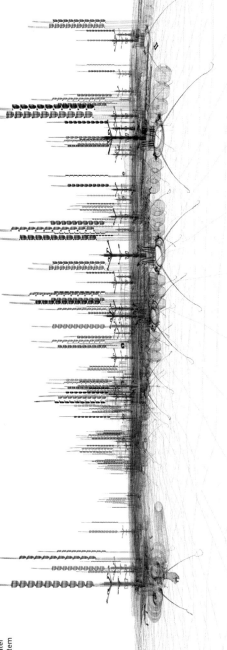

Preliminary study: plasmatic water city, reconfigurable harbour system

A **transient nomadic community** evolves annually on the ice sheet that forms each winter over the Gulf of Finland. This 'suburb' consists of many autonomous mobile parts that migrate from their summer hibernation in Helsinki's numerous harbours out to sea on the ice sheet as it forms. The components configure and self-organise in the ice due to the social and functional behaviours of their nomadic inhabitants to create *dynamic and ephemeral/architectural* urban and social structures. Depending on the severity of the ice season the suburb will exist for 5 months of each year. The variable nature of the ice winter results in an unpredictable and constantly changing seasonal architecture. The suburb operates as a scientific base for ice research, as a staging post for the Baltic Sea icebreaker and fishing fleets and as an industrial fish smoking factory.

Ice is used as a quick and efficient material for combing the building components into emergent architectures. It provides a free-form, malleable and unpredictable structure with plasmatic qualities. The community is compact and mobile when the ice sheet is unstable (early and late winter) and fragmented and spread out when the ice is stable (mid-winter). In intermittent periods and regions of localised ice decay or build up, both the community and architecture instinctively respond and react to their physical environment, continually and infinitely inventing and re-inventing themselves.

The longer the amount of time the suburb remains on one site, the more developed and complex it will become and the boundaries between architecture and ice, building and site, man-made and natural will appear increasingly less defined.

The project aims to explore **ambiguous time-dependant** narratives between ice and architecture, land and sea, chaos and order.

Ice carved conveyer belt

Helsinki archipelago during peak ice conditions (mid february)

Decay of ice sheet

87

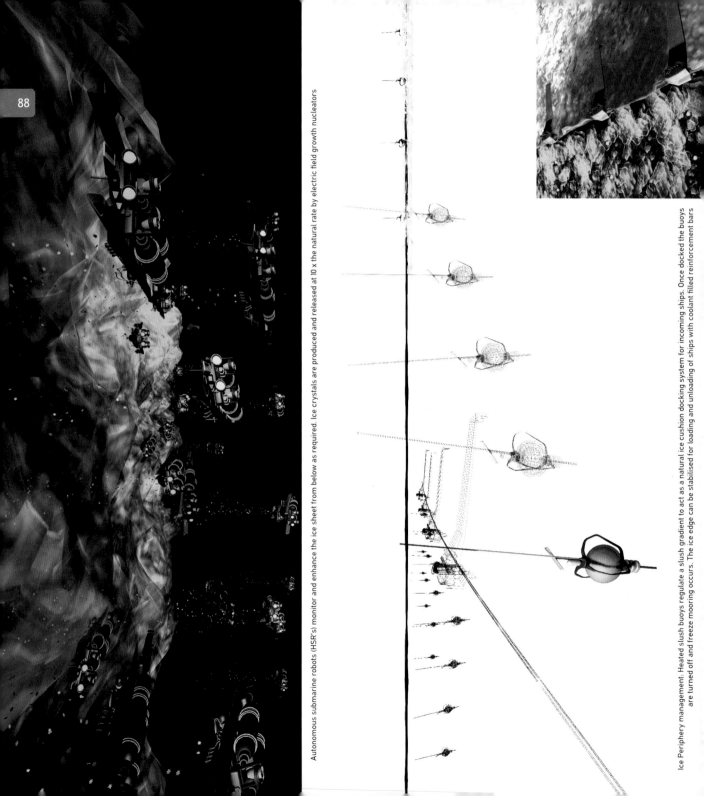

Autonomous submarine robots (HSR's) monitor and enhance the ice sheet from below as required. Ice crystals are produced and released at 10 x the natural rate by electric field growth nucleators

Ice Periphery management: Heated slush buoys regulate a slush gradient to act as a natural ice cushion docking system for incoming ships. Once docked the buoys are turned off and freeze mooring occurs. The ice edge can be stabilised for loading and unloading of ships with coolant filled reinforcement bars

HSR smoking production line • waste management communications and desalination plants break away from mother ship as production line unfolds. Ice cellars are dug into the enhanced ice sheet for storage of produce. Ambiguity between ice and architecture emerges.

HSR's recharge and download data to mobile energy plants in ice. Energy can be generated from high winter winds and sea / ice movements

Construction components combine with ice to create a dry dock for maintenance and self-replication of architectural and marine systems.

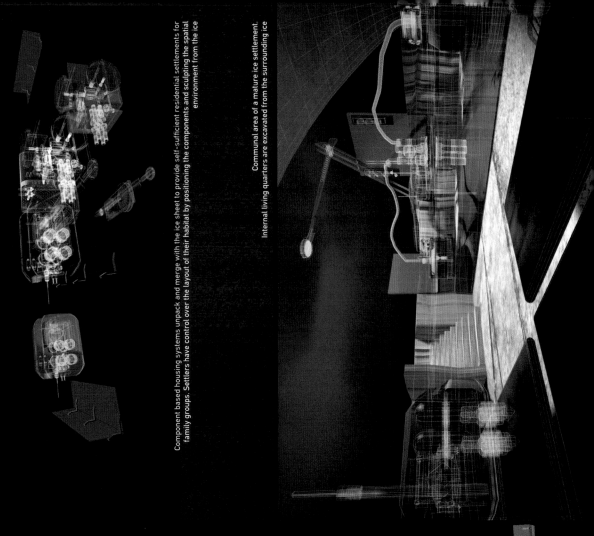

Component based housing systems unpack and merge with the ice sheet to provide self-sufficient residential settlements for family groups. Settlers have control over the layout of their habitat by positioning the components and sculpting the spatial environment from the ice

Communal area of a mature ice settlement.
Internal living quarters are excavated from the surrounding ice

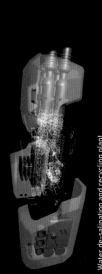

Water de-salination and recycling plant

Waste management systems

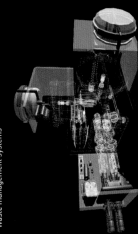

Energy storage batteries, data control systems and cooking facilities

Housing Systems ready to travel

Functions of Ice Suburb:

[01] Management of marine ecosystems - fisheries / bird nesting
[02] Monitoring / assessment / research of sea ice / environment / oceanographic conditions.
      Collection, archiving and distribution of data
[03] Maintain economically important shipping lanes and provide coast guard facilities
[04] Increase Helsinki inhabitant's awareness of the science, poetry and value of their sea
[05] Provide habitable water communities
[06] Small-scale sea based industries – Fish Smoking
[07] Self-maintenance and self-replication facilities to allow growth and evolution of suburb

Shelter is provided by a spray ice membrane

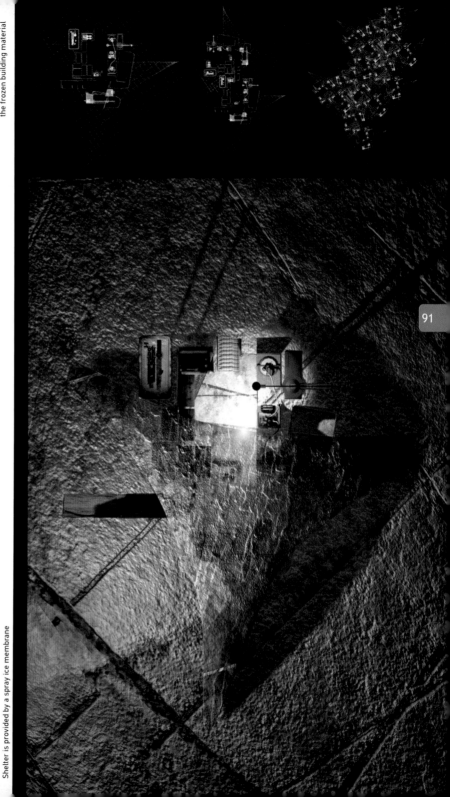

Ice camps develop in complexity and size over time as settlers combine and share resources to cope with the harsh environment and make better use of the frozen building material

Industrial and agricultural ice landscape. Fish drying fields and smoking kilns within ice sheet.

Aerial view of immature ice suburb. Early January

"Architecture is music in space, as if it were a frozen music"
Freidrich von Schelling. 'Philosphie der Kunst' (1803-1817)

Selected references:
"The Structure and Mechanical Behaviour of Ice" Schulson, Ernald M. (JOM, 51(2)1999)

"Ice Palaces" Anderes & Agranoff (Macmillan of Canada, 1983)

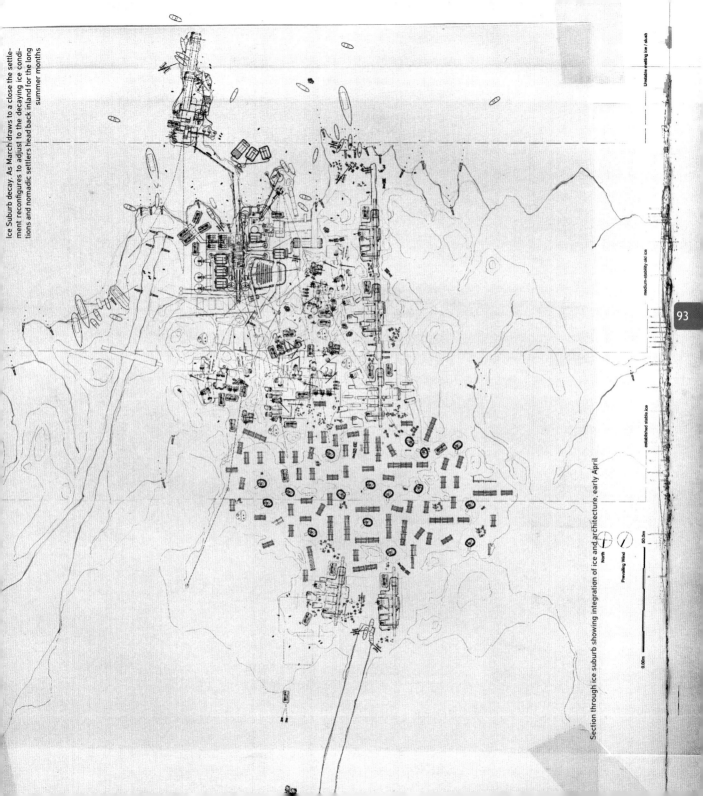

Ice Suburb decay. As March draws to a close the settlement reconfigures to adjust to the decaying ice conditions and nomadic settlers head back inland for the long summer months

Section through ice suburb showing integration of ice and architecture, early April

North

Prevailing Wind

0.0m   50.0m

established stable ice   medium-stability old ice   Unstable melting ice / slush

93

The Physical sciences are "nomothetic"; they seek to establish explanatory laws, and these laws are most useful and enlightening when they deal with relationships between the invisibles and intangibles underlying appearances. These invisibles and intangibles cannot be described, for they are not objects of immediate experience; they are known only by inferences drawn from immediate experiences on the level of ordinary appearance. Literature is not "nomothetic"

but "idiographic"; its concern
is not with regularities and
explanatory laws, but with
descriptions of appearances
and the discerned qualities of
objects perceived as wholes,
with judgments, comparisons
and discriminations, with
"inscapes" and essences, and
finally with the Istigkeit of
things, the Not-thought in
thoughts, the timeless Suchness
in an infinity of perpetual
perishings and perpetual
renewals.

dous Huxley Literature & Science. 1963 pub. Chatto&Windus. London (Page 10)

Decycle
dirty rotten architecture
Decycle Arquitectura en descomposición
Annika Schollin
London, U.K. 2001-2002

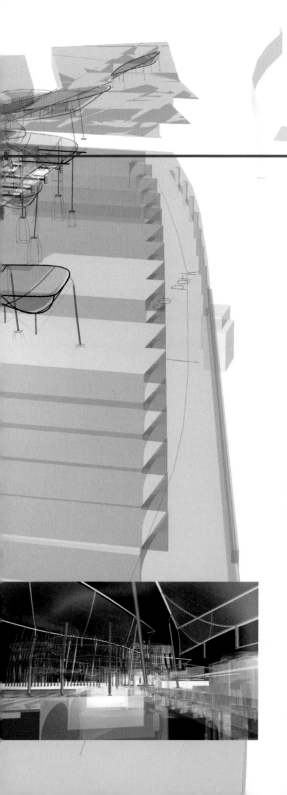

The reconfiguring market place clings to and scatters itself over the derelict goods yard in the manufacturing area of Brick Lane in London.

Architecture tends to deal with the 'new' without taking into account how buildings and structures are affected by external forces. Some materials respond to ageing very badly while others are enhanced by the effects of time.

The perpetually reconfiguring marketplace, placed in the ever-changing area of Brick Lane, London, explores themes of **decay resiliency**. The juxtaposition of old and new, clean and dirty, urban and jungle/vegetation creates the backdrop for an unpredictable journey through the site where things can fall apart in front of your eyes.

Using soft and hard materials (wood and steel) that respectively perished, disintegrated or resisted over time, a system was obtained in which **designing decay** became essential for the development of the marketplace as an overall organism.

Features for aggravating circumstances are implanted within the everlasting metal frame structure: **hydrocollectors**, **water-dispersing gutters** and **collectors of debris** create a cycle in which wood responds to its environment by decaying in an enhanced ratio of 2/3 years.

The cladding system and the joinery detailing promote rather than prevent the infestation of decay.

The stalls of the market are let to merchants on a 'it's yours till it falls down' basis, ensuring constant regeneration of the commercial range of the market.

When **material decomposition** of the individual stalls starts taking place, the appearance and texture of the wood will change, creating a protective green patina, later becoming structurally **unstable** through insect infestation.

Colonies of weed plants, intertwining the site, will parasite and ultimately take over wood structures. In the final stages the space will form ***micro-jungles*** within the urban structure. As materials go through the cycle of transformation, the building is no longer constant, instead it assimilates to the **scar of time** through its death and rebirth.

Celebrating decay as the organic inhabitants of the site begin to take over, weaving through, ambivalently undermining and reinforcing the built structure.

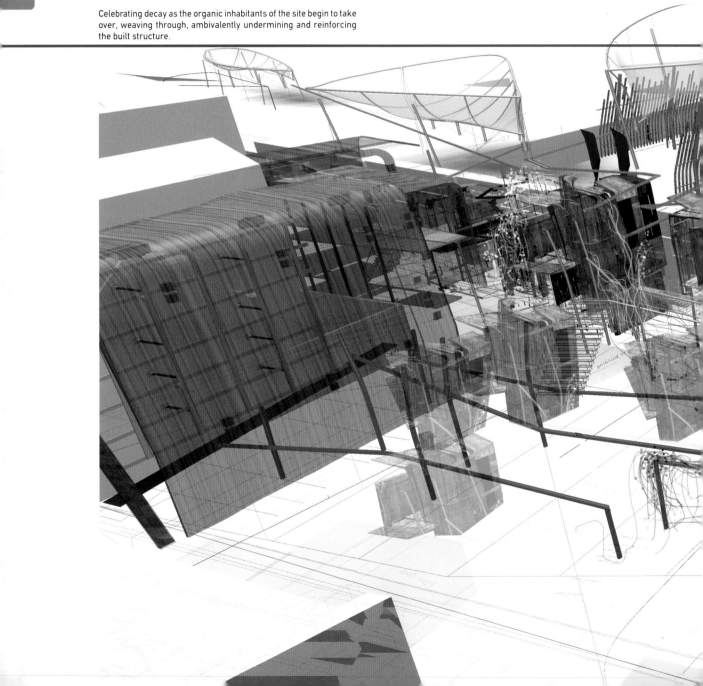

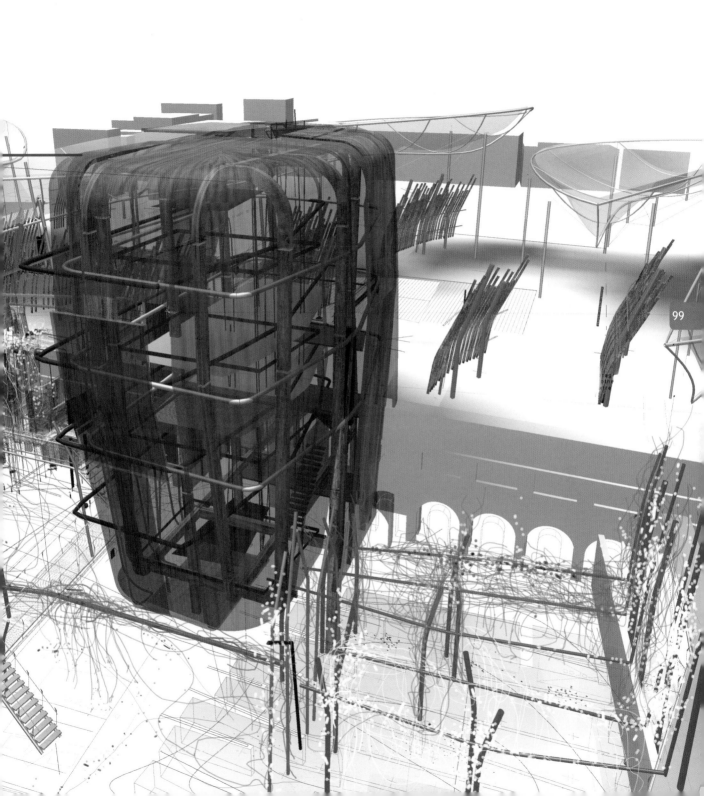

After the event: desolate and detached, the marketplace is reeking of rot and humidity in this intermediary stage of decycle.

Plan
1. Hydrocollectors
2. Water dispensing ducts
3. Wall of marketstalls
4. New, functional marketstall
5. Patinated, but still functional marketstall
6. Dilapidated, derelict marketstall
7. Timber workshop and private quarters for car penter who produces new elements to the market

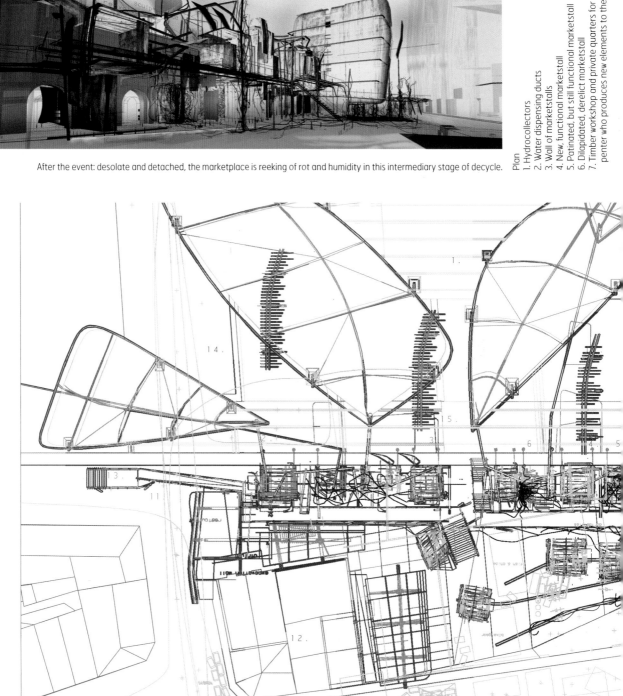

8. Intake of recycled wood
9. Weedpark/compost for old marketstalls
10. Structures for the dispersion of weed runners and climbers/ attachment for future wood membranes
11. Main entrance to the market from Brick lane facilitating bars and cafes
12. Community bank and flats
13. Access ramps to upper level of wall and to the top of Bishopsgate Goodsyard
14. Inside Bishopsgate: temporary canvas structures for stalls and storage
15. Top of Bishopsgate Goodsyard:
16. Area for car boot sales
17. Windbreakers
18. Footprint of existing market

The upper levels of the wall of stalls reached via ramps cutting through the site.

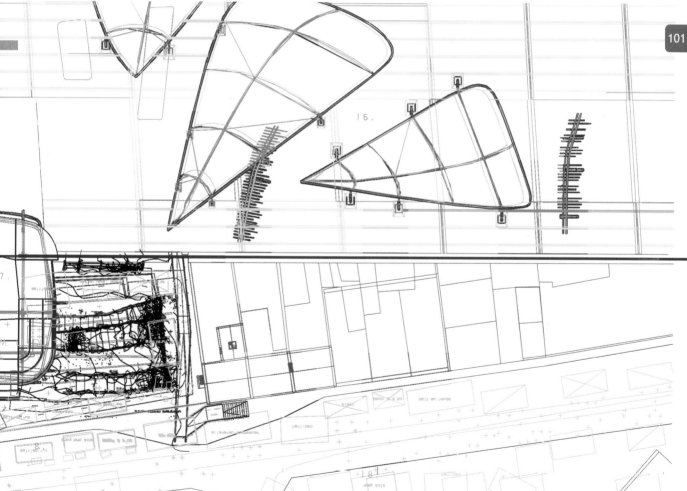

Elevation of wall of marketstalls

1. Bishopsgate Arcade (existing)
2. Hydro collectors
3. Water dispensing ducts
4. Hydraulic system adjusting hydro percolation
5. Outline of movement
6. Hydro percolating roof
7. Permanent metal skeleton
8. Short-lived vulnerable timber cladding
9. Cantilevered beam
10. Adjustable counterweight catering for changes in load and use of beams
11. Solar panels
12. Newly constructed stall
13. Debris after collapsed stall
14. Metal hinges
15. Hydro dispersing structural member
16. Salt vessels; microincisions of derogative saline water for detailed control of disintegration
17. Gutter
18. Empty space for future occupation
19. Tilting surface for maximum hydro detention
20. Ramps and stairs for upper level access
21. Workshop for the manufacture of wooden parts.
22. Storage of recycled wood

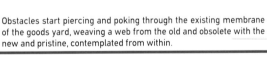

Obstacles start piercing and poking through the existing membrane of the goods yard, weaving a web from the old and obsolete with the new and pristine, contemplated from within.

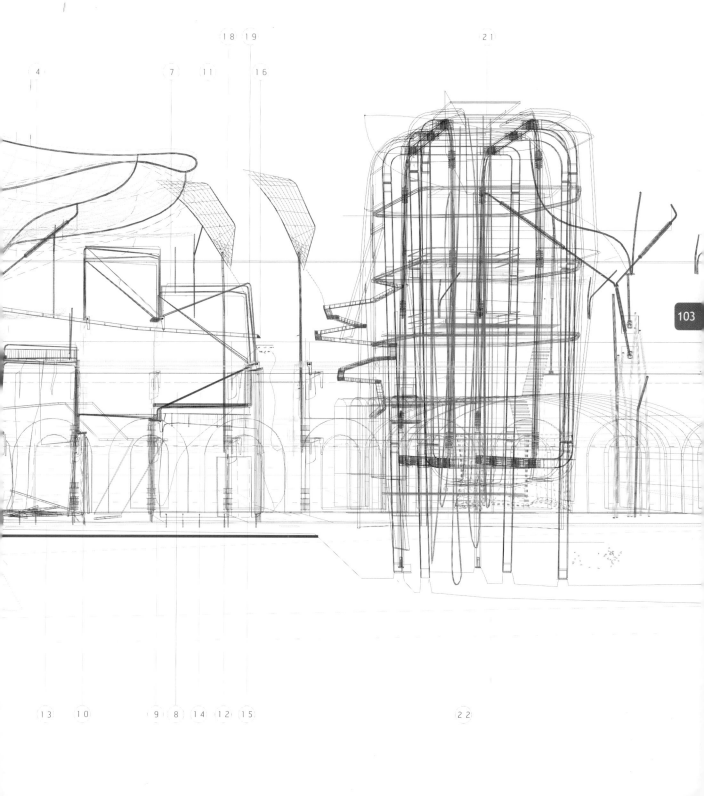

Nocturnal view of the market, seen from the Brick Lane entrance. The wooden structures are newly erected and the pods has just begun to harness water.

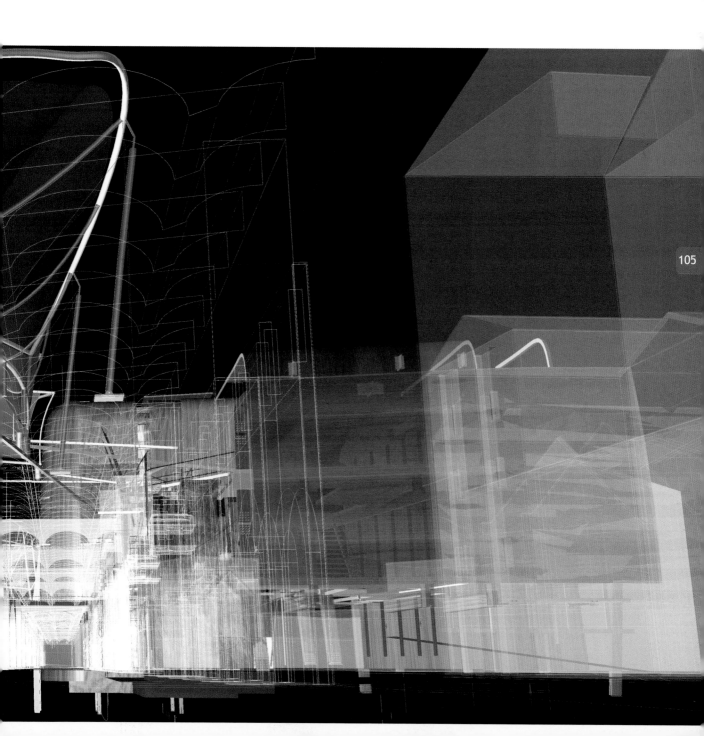

interdisciplinary week

Algaetecture
Helsinki, Finland, 2000-2001

Steve Pike

COMPONENT MANUFACTURE

The design and form of the monitor vessels and the transformation vessel was conscious of the eventual application of the component to an architectural intervention. Although high transparency acrylic was used to form the prototypes, the intended eventual material was glass. Adopting the principle of a form of 'vessel cladding', initial research considered 'blown glass' techniques as a possible means of achieving fluid volumes for bacteria containment. Observation of industrial blown glass manufacture at the Iittala factory in Finland and subsequent first hand experience at the workshops of the Royal College of Art in London, discounted this approach as one applicable to architectural construction. This was due to the necessary vessel scale, form consistency and the composition of the glass required.

A more viable approach would be the technology utilised when manufacturing automobile windshields or household items, such as televisions. 'Cerane' glass can be used to produce watertight vessels, similar to those used in television tubes. Current production methods allow for units up to two metres in length with angles formed between ninety and one hundred and eighty degrees. Perhaps a more appropriate model for production is the automobile industry where 'sag bending' is the most widely used process to create the curvilinear forms of windshields. The glass is supported along its edges and is heated until it sags under its own weight. The resulting shape is controlled by the precise delivery of heat in terms of amount and distribution across the surface. The vessel would consist of two halves, similar to the acrylic prototype, which raises the possibility of manufacturing the glass forms with 'bending moulds'. When the heated glass reaches its plastic deformation stage, at around 600°c depending on the type of the glass, these moulds can be applied to control the form. The advantage of this technique lies in the consistency of the shape and the wide variety of glass types that can be utilised. Laminated glass for increased strength can be used addressing such issues as windloads, as well as 'Low E' glass to reduce surface emissivity in vessels that may contain fragile cultures, sensitive to excessive sunlight.

The eventual manufactured vessels would have no substantial structural integrity beyond maintaining their own form under wind pressure and structural movement. Establishing a building envelope would rely upon a ribbed or meshed underlying structure, similar to many contemporary glazed canopies. Advances in linking computer modelling to component manufacture have enabled precise control of the length and girth of each structural bar and the angles of individual connecting node. Complex, fluid curvatures can be accurately plotted, producing the most efficient structure under the given criteria.

As the vessels have their own intrinsic function, exerting considerable influence on their form, they are not as flexible to shifts in geometry as simple glazing panels. For the more complicated parts of the intervention, where occupational clusters and communication routes collide, complex geometries result, precluding the application of rigid transformer vessels. In these instances, a flexible membrane would be a more suitable envelope. Transparent ETFE cushions provide an interesting precedent and a suitable solution. As a material, ETFE is highly appropriate for producing a flexible version of the transformer vessel, a 'green lung'. It is a fluoropolymer sheet providing transparency, resisting chemical and biological attack and allowing light to penetrate. As a building envelope, it is water tight, bears weather and ultraviolet exposure, diffuses glare and can achieve good fire resistance. Limitations are primarily concerned with its manufactured proportions. Standard material width is one and a half metres and at a thickness of 0.2 mm, the tearing strength is about 500N / 5cm, reducing the span of the load transmitting membranes. Its estimated life span is thirty years.

The Eden Project, by Nicholas Grimshaw and Partners is a contemporary example of a greenhouse. It is of interest for the nature of its external envelope, which consists of pockets of compressed air contained within transparent ETFE layers. The familiar 'soap bubble' geometry owing much to Fuller, though successful in creating uninterrupted volumes, is fairly limiting in flexibility of form. The dimensions of the air pockets are considerable, reaching diameters of eleven metres and a central thickness of two metres. Compared to glass they are light in weight, more energy efficient in manufacture and transmit greater levels of ultra violet. In the context of this study the principle of a multiple layered transparent envelope has great potential for developing a living membrane.

ETFE lends itself to the construction of pneumatic membrane structures. By tailoring the material, arranged in a cellular formation, fluid self-supporting envelopes could be achieved. A ribbed steel structure can be used to anchor the membrane and provide additional support. By alternating regions of compressed air cells and cavities for growth plane suspension, a soft envelope can be assembled that incorporates integral stability, translucency and transparency, lightness and mechanisms of air modification.

Pneumatic structures have a long and familiar relationship with architecture, but some of the more progressive investigations have taken place within the context of space inhabitation. The Advanced Development Office NASA has been progressing the technical specifications of inflatable habitation through the ISS TransHAB programme running from1997 to 2004. Designed as a habitation unit for the future Mars transit vehicle, it employs a pressurised inflatable shell. The lightweight transportability of this approach is appropriate to a project that must consider the escape of Earth's gravitational field. However, the numerous small objects, travelling at great speed, that are encountered in space pose a threat to the outer membrane. To solve the problem, 25mm wide kevlar straps were incorporated into the fabric, achieving new standards in durability.

"This system has been found in testing to resist impacts by a 17mm ball fired at 7km/s (15600mph or 25105kph)."
(Kronenburg, Robert, Portable Architecture (Architectural Press 2000) pg.158)

Although such high impact resistance is not necessary for the proposed Helsinki intervention, this demonstrates the current levels of material specification that can be applied, dispelling many of the traditional concerns over the stability of pneumatic constructions. Further research, regarding NASA's development of inflatable lenses, reflects the precision now achievable.

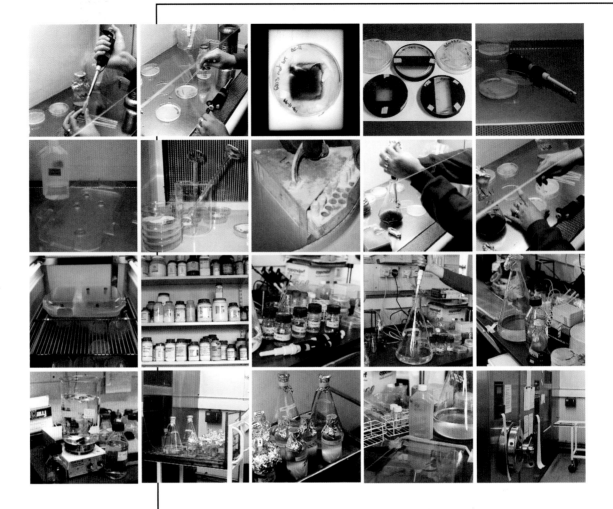

Utilising microorganisims and their inherent mechanisms in an architectural context raises the issue of control. The environmental conditions we present in terms of light, temperature, humidity and nutrition have marked effects upon their colonial behaviour. The inhibitors and facilitators we apply mark the difference between a valuable constructive material and an unrestricted colonisation operating to its own end.

The initial investigations undertaken were primarily concerned with the basic techniques of establishing and growing small colonies of cyanobacteria. Their purpose was largely as an introduction to the principles of arranging a sterile environment via a small petri-dish of agar growth medium, introducing a sample of bacteria, and providing the conditions to facilitate the growth of a colony. In general these are the most basic principles of microbiological practice, but the experience demonstrated the importance of environmental conditions when attempting to propagate a specific culture. Of the early investigations, the most meaningful was that which consisted of growing photosensitive bacteria in a petri-dish covered with a black card mask with a central square aperture. After a period of approximately two weeks the corresponding shape could clearly be seen as the area of colonial growth, demonstrating how light can be applied to influence the occupational behaviour of an appropriate bacteria. Issues of growth and control were only touched upon in these early investigations. The eventual outcomes were generally predictable and so devalued the information gained.

Interaction Vessel
The next experiment was designed to address a more complicated and less determined condition. The 'interaction vessel' provided a contained environment into which four different microorganisms were introduced. As a departure from the specific process of isolating one bacteria, this investigation attempted to draw parallels with the naturally occurring variety of microorganisms and the less predictable situation of multiple colonial occupation. Metaphorical comparisons regarding issues of territorial conquest, encounter and occupation are raised, as well as the direct observation of the colonial behaviour and eventual outcome. Cyanobacteria were employed again; 'Synechococcus 7942' that produces a vivid green field of growth and 'Fremyella Diphosyphon FD 7601' where cells are arranged in a filamentary formation, giving it a distinctly different occupational appearance. Both are 'phototropic', require a moist environment and profit from growing on a medium of agar and BG11. Fungi, a totally different category of microorganism, were introduced in the form of 'Alternaria Brassicicola' and 'Penicillium Digitatum'. They prefer a growth medium of potato dextrose agar but will also grow upon the BG11 medium. In addition, they produce spores utilising the flow of air to progress territorially. The standard containers commonly used for growth were no longer appropriate, so the arrangement and form of the interaction vessel had to be considered. Although the traditional materials of steel, clear glass and transparent plastic were employed for their ease of sterilisation and visual clarity, the vessel took its lead from the known characteristics of the organisms.

Essentially the vessel provided a horizontal plane of bacteria orientated growth medium, with the cyanobacteria introduced at either end. The fungi were located on the top of two glass 'sporangiophore', designed to mimic the component found in many fungi responsible for spore propagation. In an elevated position, in the air above the growth medium, the fungi could be agitated via the glass stems of the sporangiophores to encourage the release of spores. A cover enclosed the vessel, with the interior volume only punctured by two apertures. These were to allow for the measured application of a liquid inhibitor and a liquid facilitator as an additional means of control. The reasoning behind these elements was to explore the extent to which chemical control would effect the growth of the various colonies. Initially the facilitator was to consist of a glycerine and water solution to hydrate and provide 'fuel' for the growth; eventually only distilled water was added to prevent the material from dehydrating. The inhibitor was to be a fungal growth control such as TMV2 extract, a phytoalexin derived from groundnut leaves and a natural fungal growth restrictor. In practice, a weak solution of bleach was used as a more general means of limiting colonial development.

All of the components of the interaction vessel were sterilised using a 70% ethanol solution, before the growth medium was introduced in a liquid form. The cyanobacteria were introduced once the agar had cooled and set. After two days, allowing the bacteria time to consolidate, the fungi were added, located upon discs of potato dextrose agar. The entire vessel was sealed with a sterile elastic tape, before being placed in an incubator for approximately two weeks. The inhibitor and facilitator were added twice during this period, utilising only a few drops of each.

From the point of view of a microbiologist, considering the strict criteria required for proper scientific investigation, this experiment could hardly be considered accurately conclusive. Nevertheless, observation of how the microorganisms negotiated and occupied the environment proved interesting. The fungi, in particular the Penicillium Digitatum, were successful in their sporation, starting new colonies on the horizontal media below. The airborne route from elevated source to new outpost clearly indicated. The two cyanobacteria colonies proliligated, the Synechococcus occupying about twenty five percent of the surface with almost complete exception of all other growth; whereas the Fremyella Diphosyphon appeared to co-exist with other bacteria and fungi alike. The regions relative to the introduction of facilitator and inhibitor were demonstratively contrasting. The area influenced by the facilitator was rich in cyanobacteria growth, whereas the corresponding area for the inhibitor was sparsely occupied. The interaction vessel was successful in demonstrating the ability of differing microorganisms to coexist, the potential of certain applied controls to modify the colonial occupation, and the relation between the mechanisms of the microorganisms and the design of their environment.

Composition of BG11 for Synechocystis 6803

To make 1 litre of BG11 add the following stocks and autoclave:

X 100 Bg 11 stock	10 ml
Trace elements	1 ml
Iron stock	1 ml
Phosphate stock	1 ml
$Na_2 CO_3$ stock	1 ml
TES buffer	10 ml
Sodium Thiosulphate (solid)	3 g
1M $NaHCO_2$	10 ml

Rinse all glassware before use. Add filter-sterilised glucose (from 2M stock, to 5mM) if needed.

Stock solutions made as follows:

1 litre of x 100 Bg11 stock

$NaNO_3$	149.6 g
$MgSO_4.7H_2O$	7.49 g
$CaCl_2$	3.60 g
Citric acid	0.60 g
Na_2EDTA	1.12 ml of 0.25M solution @pH 8.0

100 ml of trace elements

H_3BO_3	0.286 g
$MnCl_2 4H_2O$	0.181 g
$ZnSO_4 7H_2O$	0.022 g
$Na_2MoO_4 2H_2O$	0.039 g
$Co(NO_3)_2 6H_2O$	0.005 g
$CuSO_4 5H_2O$	0.008 g

100 ml of iron stock

0.6 g of ferric citrate or 1.11 g of ferric ammonium citrate

100 ml of phosphate stock

3.05 g of $K_2 HPO_4$

100ml of $Na_2 CO_3$

2.0 g of $Na_2 CO_3$

TES Buffer

22.9 g of TES @pH 8.2

Agar:
Make double strength BG11 and 3% agar, then mix before pouring plates.

Growth:
Cells in liquid culture are grown shaking (not overly fast) @ 30°c.
Plates grown in illuminated incubator @ 30°c
(put beaker of dH_2O in incubator to maintain humidity)

Autoclave:
@ 121°c for 15 mins.

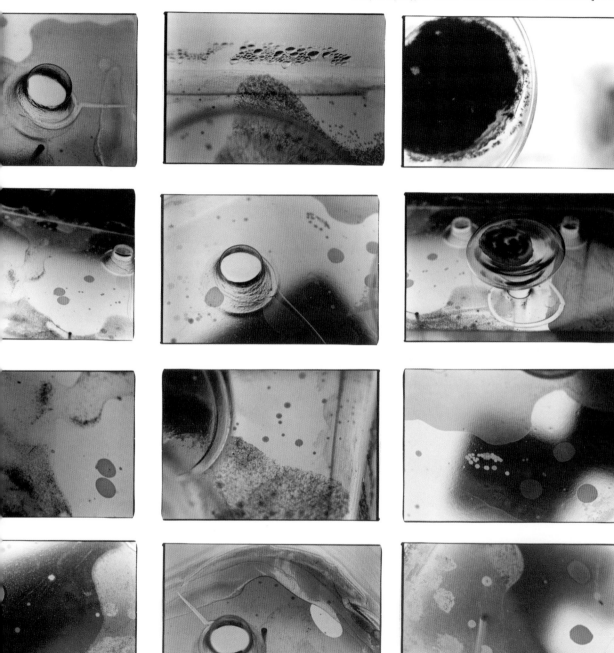

5 Interaction vessels incorporating vitreous sporangiophores and facilitator / inhibitor nodes.
Introduced Cyanobacteria and fungi: - Synechococcus 7942
Fremyella Diphosyphon FD 7601 - Alternaria Brassicicola - Penicillium Digitatum.

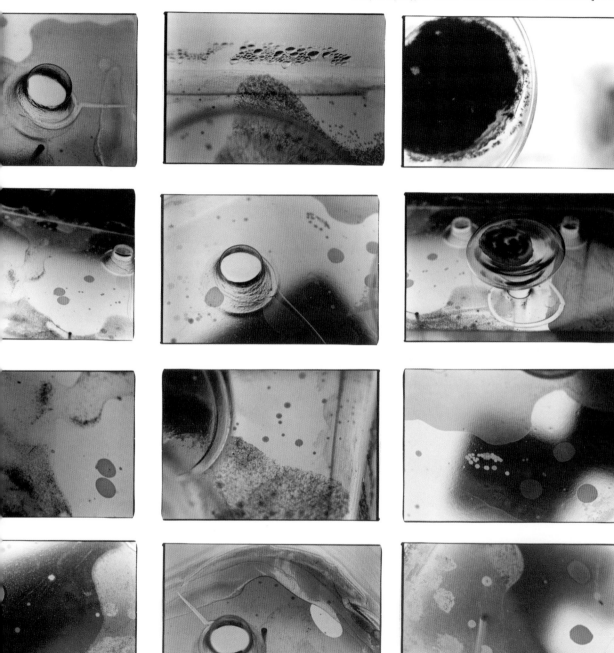

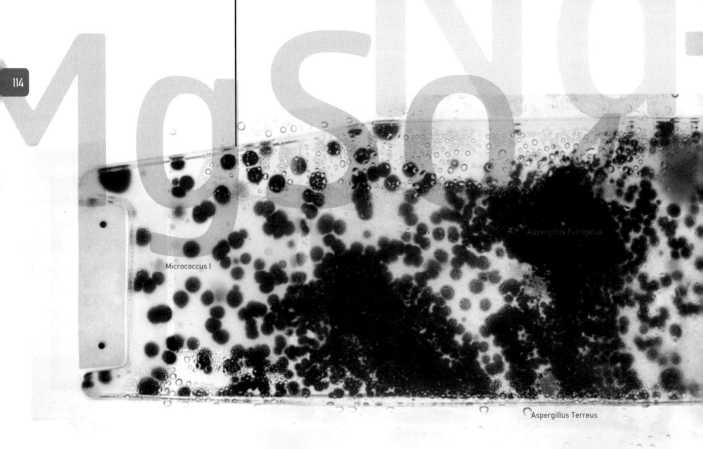

Micrococcus I

Aspergillus Fumigatus

Aspergillus Terreus

ALGAETECTURE.

Abundant, anonymous populations of microorganisms share the space we occupy. Through normal perception we cannot see them or detect their prolific microbial activity. Though they constantly surround us, they are invisible at their microscopic scale. By capturing and propagating microbes on a suitable growth medium, we can reveal their accumulated presence. As the colonies develop, the multiplicity of the individual organisms makes the whole recognisable. A series of vessels were created establishing the principles of control and growth manipulation. Interaction Vessels, Monitor Vessels and Transformer Vessels explore the forms and conditions required to facilitate or inhibit microbial behaviour. Vertical mobile growth,

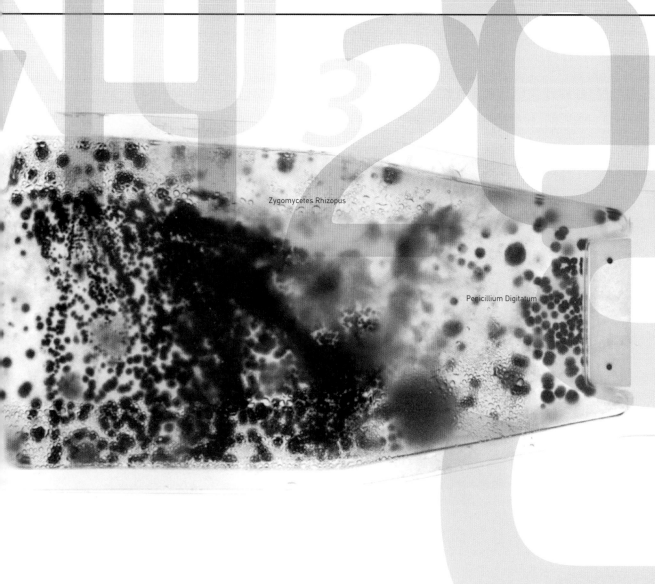

Zygomycetes Rhizopus

Penicillium Digitatum

environment response and colony regulation are addressed in order to determine potential value as an architectural component. Whilst resultant colonisation describes metaphorical parallels to human occupation.

The Helsinki algaetectural intervention presents an opportunity to engage and explore the human/microbe relationship. A new platform canopy to Helsinki Railway Station monitors the presence of environmental microorganisms by capturing, incubating and developing colonial growth. An associated Microbiological institute harnesses the mechanisms of cyanobacteria in the fabric of its construction, transforming carbon dioxide to oxygen, modifying the air of the Finnish capital. The composition and aesthetic of the intervention emerges and alters as it reacts to its non-sterile environment.

20

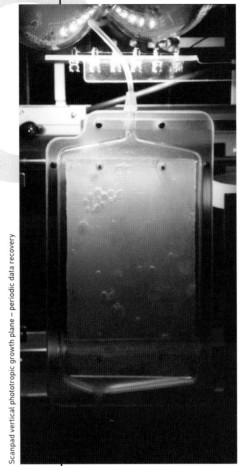

Scanpad vertical phototropic growth plane – periodic data recovery

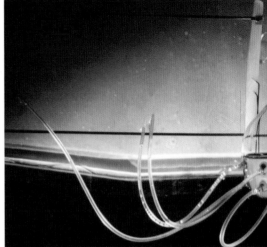

Monitor vessel growth facilitator.

Zygomycetes Rhizopus – Unit 20 monitor vessel.

Vertical colonisation apparatus.

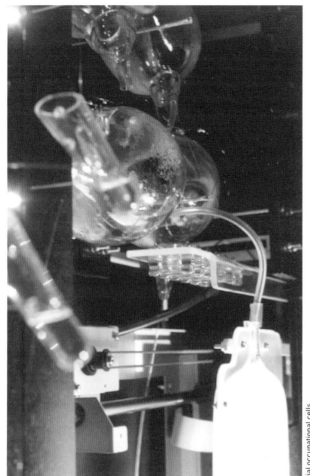

Vitreous growth facilitators and inhibitors.

Vitreous occupational chambers.

Solovial occupational cells.

Monitor vessel support infrastructure.

Vertical colonisation apparatus.

Suspended transformer vessel control mechanism.

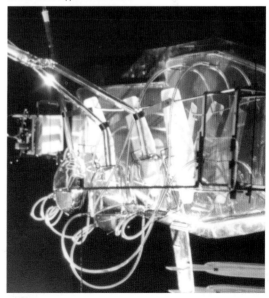

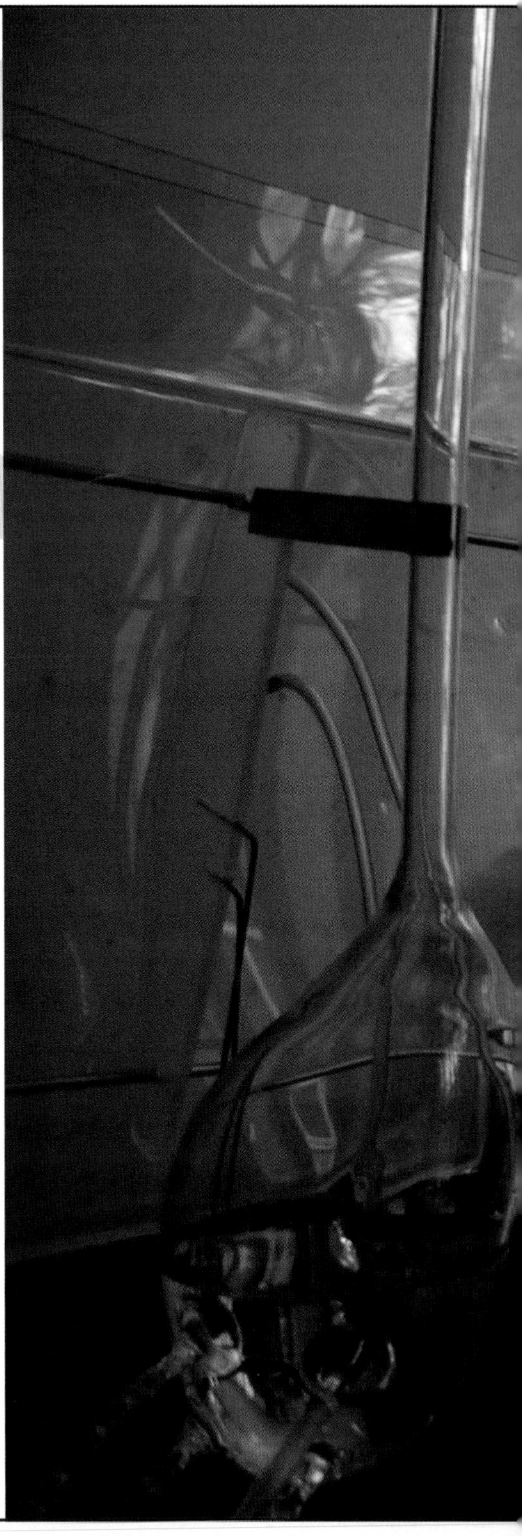

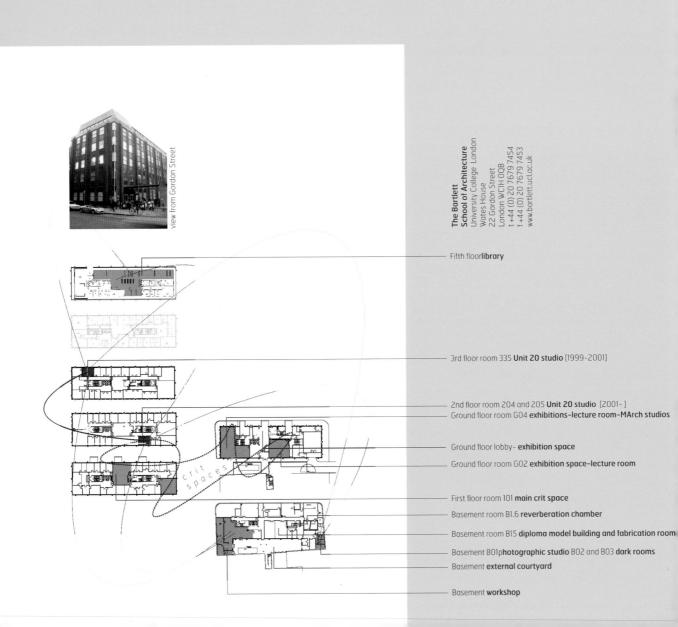

view from Gordon Street

**The Bartlett
School of Architecture**
University College London
Wates House
22 Gordon Street
London WC1H 0QB
t +44 (0) 20 7679 7454
f +44 (0) 20 7679 7453
www.bartlett.ucl.ac.uk

Fifth floor**library**

3rd floor room 335 **Unit 20 studio** [1999-2001]

2nd floor room 204 and 205 **Unit 20 studio** [2001-]
Ground floor room G04 **exhibitions-lecture room-MArch studios**

Ground floor lobby- **exhibition space**

Ground floor room G02 **exhibition space-lecture room**

First floor room 101 **main crit space**

Basement room B1.6 **reverberation chamber**

Basement room B15 **diploma model building and fabrication room**

Basement B01p**hotographic studio** B02 and B03 **dark rooms**

Basement **external courtyard**

Basement **workshop**

crit spaces

London latest street market

Mark Mueckenheim

London Urban farming

Uk, 2000-2001

Granja urbana Londres

Metropolitans have no attachment to the countryside. We do not know what we eat. The BSE crisis and the recent outbreak of foot and mouth disease has exposed that during the last few decades farming in the EU has transformed into a troubled industry. The need for agricultural goods and farmland increases. An average of 0.23 hectare of farmland per EU citizen [UK = 0.12 hectare] is the taillight to other industrialized nations and the world average of 0.35 hectare. 840 000 hectare of farmland is necessary to support the population of London.

Urban Farming is a project, addressing the above stated issues to bring farming into the urban fabric in order to create a dense and diverse environment, where the awareness of what we eat and our relationship to the nature of daily nourishment is more present. The existing Soho food market on Berwick Street, London is transformed into a future market, which is supplied through a food processing plant located in the adjacent Kemp House with a fish hatchery attached to its façade. For the construction specifically engineered composites are used to enable adjustments to the different stages within the process of preparing, storing and the distribution of food. Though the project form completely derives from functional constraints, the spectacle and beauty of a **24-hour market cycle** could potentially become an attraction of its own.

The skin of the shells, a composite material of glass fibres and a smart computer controlled resin, is capable of influencing their shape, so that food can be stored inside the skin.

the new market in operation seen at street level: the residential tower of the Kemp house with the fish hatchery attached to its façade is visible in the background

Pedestrian view of the market at Berwick street: market stands are lowered to street level

Interior of the food processing plant, which supplies the market during the nighttime

the site : Berwicks ctreet in Soho. unlike the surroundings, the street is not overtaken by tourist activities. It is a lively and functional London neighbourhood as the rest of Soho once was

volumetric site analysis: open spaces and voids within the urban fabric

open spaces and voids within the urban fabric

are ordered by certain boundary conditions which were observed on the site

the analysis gives a specific order in which to organise the later architectural intervention: the market

Berwick Street Market at night – a fish hatchery is implemented onto the façade of the Kemp house

planimetric view of three hatchery units

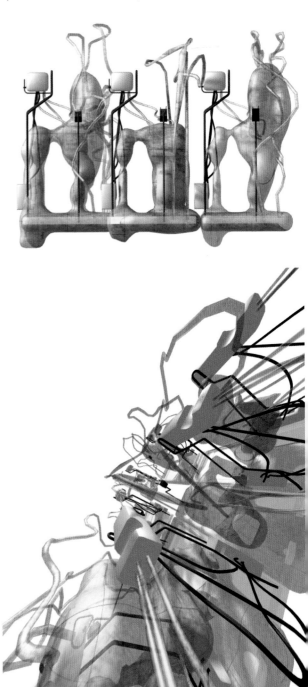

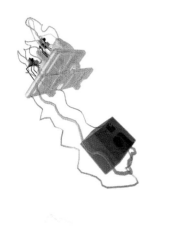

during a 24h market cycle, the components are performing an 'architectural ballet' which will add to the vibrant energy of the site, potentially becoming an attaction of its own.

details of single components of the fish hatcheries

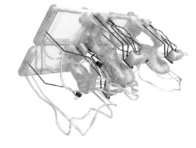

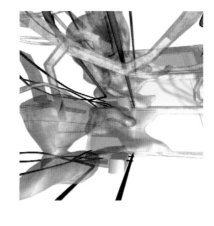

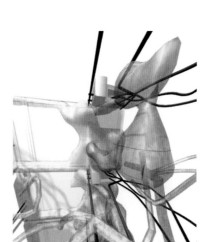

Façade details

perspective section through façade of Kemp House

Perspective section through market stands

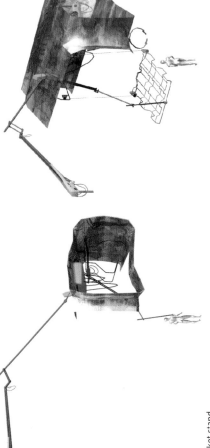

single market stand

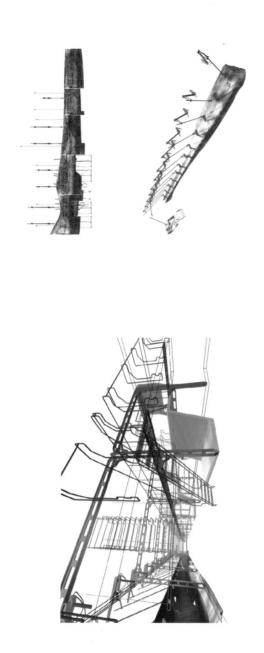

food processing facility inside Kemp House

The skin of the shells: it consists of a composite material which is composed of smart computer controlled resin and glass fibres capable of influencing the shape of the shells, so that food can be stored inside the skin.

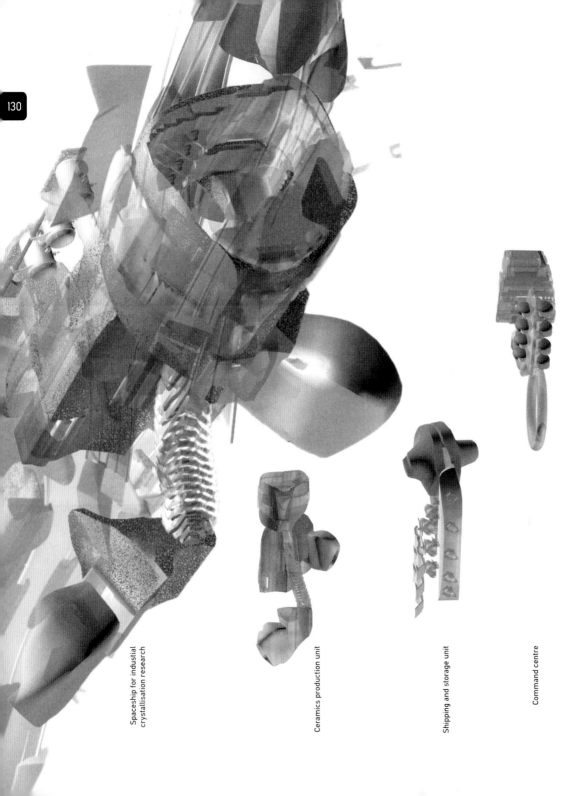

2000-2001_Zoran Orescanin_S[ci] [o]rbital

Spaceship for industial
crystallisation research

Ceramics production unit

Shipping and storage unit

Command centre

Laboratory for biological studies.

Material science is on the brink of a new era – the manipulation of materials at molecular level. The aim is to better understand the physical properties of materials like metal alloys, ceramics, plastics, or composites. However, there is one type of matter, which is embodied with more mystery than all others – proteins, the matter of life.

Proteins are the most complex molecular structures and are essential for biological functioning. Many of the drugs produced by the pharmaceutical industry are either proteins, or act by binding to proteins. They are essential for the further development of medical science.

Crystal growth or crystallisation is used to provide a single protein crystal that can be examined to determine it's structural properties. The most disadvantageous restriction to the crystal growth process is multi-seeded formation, meaning numerous small crystallites are formed instead of a single crystal. This is mainly due to convection caused by gravitational forces.

Lithography unit and energy generator

Protein synthesis unit

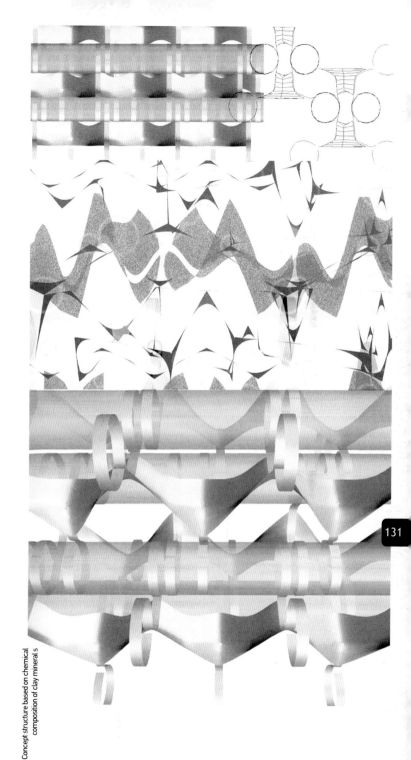

Concept structure based on chemical composition of clay minerals

131

In order to overcome this, experiments are undertaken in conditions of micro gravity. The success of these experiments has led scientists to believe that further development of crystal growth technology should be conducted in outer space as the **absence of gravity enhances crystal growth.**

The proposal:
Design of a spaceship for industrial crystallisation research purposes, which will be able to interact with its internal and external environment in a dynamic manner, aiming to provide researchers with facilities for investigation on protein crystal growth and their application in medical and material science.

The design criteria:
Structure of a spaceship is to fulfil several requirements:
It can absorb external stresses and be deformed to a certain degree.
Spaces created between structural systems are inhabitable.
Failure of one element within the system does not result in a collapse of the whole system.

Preliminary studies of:

Quantum dynamics

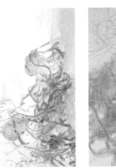

Microcosmic landscape

Electron fields' interaction

Crystal structure 1

Crystal structure 2

Differentiation of internal spaces is provided with a non-uniform structural system.

The model of an earthworm

was chosen as a starting point for the project, since it exhibits similar properties that are required by the brief such as its relationship to its surrounding environment. An earthworm belongs to a group of soft-bodied creatures, utilising a fluid skeleton both as a mechanism of locomotion and structure. The support it receives from the soil means that it is not dependent on having a rigid skeletal structure in order to deform and propagate through the soil. Orientation does not play a fundamental role in the morphology of an earthworm; just as in space, gravity is not an issue.

Furthermore, an earthworm is composed of self-sustainable units which are able to operate independently if split apart. A segmented body also results in a highly integrated structure with adequate amount of connective tissue.

Spaceship: production units and structural elements

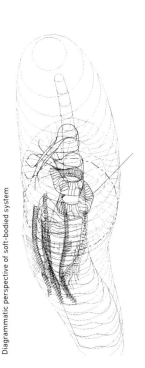

Diagrammatic section of soft-bodied system

133

Diagrammatic perspective of soft-bodied system

The architectural design requires modification of the earthworm model and the development of a system that will provide for limited flexibility of the spaceship body. However, the design is to maintain structural integrity and a degree of connectedness between constituent elements as its main objective.

The network pattern of clay crystal structure was chosen as a source of geometric principles that govern the structural system of the spaceship. The position of atoms is fixed within a crystal lattice, but the relationship between atoms is not rigid as they oscillate relative to each other. In a similar manner the structural elements of a spaceship should be in a defined, yet loose, position in respect to each other. Andalusite clay crystals are used as a structural matrix for insertion into the spaceship body. Andalusite is an alumino-silicate with separate SiO4 groups (island structure) in which aluminium atoms are in the centre and at the corners of the unite cells. This configuration of the unite cell was particularly suitable for the cross-section of the spaceship, because it has a well-defined core of the cell – an aluminium atom that is in connection with six oxygen atoms. It is also important that the pattern profile repeats itself along the z-axis.

The appropriation of the earthworm morphology and the crystal pattern was principally for functional reasons. The crystal structure of andalusite has been applied at a diagrammatic level and has served as a generator for the development of spatial organisation.

Spaceship: Interior view of protein synthesis unit

Longitudinal section through space vessel

Cross-section through space vessel

Generation of section profiles

Extraction of intersection zones

Extraction of intersection zones between chambers

Plate structure

Selected References

"The Locomotion of Soft-Bodied Animals" Trueman, E.R (Edward Arnold, 1975)

"The Chemistry & Physics of Clays" Grimshaw, R.W (Jon Wiley & Sons, 1971)

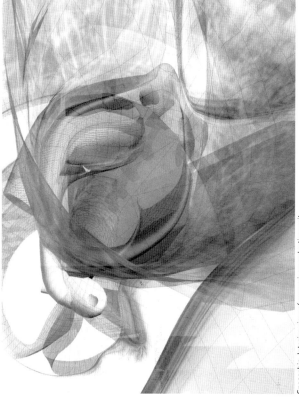

Spaceship: Interior view of ceramics production unit

Interlocking of chambers

View of cantilever from below, showing human powered vehicles plugging into building. Stationary, the vehicles allow a team of people to unfold a retractable cafe roof.

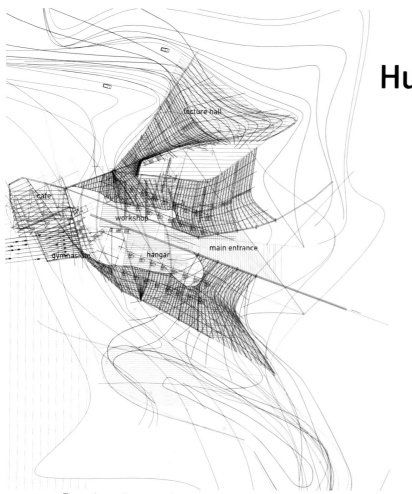

lecture hall

café

workshop

gymnasium

hangar

main entrance

James Foster
Human Power Plant
planta de energía humana
Missouri, U. S. A
2001-2002

The major project stems from an investigation into the potential power of the human body. Set on a swamp between the borders of the Missouri and Texas States, the building is the home for the International Human Powered Vehicle Association [IHPVA]. It provides enthusiasts with facilities to manufacture, research and test various types of human powered vehicles [including aeroplanes, hydrofoils, submarines and highly streamlined recumbent bicycles].

The centre is a truly public building intended as an educational demonstration project addressing issues on energy consumption.

The building is as far as possible reconfigurable and adjustable by the human hand, the café roof for example can be unfolded, but only by a team of people pedalling recumbent vehicles, which plug into the building becoming static energy generators.

Ventilation is mechanical with oscillating punkah fans driven by movement generated in the gymnasium. Lightweight human powered aeroplanes are craned onto the rooftop take off platform using human driven block and pulley systems. Within the building, piezoelectric stair treads generate enough electrical power to illuminate the route to the next level.

The scheme is intended to harvest energy from its occupants whilst they go about their daily tasks; these ideas require use of lightweight engineering and efficient mechanism design.
The building structure is complex, the hangar space is sculpted out of the landscape morphing into a large cantilever over the water which allows the café space to benefit from the dramatic, sinister panoramic view.

138

Preliminary studies of 'fibrespace'.
Investigative model and drawings that demonstrate how the physiology of human muscle fibres can influence the design of energy transfer devices.

THREE POINT LINKAGES ALLOW TRANSMISSION OF MOVEMEN
BETWEEN FIBRES. DISTANCE MOVED CAN BE MULTIPLIED FRO
ONE FIBRE TO ANOTHER

MECHANICAL ADJUSTERS ALLOW
RECONFIGURATION OF FIBRES

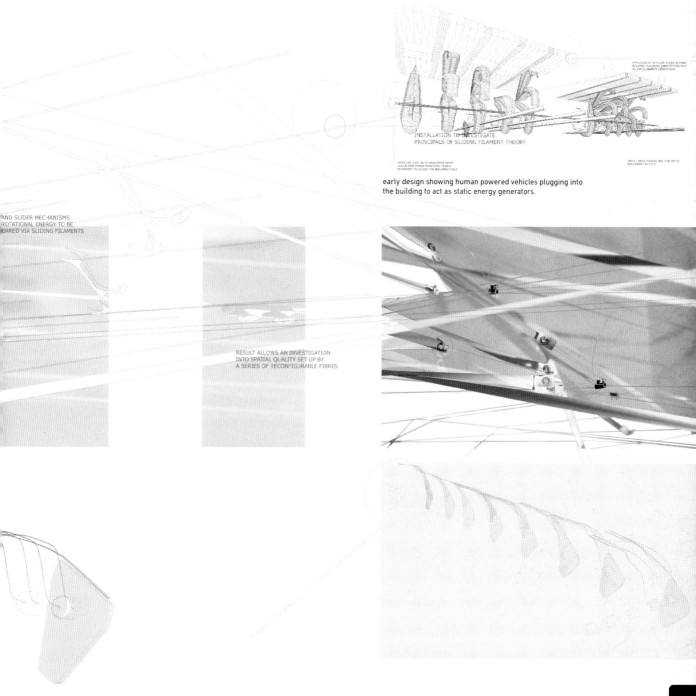

INSTALLATION TO INVESTIGATE
PRINCIPALS OF SLIDING FILAMENT THEORY

early design showing human powered vehicles plugging into
the building to act as static energy generators.

AND SLIDER MECHANISMS
ROTATIONAL ENERGY TO BE
ERRED VIA SLIDING FILAMENTS

RESULT ALLOWS AN INVESTIGATION
INTO SPATIAL QUALITY SET UP BY
A SERIES OF RECONFIGURABLE FIBRES

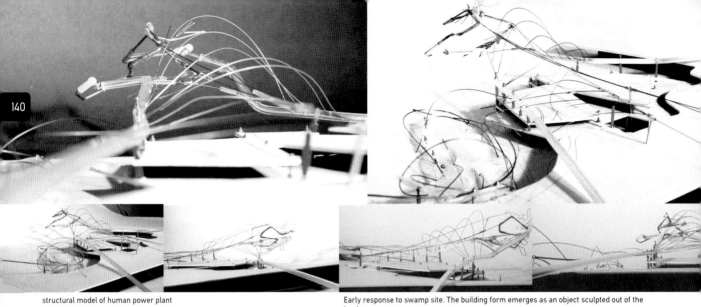

structural model of human power plant

Early response to swamp site. The building form emerges as an object sculpted out of the landscape.

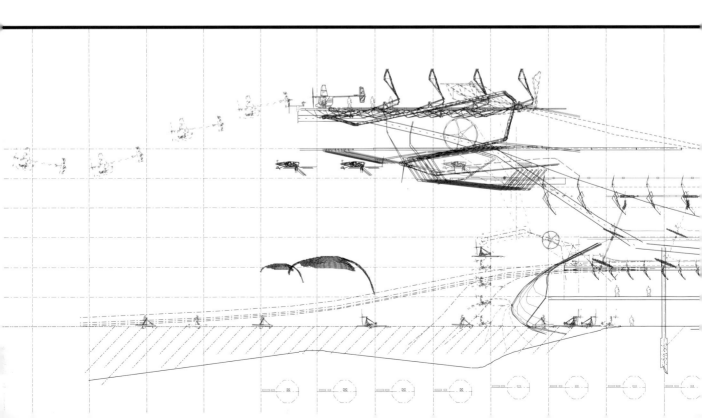

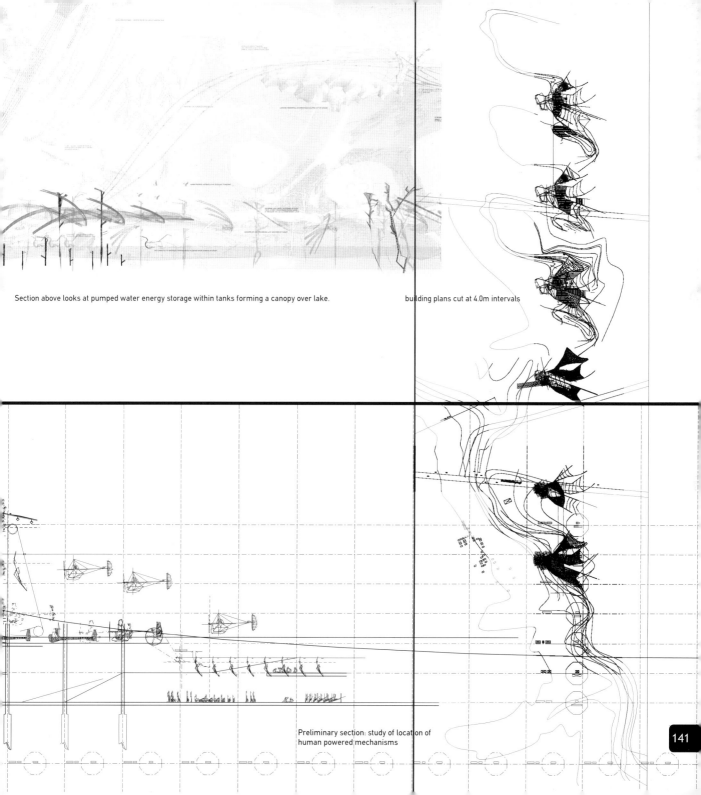

Section above looks at pumped water energy storage within tanks forming a canopy over lake.

building plans cut at 4.0m intervals

Preliminary section: study of location of
human powered mechanisms

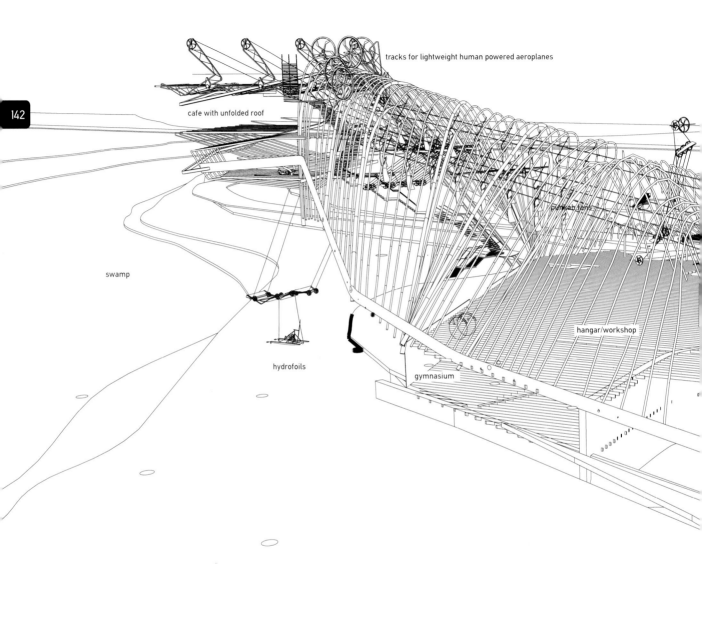

tracks for lightweight human powered aeroplanes

cafe with unfolded roof

swamp

hydrofoils

punkab jans

hangar/workshop

gymnasium

External perspective showing structural and mechanical systems with cafe and human powered vehicle tracks

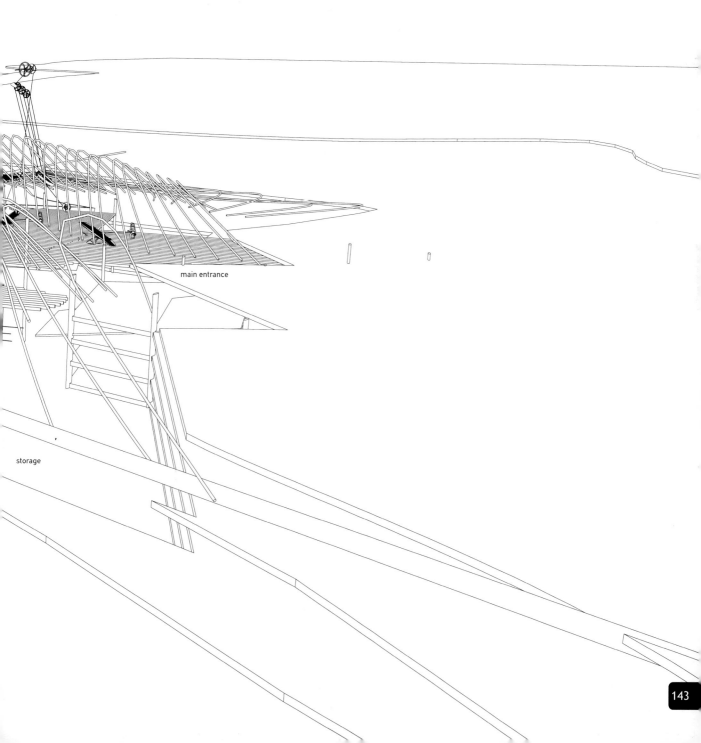

main entrance

storage

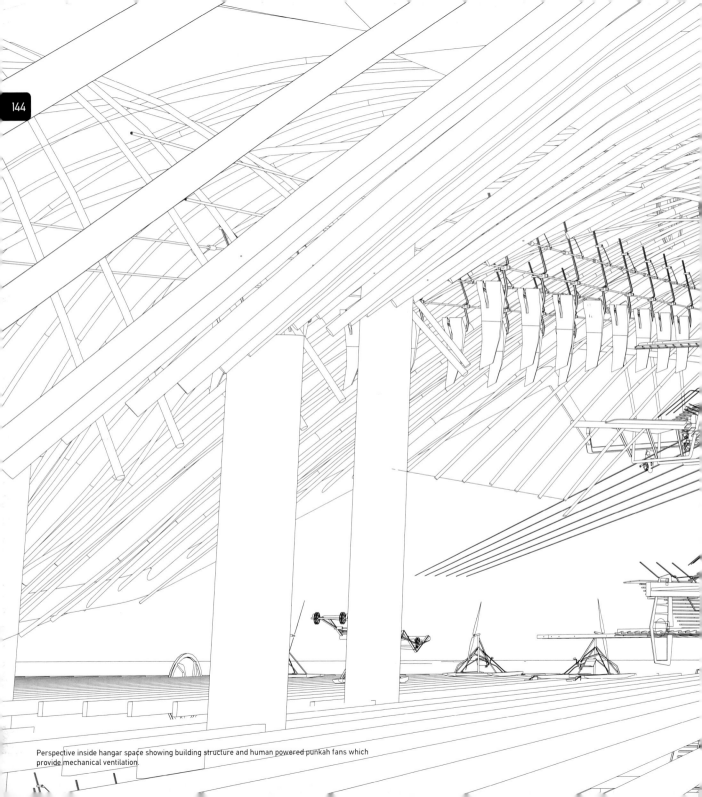

Perspective inside hangar space showing building structure and human powered punkah fans which provide mechanical ventilation.

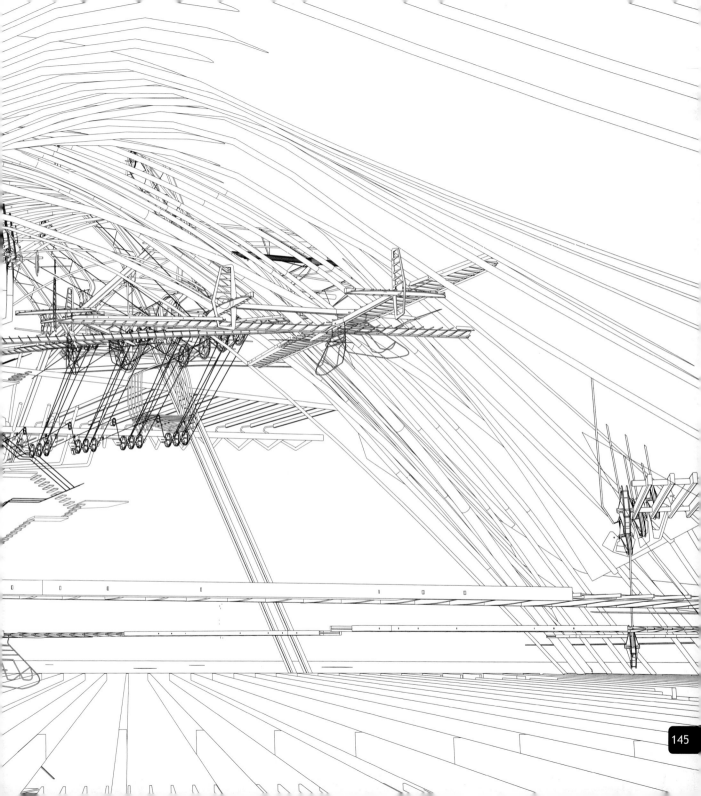

Skyline of Frank O.Gehry´s Guggenheim Museum in Bilbao in November 1999

BILBAO

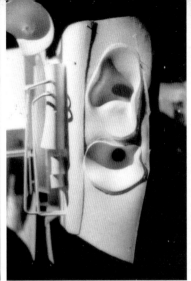

Jens Ritter
1999 - 2000

acoustic wind membrane

The Acoustic Wind Membrane is situated between the Old City of Bilbao and the end of the river Bilboko on a mountain plateau 300m above sea level. Strong winds are constantly blowing from the sea onto the mainland. The structure is located in this free flowing air stream and consists of an institute for the investigation and analysis of wind properties and an interactive public air-centre which lets people experience the dramatic wind induced architecture.

A flexible sensitive membrane about 30m by 60m is exposed to the airflow and acts as a layer for measurements and also guides air into the building. Sheltered behind this skin, laboratory workstations are positioned within the main structure. The public air-centre utilises both natural wind (exposed areas) and controlled airflow (sheltered areas).

Changing properties, density of air and the variety of natural wind patterns formed in the process, define the architectural shape. Flexible materials such as membranes, strings and cables react to the variable air movement, creating visible and physical spatial responses to invisible moving matter.

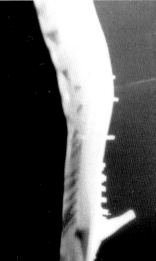
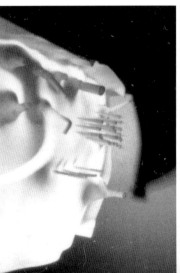

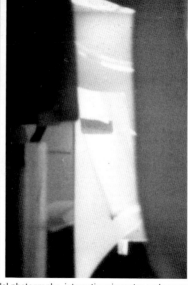

model photographs: interactive air centre and research laboratories within the structure

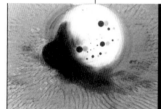

preliminary studies: experiement with mixed fluids

model photographs: soft skin with different aperture air sensible

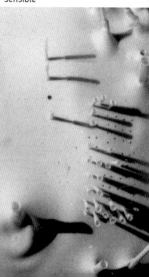

model photographs:soft sensitive skin of interactive air
centre and research laboratories within the structure

model photographs:interactive air centre
and research laboratories within the
structure

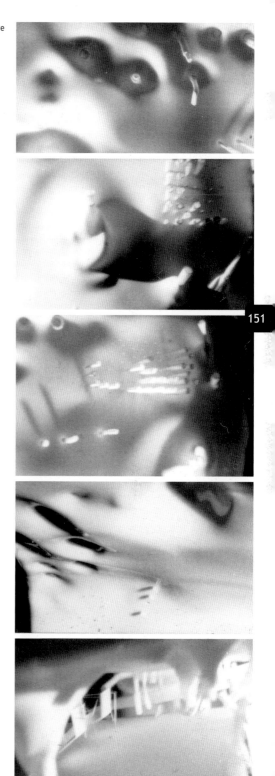

151

Perspective section through building along the Chicago River

CHICAGO
Living Propagation

V i d a   m u l t i p l i c a d a

R o b e r t   M a r i n u s   G r i n d l e y

2 0 0 1 - 2 0 0 2

Last year he made
a wall between their houses
a strong wall, solid and dependable
On her side she planted honey suckle
He choose to keep his plain, but she can see
where small things
have seeded in the cracks; moss
white stonecrop
and ivy-leaved toadflax

Jennifer Brice.
Extract from a poem titled Working In The Cracks Between, Brice, Jennifer,
Working in the Cracks Between (Buxton, Aquila Poetry (c) 1989)

A study of crack propagation formed the conceptual beginnings of the design project. The crack was seen as an opportunity, not a problem. Cracks can create openings for plants to grow, for shelter and refuge, for light to escape through and consequently for **manipulative transparency** to occur.

The site along the Chicago River was chosen for the design project because of the similarities it shared with the early conceptual work. The impact of the Chicago city grid has had a 'straightening' effect on the once winding path of the Chicago river. However the existence of the river has, in turn, distorted America's best example of a perfectly gridded city. This tense relationship between river and grid yields the site for the design project.

Suburban family housing is introduced to the narrow site along the river. This **urban crack** provides an opportunity for something new to seed and take root in the glassy-smooth, corporate and commercial downtown area.

The inherent repetition of the housing units with extensive garden areas is celebrated but experiences distortions due to the piercing path of the public route which runs along the length of the scheme. Three mobile pedestrian bridges are introduced along the river connecting both margins together and providing access to the public route along the riverside.

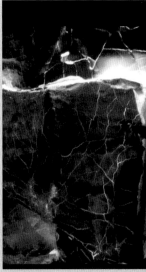

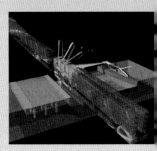

Concept model investigating crack formation on building façades

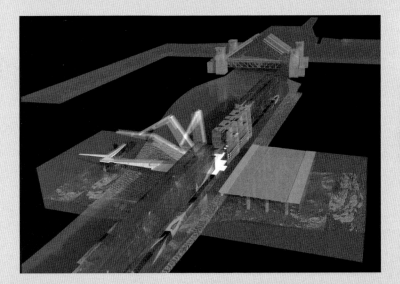

view of living propagation on the river

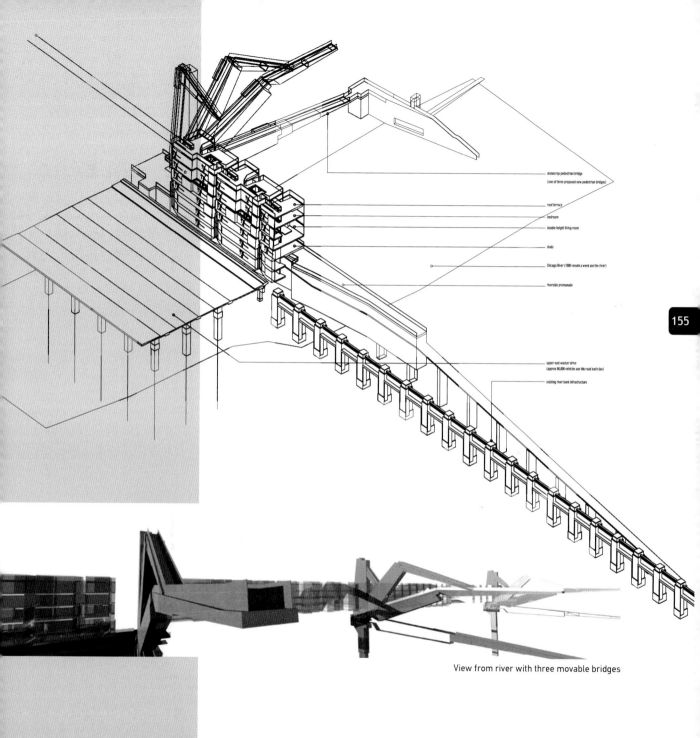

stonecrop pedestrian bridge
(one of three proposed new pedestrian bridges)

roof terrace

bedroom

double height living room

study

Chicago River (1000 vessels a week use the river)

riverside promenade

upper east wacker drive
(approx 60,000 vehicles use this road each day)

existing river bank infrastructure

View from river with three movable bridges

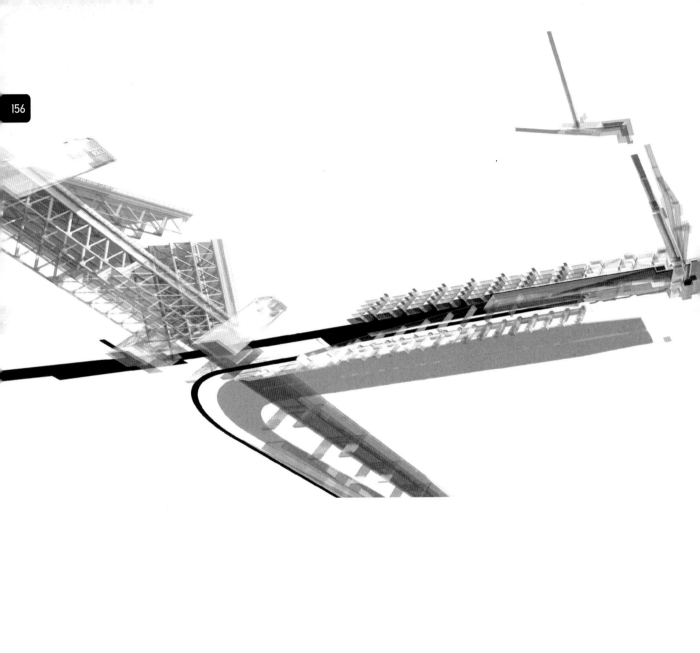

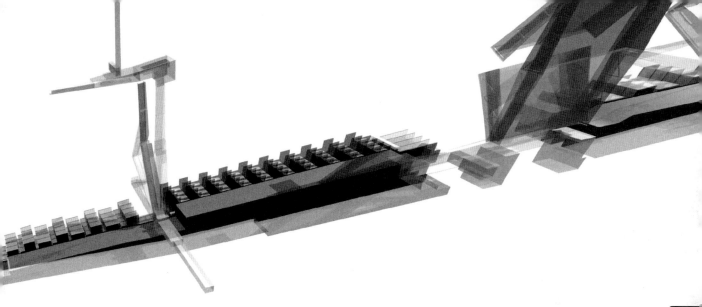

DYNAMIC TRANSPARENCY

Responsive Privacy For City Living

Downtown Chicago, a city with a river.
At one time Chicago boasted 52 moveable bridges, more than any other city in the world. Today the number is around 45 and still more than any other city . A sequence of them open to allow the taller of the 1000 vessels, that use the river each week, to pass from Michigan Lake along the river and into Chicago. These adjustable bridges form part of a simple dynamic system controlling the way those on the tall masted yachts experience the city.
The river breaks into the city and gently disrupts the geometry of the one of the purest and most developed examples of the Jeffersonian one mile grid that covers America . Occasionally the city responds directly to the curves of the river but history confirms that , along with the reversal of the flow, the watery bends too have been altered, straightened in most cases to stretch out exactly parallel to the East West roads .

Although most of the river passing through downtown Chicago has been tamed by the geometry of the grid its remaining inconvenient twists and bends generate the stretch of land that will act as the site for the architectural project. Currently unused, the site provides an opportunity for the design project to infiltrate the centre of the metropolis with housing and accommodation capable of sustaining family life. The site is 800 metres long and prises open the primarily corporate and commercial downtown area providing an opportunity to bring residential and family life to the banks of the river .

The search for privacy.
'Privacy is most urgently needed in the dwelling unit'
The major threat to privacy for the site in Chicago is the road. Upper East Wacker drive is used by 38,900 cars each day on its upper level . For two thirds of the site this road becomes two tiered with the lower level providing a route along the river for another 32,300 cars each day. There are 60,000 pedestrians that use the Wacker Drive sidewalks and 20 bus routes overlap along this road daily. These factors degrade the levels of privacy on two fronts, noise pollution and visual exposure. The visual exposure is expounded by the

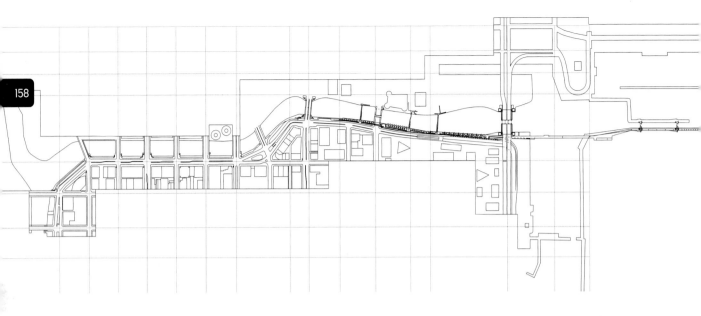

huge concentration of skyscrapers and high rise offices and those that work in them. The site is literally exposed to the eyes of millions of people.

The lack of density in suburban Chicago is probably the biggest factor in providing privacy necessary for the home environment. In fact it is a very simple equation, if you decrease density in terms of buildings, roads and people, you increase privacy, or privacy is proportional to distance from your neighbour.
The reality of putting distance into this equation is expensive, inconvenient, anti-social and breaks up communities. Endless outward expansion canÕt be and is not the answer. Therefore as soon as you increase the proximity of a threat to privacy a system needs to be introduced to protect against it. The house itself is such a system. But more than the house, land outside and other objects independent to the building are used to protect privacy.
The challenge is clear. If privacy is to be achieved on the downtown site in Chicago, with its excessive levels of traffic and dense population, the solution must lie in the adaptability and ability of the architecture to provide privacy. As land is at a premium devices in the landscape, as used in suburban Chicago, can not be implemented. Instead the solution must be generated by the architectural skin of the building. Specifically in the south facade.

Dynamic transparency
The adjective, dynamic, relates to motion, force or energy. Understanding the term dynamic is crucial to this investigation for it is a dynamic transparency that holds the key to a flexible building that is responsive to the acute need for privacy in the city. Just as the moveable bridges along the Chicago River open and close to control the flow of boats into the very heart of Chicago, the house along the river must to be granted the same privilege: a dynamic system to control what passes through, into and from the home.
The control of the opening through which vision and sight is made possible is the simplest way to adjust the level of transparency afforded. This can be done by either obstructing the opening with an opaque object or by altering the size of the opening.

An example for the first system is the opening and closing of a door or a shutter over a void in the architectural fabric. Early conceptual models using brittle plaster and light explored crack propagation and begin to represent the correlation between the growth in aperture size and transparency. The fractured surface generated was used as a conceptual proposal for the South facade of an early design to suggest a solution that responds to changing intensities of privacy [fig. 12]. This concept design represents the possibility for the facade to, in some way, mimic the ability of the crack to move across a surface, and control the way light passes through the skin.

Motion transparency

The following research looks at how transparency can be dependant on and controlled by light conditions, motion and aperture size. This information will begin to allow the concept aesthetic of a fractured surface to be applied as a plausible solution to controlling privacy and protecting the proposed homes through systems contained in the building skin.

There is an intense concentration of traffic all around the site. As stated earlier thousands of cars pass along Upper East Wacker Drive each day, not to mention the buses, pedestrians and the 1000 boats a week that cruise along the river. What is interesting here is the velocity and proximity of the moving traffic to the building in terms of the passengers perception of transparency as they move past the building. To have a hundred thousand people go pass your house at varying speeds each day can be disconcerting especially if you know they can see you. Therefore we are about to see how speed and locomotion can alter the perception of transparency. In psychological terms this phenomenon is defined as Motion Transparency.

A simple experiment in Motion Transparency can be carried out by placing your own hand in front of a computer monitor or television screen and moving it back and forth reasonably fast. The hand takes on the appearance that it has become transparent in most parts. The faster the hand moves the more transparent it seems to be. The hand in no way alters its physical structure but our perception of it certainly has.

The perception of transparency can directly influence the perception of privacy as we discussed previously. However the example of the moving hand illustrates the principle that physical transparency is not necessary for phenomenal transparency. Yet the perception of phenomenal transparency is often labile and can be switched on and off by an effort of will by the observer . However, having explored the basic principles in inducing the perception of transparency the question now is how can this be applied to architecture. Perhaps by manipulating systems in facades to generate the specific movements and other conditions such as luminance levels, an impression of depth and transparency can be 'switched on' where there is non. Unfortunately this straight forward translation does not deal directly with real transparency and therefore privacy can not actively be controlled.

Depth and transparency can be achieved in a single, flat, opaque plane. Many artists have achieved this in their work and psychologists are proving why it is possible. No doubt people will hang paintings in the homes that are proposed for the site in Chicago. The chosen image will no doubt offer them a window to the countryside or another world altogether, but the big downside to this notional perception of transparency is that it is not real transparency. No views of what really lies behind the opaque surface are given. Light does not actually pass through the opaque surface it is merely emitted or absorbed. Some experiments were done to explore the potentials of real motion transparency (RMT) in architecture.
Real motion transparency can be defined as either:

A   A surface in a fixed position that changes from opaque to transparent in response to the velocity of the observer.
B   A surface in a fixed position that increases in transparency when the observer gains velocity relative to it.
C   A surface that changes from opaque to transparent when it or its components are stimulated into motion, relative to the stationary observer.

Facing up to the city

Through these experiments we have discovered the importance of a balanced and adjustable relationship between privacy and transparency in the domestic home. When the provision of land is generous, as in the suburbs, complex levels of screening and filtering techniques control the way people see in and how those inside see out. Through a certain spatial depth that the site affords the home can create an environment that is protective and private. Therefore we have concluded that due to the unavailability of space, and due to the extreme proximity of the city to the homes proposed along the Chicago River, the relationship between transparency and privacy must be resolved within the limits of the architectural fabric. The solution must also respond to the different routines of people who use the building and to the different velocities of those who pass by and pose a threat to the privacy of those inside.

Strategic Proposals

The South facade bares the responsibility for the protection of the inhabitants. The reason for this is that the road and the tall office buildings are on the South side. The North side of the building faces just as many office buildings as the South accept here the river separates the two by a distance of between 50 and 100 metres. It is important that the residents are orientated towards the North and the river. A simple planning move strategically places all the noise and visually sensitive spaces with in the home, that is bedrooms, living, study, etc. to the North and opens them out towards the river. In effect the entire length of the South side of the building is designated as a service and circulation zone. In doing this, a visual and acoustic buffer zone is created.

A consequence of putting the service zone to the South is that the natural South light into the homes is greatly reduced or even cut off completely. However this not solely the result of the building plan as the surrounding skyscrapers already obstruct a large majority of South light as shown in the computer sun path analysis for Chicago. Further more the Chicago Plan for 2020 shows that future development of the land to the South will consequently render the majority of site in shadow. However East and West light into the scheme will be virtually unobstructed, even though the overall height of the building is only 40 metres, a fraction of the height of many of the nearby skyscrapers. This is made possible by the East West River that prevents other buildings from encroaching on the low angle sunlight. The design proposal hugs the riverbanks and harnesses this low angle sunlight by introducing openings along the entire length of the building that act as low angle light wells.

To combat visual and to some extent acoustic invasion into from the road and pavements the building is raised up 2.5 metres from road level and 4 metres from river level. This has three benefits; firstly the relationship of the lower level homes to the road is staggered, therefor reducing its impact. Secondly the building will not obstruct the view of the river from street level and thirdly the riverbank under the building is kept free for public use. It is a design intention to reinstate a relationship with the waters edge by introducing a public route in this area.

The relationship of resident and the river is a very important one and will be used as one of the main attractions to persuade suburban fami

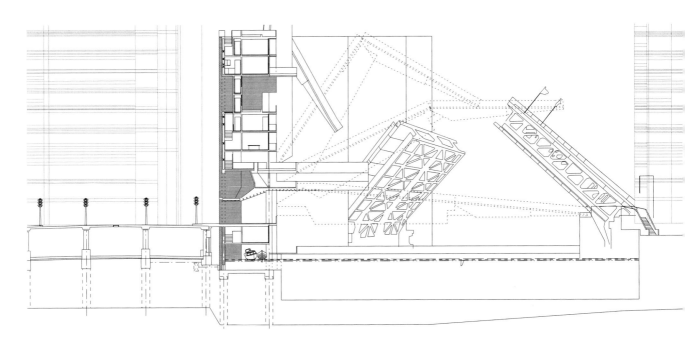

lies to reconsider the city centre site as a suitable and desirable place to live. A visual relationship has been established in the planning of the individual homes that open out towards the river. However the road currently destroys the riverside as a place to walk along and enjoy. As stated previously it is the intention that the passers by and road users are able to have visual contact with the river. If the building was to cut this off a large stretch of river would be hijacked from the collective conscience of Chicago. However, in elevating the building to allow this visual relationship with river, there is a negative effect on those who wish to use the riverside as a leisure activity. Perhaps more importantly the ability of the building to act as an acoustic barrier is breached when it is elevated to allow the visual connection.

The solution must be obtained by introducing a filter that responds to different and conflicting levels of transparency.

The public route is celebrated through the design of the south facade. Here the intention is to allow transparency from the viewpoint of those situated in the adjacent buildings to the South but to maintain an opaque surface from those using the public route through the building, thus focusing them towards the river and heightening the experience of being removed from the city. Using opaque discs, such as those used in experiment two that are fixed to the south side of a transparent screen. The discs are rotated by the wind to induce motion transparency. This produces a fluctuating transparency in the facade that follows the public route through the scheme.

The experiments in Real Motion Transparency began to quantify the conditions necessary for an opaque screen to be perceived as transparent when traveling at speed. This work helped approximate a design for a screen placed at road level that would seem transparent to the road users but opaque to those on the other side, enjoying the river and traveling at a much slower speed. The scope of these experiments was limited to the relationship between aperture size and velocity necessary for transparency. There is potential for more exploration into the other factors such as:
> aperture shape
> colour combinations
> angle of approach
> scale of aperture

A fuller understanding of all these factors would have allowed the experiments to be more comparable to the reality of East Wacker Drive.

Many of the privacy issues posed by the proximity of the new building to the road and the city were resolved in the strategic design of the plan. The service zone was crucial to establishing a visual and acoustic buffer. The location of this buffer zone was justified on the South side of the scheme because of the unusually low amount of South light available due to the existing and proposed skyscrapers. As a result the residents are orientated northward which, although thermally not ideal, does allow unobstructed East West views to the river and of the sunrise and sunset over Chicago.

Watertank at the Fluid Mechanics Labora

vil Engineering Department, UCL

interdisciplinary work

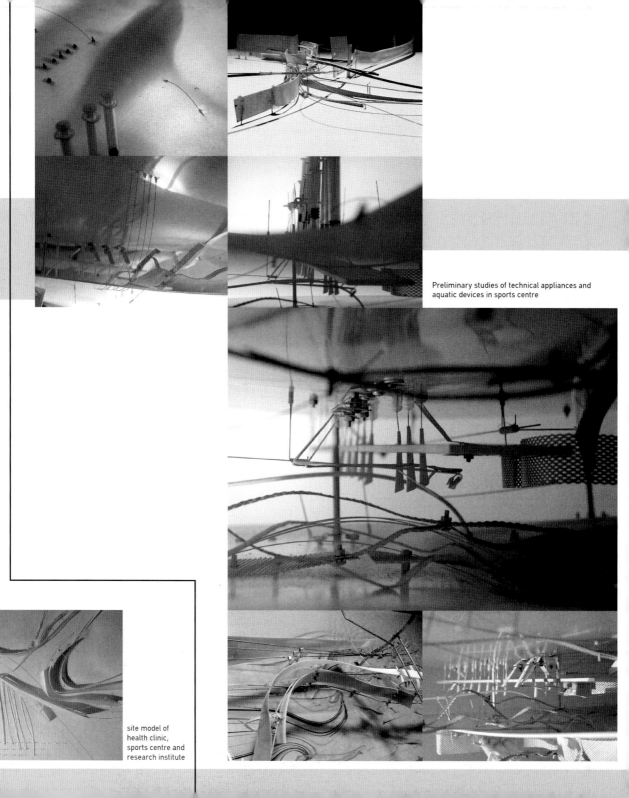

Preliminary studies of technical appliances and aquatic devices in sports centre

site model of
health clinic,
sports centre and
research institute

Jens Ritter

HEALTH CLINIC, SPORTS CENTRE
AND RESEARCH INSTITUTE
Helsinki, Finland 2000-2001

Sledge model inserted in regular water flow

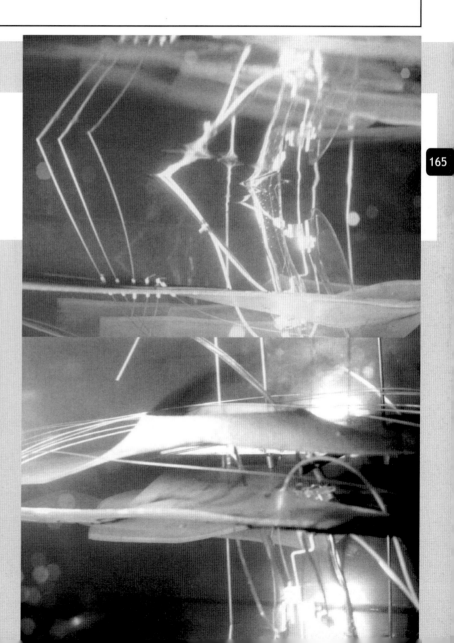

cross section through sports centre

HEALTH CLINIC, SPORTS CENTRE AND RESEARCH INSTITUTE

The starting point for the project is based on the high density of mineral particles in the air 50cm above sea level as a result of the **air-sea-exchange**. These minerals are very healthy for the human respiratory system and can greatly improve and influence the capacity of the lungs. The idea is to make this area or level accessible for people who need, or would like to claim the advantages of quality air.

The sports centre and the institute float on airbags held by cables which are attached to an island and a sandbank. The idea behind the entire shape of the complex is to place and integrate a structure in a specific given context. The first impression is of dynamism and smoothness. The structure responds to the (natural) environment and this interaction visibly determines its form.

The project consists of three parts: a health clinic for lung diseases, a wind/water sports centre, and a research institute.

Selected references:
"Boundary Layer Climate" T.R. Oke, 2nd edition, Routledge, Taylor & Francis Group, 2000
"Physical Fluid Dynamics" D.J. Tritton, Van Nostrand Reinhold Company Ltd. 1977

left image: cross section through health clinic
right image: cross section through research institute

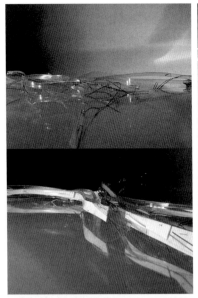

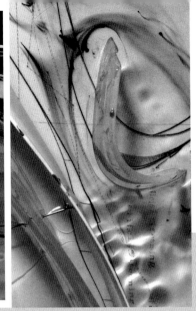

concept: models transformation of structural shape of fluids into
architectural forms
-test studies of behaviour ofmanipulated fluid behaviour

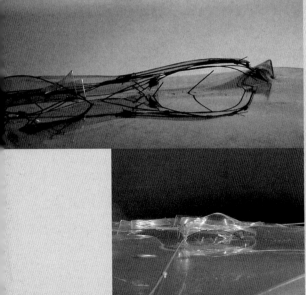

experiments on
water movement
between fins (see
text on page 171)

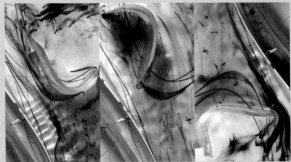

Model built into watertankinterferring with constant waterflow

model positioned on watersurface
with flow simulation in water an air

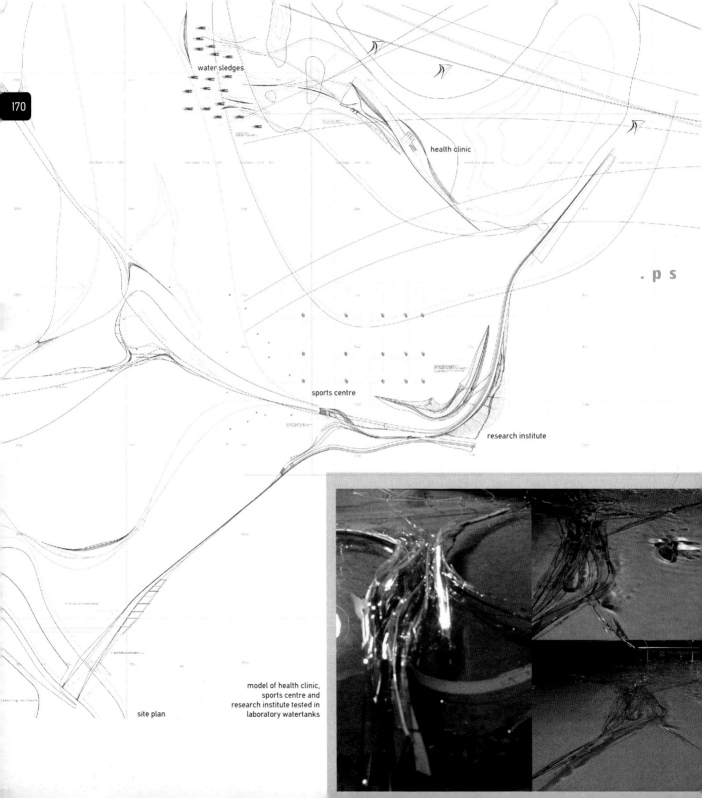

water sledges

health clinic

. p s

sports centre

research institute

site plan

model of health clinic,
sports centre and
research institute tested in
laboratory watertanks

possible pathway

pressure center to equalize the
different pressure between air and water

plan of sports centre

xperiments were carried out at the Fluid Mechanics Laboratory of the Civil
eering Department at University College London.

Tank used for experimentation with lamina flows:

velocity:	30cm/s
water height in the tank:	220mm
water height in the testing area:	55mm
of the boundary layer (max velocity/ in section):	5mm
of free stream:	50mm
th of the testing zone:	
mm	
th of the water tank:	
mm	
of testing zone:	580mm
of boundary layer (max velocity /in plan, on each side):	60mm
of free stream:	460mm

fluence of air movement on the water surface can be neglected. Its frictional

ence is very small and the experiments are carried out 55mm below the surface

water on a glass sheet.

iment of water movement between fins:
ation of Flow (extract of technical studies)

The basic intention of these studies is to observe and control the movement of
a fluid between and around vertical fins inserted within the boundary layer. They
create open spaces with turbulent fast moving air, or sheltered spaces with slowly
circulating or almost still air. Their architectural quality is intended to be open,
aggressive and public, or calm protected and private.
One important sheltered space within the boundary layer is a protected swimming
area in the open sea.

Test Model (images on page 168)
On top of the glass sheet I introduced a white acrylic sheet, which acts as the
support for the model. On this sheet vertical transparent acrylic stripes (simulating the fins) are attached by pins. This slight attachment is sufficient because the
stripes are positioned longitudinally to the water flow. so the frontal force of the fins
directly obstructing the current is minimal. The fins predominantly influence water
passing by them longitudinally.
Firstly there is a fixed straight element which is positioned in line with the flow. The
disturbance causes by this element is relatively small. It exerts little frontal resistance against the current. Its diameter d is 2mm and it has a pointed shape. It only
exerts a subtle influence on the flow. The change in water movement is not abrupt.

The other fin is movable and curved. This is a major difference because according
to its position, its surface faces into the water flow. The intervention is not linear, so
the space around it opens and closes (widens and narrows) during the continuous of
the flow. The speed and direction of the water flow can change abruptly. The line of
the movable element in plan could be described as indeterminate or meandering. It
creates one main concave situation and one main convex situation on either side.

JAMES FOSTER

NATALIA TRAVERSO CARAUNA

174

peter cook _vicente vidal _j.maria lozano _unit text salvador perez arroyo and marco
Architecture _James Foster//The Humanpower Architectural Transformation_exhib

rens holm _briefs _fieldtrips _technical dissertations_Natalia Traverso//FerroFluidic
·itics_bartfolio_lecture series _thanks UL²⁰]'s _students _cirriculum viteas _index

175

Human power architectural transformations

Introduction

Modern society has become accustomed to a using a ´sledgehammer to crack a nut´ approach to energy usage. Confronted with a situation where man power provides the only source of useful energy, one is forced to be innovative and inventive. The term human power can be interpreted in several ways from bruit force applied to mechanical devices to the potential of human generated electricity, leading to proposals and functions which range from the practical or energy saving to more trivial demonstration devices designed to make people realise their own capability.

"In technologically advanced countries, we can avail ourselves of energy in the form of engines powered by fossil fuel and devices

drawing on electricity. The result is a large number of couch potatoes; a large number of athletes, joggers and health enthusiasts,

and a still larger number of persons who fall between these two groups".

Abbott, A., Wilson, D., Human Powered Vehicles, Human Kinetics 1995, USA (p.267)

Until about two centuries ago, the majority of the worlds work was carried out by muscle power, this category can be further subdivided into human and animal muscle power. It is proposed to investigate the human side of this concept, and discuss the relevance of the idea today, an in particular the opportunity of human power within building.

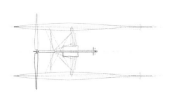

Bicycle transportation is perhaps the most obvious application of human power, and remains a thriving form of transportation, in all extremes of society, from the third world where it is used for transportation primarily because of a lack of alternatives, to the modern hi-tech city, where bicycle messengers provide the most effective method of getting a physical object from A to B quickly.

The International Human Powered Vehicle Association [IHPVA] is an organisation set up in Southern California in 1975 by Chester Kyle and Jack Lambie. The association has overseen significant technological developments in human powered water, land and air vehicles and is intent on promoting human power as both a viable transport solution and an exciting sporting or recreational interest.

It is useful to provide an outline of the background and philosophy of the IHPVA and its members. The pursuit of HPV enthusiasts can, in ways be likened to an extreme sport. However, participants are often scientists and engineers with an enthusiasm for the obscure, eccentric inventors set on achieving success with their own unconventional design.

Despite the unconventional obsession, the science behind hpv technology is high-level, encompassing disciplines of aerodynamics, materials science, hydrodynamics in addition to the ergonomic considerations and necessary physiological knowledge.

Sporting and competitive applications act to drive technological advances. It is often the case that sporting bodies restrict technical progress, theoretically to provide better or more entertaining competitions, keeping the competitors more evenly matched. It is rarely that a sport encourages, technological advances without restrictions. This was one of the goals of the IHPVA; to encourage development not bounded by arbitrary restrictions of officially sanctioned events. This provides an ideal environment to combine sporting competitiveness and creative invention.

Ideas of human power applied to various forms of transportation have always existed, man powered flight is an age old idea, only ever realised in recent decades as technology allowed a suitable machine to be developed. The technology, despite using an ancient principal, can be very sophisticated. Materials technology, physical, aerodynamic and ergonomic principals have been refined by determined enthusiasts striving for obscure goals of fastest speeds and longest flights.

Novel Applications
Applications of human powered technology to space exploration have been subject to a considerable amount of research, firstly because of the energy conscious nature of space travel and secondly because of the need to exercise to avoid the kind of muscle wastage that can occur when spending long periods of time in a micro gravitational environment.

Because force and acceleration represent two distinct entities, simply applying a force to an object [eg. bungee cord or lower body negative-pressure device] in micro gravity does not mean that it regulates a beneficial loading of the skeleton similar to that with exercise on earth. An animal or human placed in a rotating centrifuge does experience the force benefits produced by a sustained acceleration gravity field.

Exercise Physiology: Energy, Nutrition and Human Performance, 5th EditionW. D. McArdle, F. I. Katch, V. L. Katch, p.723

The spacecycle is a human powered centrifuge producing artificially induced gravity, providing exercise for two astronauts at once, their pedalling motion rotates the whole device at the same time, thus simulating the force benefits of exercising within the earths gravitational field.

A further potential of the spacecycle has yet to be proven a success; theoretically training in 2g is better than training in 1g, and could give the user the benefits of an hours exercise in thirty minutes.

In architectural terms it is, at first difficult to see the relevance of such principals, buildings rarely need to move as objects, aerodynamic principals and hydrodynamic principals have limited applications in the majority of buildings. However, at the detail level, and in terms of constructional principals, the use of materials, weight saving techniques and the basic mechanistics may provide valuable lessons. It may be possible to borrow from the technology and apply ideas to human powered buildings in terms of moving components within buildings, and also in terms of ideas relating to self build projects and transportable structures.

rens holm _briefs _fieldtrips _technical dissertations_Natalia Traverso//FerroFluidic
ritics_bartfolio_lecture series _thanks Ul[20]'s _students _cirriculum viteas _index

177

How can ideas of human power influence design, function and energy consumption? How can buildings be adjusted, reconfigured and tailored either on a long or short term basis? The ultimate human powered building is one which can be physically moved using the strength of one man.

In 1995 the total energy consumption in the UK was 6367 PJ of which 2878 PJ was used in buildings. This represents a proportion of 45.2%.

How much energy can a person produce?

The graph output figures shows the way in which power output diminishes as the duration of exercise increases. The data demonstrates that for a very short period of time an extremely high power output can be achieved whilst the muscles function anerobically, the value then decreases rapidly. The output then reaches a more steady value as the aerobic metabolism supplys the energy. This level does decrease gradually due to fatigue, the most important piece of information that can be taken from an experiment of this type is the power that can be maintained for a significant length of time.

The simplest, and possibly most useful set of conclusions to be gained from the graph is that leg cranking provides the most power effective output from the human body, and that people of average fitness should be capable producing 300 - 400 W which is equal to 0.4 - 0.5 horsepower for periods of upto one hour.

The key challenge in applying the principals of human powered vehicle design are concerned with appropriate material selection and component design in order to allow movement with the minimum of force.

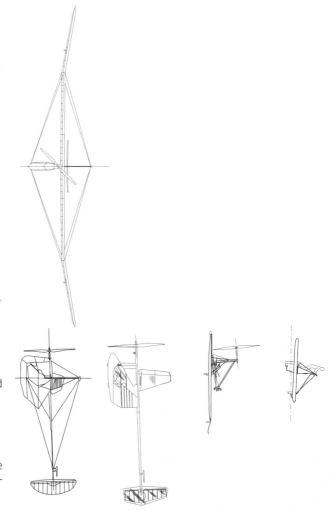

Human Power and Architecture

Buildings tend to be considered static, inanimate objects. Moving components within buildings generally exist on a small detail level. The idea that moving components can exist on an architectural scale, moving walls, roofs, floors allowing spaces to be reconfigured to suit different functions, different climatic conditions, different events can provide many new and interesting directions for architects.

Applying the principal of a convertible car to a building is interesting, allowing an entire space to transform from an indoor to outdoor area with changes in climate. In a situation where this transformation would occur less than a couple of times per day, using human power to perform the transformation would be a lot more realistic than installing expensive electrical systems. There is also the satisfaction associated with making such a large scale transformation using muscle power alone. The speed of such changes does not need to be rapid, therefore mechanistic approaches can be tailored to low power over several minutes.

Moving large components using muscle power can be made easier by designing systems with a certain mechanical advantage. A simple method combining block and pulley systems with leg or hand cranking mechanisms allows less force to move a large load, at the expense of distance travelled; in this case, the number of revolutions of the cranking mechanism.

Such mechanisms can be combined with varying counterweight systems. A counterweight attached to a mechanism locked in place would propel the mechanism in the desired direction according to gravitational force on release of the locking mechanism. If the counterweight were then reduced the mechanism would then return to its original position. This variable counterweight could be created using a pumped water system, the demands on the human operative being limited to pumping the water.

The potential of movements and transformations that already exist within a building: doors and windows opening and closing, being the most obvious and the most frequently used.
Used locally, their movement could be converted to potential energy for another application.

Natural Ventilation
After studying human powered air and water vehicles, perhaps one of the most obvious applications of kinetic energy stolen from human movement is in powering a series of propellers for use in increasing the air change rate within a space, and potentially eliminating the necessity for air conditioning. The most suitable space for such an application is within a gymnasium, the kind of space so frequently overheating with large numbers of human engines working to maximum capability in close confinement. An increase in ventilation rate increases the rate of evaporation of perspiration, ie. Improves the effective cooling thus improving exercise performance.

rens holm _briefs _fieldtrips _technical dissertations_Natalia Traverso//FerroFluidic
itics_bartfolio_lecture series _thanks UI[20]'s _students _cirriculum viteas _index

179

Other building services
A piezoelectric material generates an electric charge when mechanically deformed. The technology is still in its
infancy, however as a proposition, the idea has a range of applications. Piezoelectric materials have already been
investigated as a material inserted into the soles of training shoes to capture the energy dissipated on contact
with the ground. Obviously, the quantities of power involved are very low, proposals for use are limited to low power
personal electronic devices such as mobile phone recharging. Applica-
tions of the piezoelectric principal to building surfaces, more specifically
floor surfaces could be used to capture energy. The cost of applying a
sophisticated material to all floor surfaces would be uneconomical, the
application could be concentrated within areas of high usage, circulation
zones and particularly stair treads. In the case of stair treads, it is easier to
predict with a smaller margin for error where the feet will land,. Generally,
due to the effect of gravity, greater forces are involved, therefore the ratio
of energy gained to area of piezoelectric wafer invested in is greater.

Coupling of this kind of piezoelectric system with a low power lighting
system, used locally, lighting systems could be entirely self powered,
providing light only where strictly necessary within the occupied area. This
simplified overview suggests methods of energy savings, combined with
low energy systems which represent a positive step in renewable energy
systems.

The idea of heat gain from body heat is another potential interpretation of human power. Putting this idea into
practice would be problematic, as precise control of such a system may require complex control and feedback
mechanisms. The main requirements of an environment of this type would be a space sufficiently insulated so as
to gain the lowest possible u-value, to maximise the effect of the body heat within. Programmatic considerations
are important, the space would have to contain sufficient people to provide enough heat gain, and the patterns of
occupation should be as even as possible. If the complexity of such systems

Punkah fans
Oscillating blades, of differing sizes are constructed of fibreglass with a lightweight aluminium frame fold away to
form an additional layer to the building skin. To increase air circulation rate within building, these pieces become
unfolded and oscillate. Drive comes from body conditioning gym, the area of the building producing the most con-

180

peter cook _vicente vidal _j.maria lozano _unit text salvador perez arroyo and marcc
Architecture _James Foster//The Humanpower Architectural Transformation_exhil

sistent supply of kinetic energy. Crank and slider driven, the air change rate is directly proportional to number of people using gym. Crankshafts can be adjusted to control rate of energy transfer, degrees of movement of blades.

Energy Storage
Pressurised energy storage Peristaltic pumps provide a simple method of quietly and smoothly moving a liquid from one volume to another. An input of rotary motion which comes human pedalling provides water transfer from lake, via filter to overhead water storage tanks. Water in these storage vessels, made from an expanding silicone based membrane becomes pressurised, the liquid becoming laden with potential energy. The pressurised liquid is then used to drive hydraulic devices within the building.

Lightweight Engineering
Weight critical fields and technologies are one of the most significant factors in reduction of energy requirements of moving components. Bicycling technology has seen massive advances in speeds achieved, the participants owe a lot of this to the materials technologists and design engineers who have pushed the boundaries in terms of weight and aerodynamics. Applications of some of these principals to moving components can be a significant contributor in reducing the weight and power consumption necessary to create movement. Consider as an example a system of louvres applied to the outside of a building. Analysed very simplistically, power is directly proportional to weight, therefore halving the weight of each louvre component allows the same movement to be achieved with 50% less power. This may not be significant when applied to a single louvre, but if the building skin were made up of 1000 louvres, then the energy saving becomes considerable.

It is useful to analyse the technologies adopted by human powered vehicle technologists, where weight savings and aerodynamic improvements have lead to significant advances in speed and time trial events. The developments themselves have evolved from aeronautic, automotive and marine technologies, and include composites, sandwich construction and Fibreglass. Whilst a detailed study of individual materials technologies and properties is beyond the scope of this dissertation, some further analysis is useful in order to establish the weight saving benefits gained from adopting techniques from other fields.

Lightweight Engineering
Weight critical fields and technologies are one of the most significant factors in reduction of energy requirements of moving components. Bicycling technology has seen massive advances in speeds achieved, the participants owe a lot of this to the materials technologists and design engineers who have pushed the boundaries in terms of weight and aerodynamics. Applications of some of these principals to moving components can be a significant contributor in reducing the weight and power consumption necessary to create movement. Consider as an example a system of louvres applied to the outside of a building. Analysed very simplistically, power is directly proportional to weight, therefore halving the weight of each louvre component allows the same movement to be achieved with 50% less power. This may not be significant when applied to a single louvre, but if the building skin were made up of 1000 louvres, then the energy saving becomes considerable.

Ergonomic Design
Designers of human powered vehicles, particularly those aimed at achieving high performance in terms of speed, endurance and distance consider the ergonomics of the device and controls of ultimate importance.

rens holm _briefs _fieldtrips _technical dissertations _Natalia Traverso//FerroFluidic
itics_bartfolio_lecture series _thanks UI[20]'s _students _cirriculum viteas _index

181

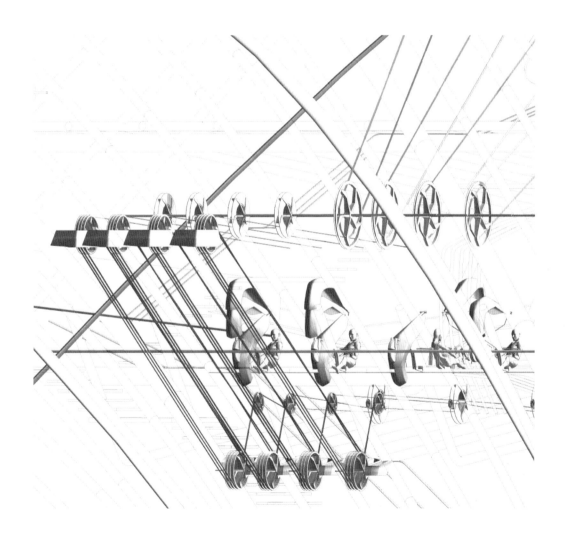

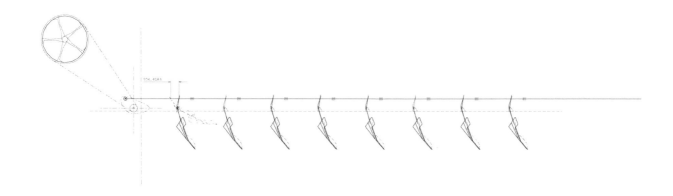

rens holm _briefs _fieldtrips _technical dissertations_Natalia Traverso//FerroFluidic
itics_bartfolio_lecture series _thanks U[20]'s _students _cirriculum viteas _index

183

It is this attention to ergonomic detail that can provide valuable lessons to architectural design; High end bicycling technology is concerned with the interaction of the bicycle and the body, the machine becomes an extension of the body. Therefore, the connection points between the human machine and the mechanical one are of the utmost importance, as are gearing ratios, crank lengths, even the degree of ovalisation of the chainwheels. The science behind this biomechanical fusion is complex. It is rare that points of contact within buildings receive such consideration, however it has been proven that increases in performance and efficiency are a direct consequence of time invested. Application of such lessons to building components could produce similar increases in capability and potential applications of human power.

Low energy design
As the power requirements for microelectronics continue decreasing , it is no longer unfeasible to harvest a useful amount of energy ëparasiticallyí from normal human activity.

Using everyday technology, the conversion of small quantities of energy generated by subtle human movements into electrical energy is an inefficient process, each time an energy conversion occurs, there is a significant energy loss. Direct driving of suitably matched mechanical devices, keeping energy in form of the potential or kinetic provides a more realistic approach to human powered systems with current technology. However the necessity to reduce energy usage in general, especially within the built environment which eats up so much, acts as a driving force to reduce consumption. The necessary requirement of human powered systems for low power operation becomes another driving force for this reduction. Coupled with the development of more efficient methods of energy conversion, the future holds many possibilities for ideas of harvesting power from a buildings occupants.

Sustainable Building
As a realistic proposal, the idea of a purely human powered building is novel, and at least in the western world, somewhat extreme.

Ideas of sustainable building have existed for some decades now, with concepts that range from renewable natural power sources [wind, water, solar etc] and supposedly zero energy buildings, to in depth analysis of embodied energy of construction materials. Despite the continued topical nature of sustainability, in many architectural situations the idea is reduced to little more than a trend; the inclusion of photovoltaic technology or wind generation becomes a token gesture on the faÁade or roof. Within the building industry mainstream, little has changed.

The application of human power technology, either directly or indirectly [incorporating ideas of low energy design from the previous section] coupled with advanced methods of sustainable energy generation would represent several dissertation in itself, suffice to say that a combination of methods would allow more power to be gained for more of the time, whilst the human power aspect would encourage interest and innovation to the more mundane sustainable systems.

184

peter cook _vicente vidal _j.maria lozano _unit text salvador perez arroyo and marcc
Architecture _James Foster//The Humanpower Architectural Transformation_exhi

Ferrofluidic architecture: designing a liquid pulse

An investigation seeks to represent the fluctuating oil market prices onto a hydrocarbon based ferrofluid panel.

Ferrofluids are magnetic fluids which may be controlled by a magnetic field. The fluid may become attracted at an instant to a magnet, transforming from a regular liquid to a dense magnetic mass. Ferrofluids are "gryphons" in the world of materials, part liquid, part magnet,

The aim is to investigate these qualities through the process of experimentation, and create a panel which can be manipulated by a varying magnetic field into the pulsating effect required of the panel.

An area covered by these panels will create a dramatic pulsating canopy, in tune with the rhythm of the fluctuating stocks, visually conveying the state of oil affairs.

The investigation opens up possibilities of creating a solar panel, which like electrochromic glass may alter the translucency of the panel. Unlike the electrochromic panel, ferrofluids have an immediate response and give the possibility of a complete blackout, none of which can be achieved by the present electrochromic panels.

A ferrofluid proposition is therefore put forward as a new architectural material, for usage, manipulation and to create effects not yet achieved by contemporary architecture.

Patern creation of ferrofluids

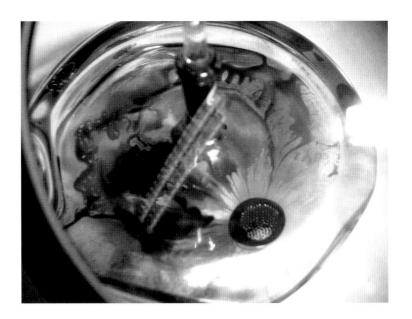

rens holm _briefs _fieldtrips _technical dissertations_Natalia Traverso//FerroFluidic
ritics_bartfolio_lecture series _thanks Ul20]'s _students _cirriculum viteas _index

185

Ferrofluid origins

Ferrofluids developed as a result of the "US Space research Program". They were invented by NASA as a way to control the flow of liquid fuels in space. Ferrofluids were conceived as a novel answer to problems of zero gravity in outer space application in space shuttles.

Contemporary uses for ferrofluids include:
Use as active components that contribute towards the enhanced performance of devices. These devices are either mechanical as in seals bearings and dampers or electromechanical, e.g. loudspeakers stepper motors, and sensors. Their role became increasingly important used in CD drives, For inkjet printing and sink float separation recovering resources from waste materials (metals).

Ferrofluids have 3 unique properties:
A ferrofluid will stick to a magnet.
A ferrofluid will take the 3-dimensional shape of the magnetic field that passes through it.
A ferrofluid changes its apparent density in proportion to the strength of the magnetic field that is applied to it.

Ferrofluid ingredients
There are 3 primary components in Ferro fluids. These are 'the carrier', 'ferromagnetic particles', and 'surfactant'.
A Ferrofluid is a stable colloidal suspension of sub-domain magnetic particles (usually ferromagnetic particles) in a liquid carrier. The carrier liquid can be a hydrocarbon based carrier, ester, water based, etc. depending on the product needs. Particles are highly ferromagnetic and as such are attracted to the poles of magnets or any magnetic field. When placed in a magnetic field, the conflicting attractions of gravity, magnetism, and surface tension shape the ferrofluid. They will move to form interesting patterns (spiking effects) when brought near a magnetic field.

An attractive feature of ferrofluids is the visible spiking up of the substance when a substantial magnetic field is applied. They stand up on end like iron filings would. This is due to their chemical make up which involves an immediate attraction of the ferromagnetic particles, but a prevention to agglomerate by the surfactant which keeps them apart.
The surfactant is added to surround the small particles at a distance from each other, and overcome their attractive tendencies.

A typical ferrofluid may contain by volume 5% magnetic solid, 10% surfactant and 85% carrier.

Responsiveness of ferrofluids
When a magnetic field is applied to a ferrofluid, the magnetic moments of the particles orient along the field lines almost instantly. When magnetized, the ferrofluid responds immediately as a homogeneous entity. When the applied field is removed, the moments randomize quickly.

Testing liquid consistency of ferrofluids: attempt to create an immediate response and return after magnetisation.

The ferrofluid was placed into a specifically glass blown container with a syringe. With the use of a button magnet, the ferrofluid was tested for reaction. There was an instantaneous response and attraction towards the magnet.

186

peter cook _vicente vidal _j.maria lozano _unit text salvador perez arroyo and marco
Architecture _James Foster//The Humanpower Architectural Transformation_exhi

At the same time however, a problem was encountered. The fluid did not flow quickly enough around the container. The ferrofluid was also so densely dark that the sides of the container became opaque immediately and took minutes to clear again.

The viscosity of the hydrocarbon based ferrofluid is too great for the desired effect, hence, although the attraction to the magnetic field (magnet) is immediate fluid takes about 3 minutes to completely return to a stable liquid form.

During this period, the dark ferrofluid temporarily stains the glass container it is in, obscuring the desired transparency of the panel during magnetisation. This is a problem with ferrofluids which as they are produced, cannot be resolved. A solution by adding another liquid to try to reduce the viscosity of the ferrofluid, however maintaining its responsive nature was the next investigation. A test using oil was the immediate reaction, but water was later found to be far less dense and less viscous than oil. It proved more effective, allowing the ferrofluid to flow much more freely through the aqueous based liquid.

The differing densities of the ferrofluid (hydrocarbon) and water also meant that although the fluids flowed extremely well, the ferrofluid was not diluted as the oil and water did not bond chemically. The water therefore acted as a catalyst in the flow of the ferro-

rens holm _briefs _fieldtrips _technical dissertations_Natalia Traverso//FerroFluidic
ritics_bartfolio_lecture series _thanks Ul[20]'s _students _cirriculum viteas _index

187

fluid and not so much as a diluting agent.

Testing the type and shape of the magnet

Several magnet types were tested using various shapes, sizes and materials. Magnets have varying forms and these all reflect on the magnetic field they give off hence directly affecting the intensity of the magnetization and the visual response of the ferrofluid.

The significant tests included those with a button magnet, and various electromagnets with different voltages and currents powering it.

Experiment
A constant amount of ferrofluid in a petri-dish was tested with various magnets of differing intensities and shapes. The strongest magnets were the button magnets, and the most concentrated magnetic field occurred when a magnet was placed above and below the ferrofluid panel, the magnets sandwiching the ferrofluid panel where the opposite poles attract directly.

Testing the gradient
The maximum gradient resisted by the magnetic attraction was also tested. The button magnet would 'stick' magnetically to the ferro-fluid in the petri-dish and the gradient of this petri-dish would be increased at 10 degree intervals. The investigation proved that the amount of ferrofluid 0.9ml and the button magnet had a greater magnetic attraction than gravity itself. The ferrofluid could be held upside down in the panel with without detaching itself from the button magnet.

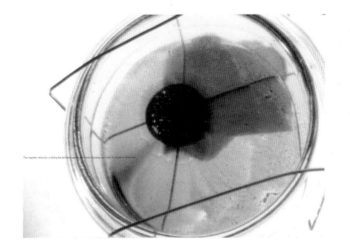

The figure shows the dish at almost 90 degrees, withstanding the weight of 2 magnets

Testing the ferrofluidic strength

The strength of the ferrofluid was also tested observing how many button magnets could be held by the magnetic field between them before falling and responding to the force of gravity. 3 magnets each weighing 3 grams were held by 3ml of ferrofluid (new mixture).

The versatility of an electromagnet

A power supply with a maximum emission of 20 volts and 20 amps was used.

An electromagnet was tested at varying voltages and amps to see what the ideal electric input would be for the ferrofluid. What was found is that varying the voltage was far more influential in determining the magnitude of the current than varying the current. However reducing the current below 0.5 amps also had detrimental effects! (There was not enough power to create a magnetic field strong enough to have an effect on the ferrofluid!)
"There is a directly proportional relationship between voltage increase and number of spikes with a current of at least 2 amps."
A maximum of 36 spikes at 20 volts was found. Increasing the voltage would also increase the number of spikes, however testing this was not possible as the power supply only went up to 20 volts.
Increasing the current over 12 amps just melted the plastic insulating the cable!

The spiking response
The distance of the magnet form the ferrofluid was vital for achieving the effects required. If the magnet was too far away, the ferrofluid barely responded (over 1cm). When the magnet was touching the panel, the ferrofluid concentrated at its maximum to agglomerate over the surface area of the magnet. When held between 1mm to 9mm from the ferrofluid panel, spikes emerged, increasing in size from 9mm to 4mm and then becoming smaller and more numerous and concentrated as the distance to the ferrofluid panel was decreased.

rens holm _briefs _fieldtrips _technical dissertations_Natalia Traverso//FerroFluidic
ritics_bartfolio_lecture series _thanks U[20]'s _students _cirriculum viteas _index

189

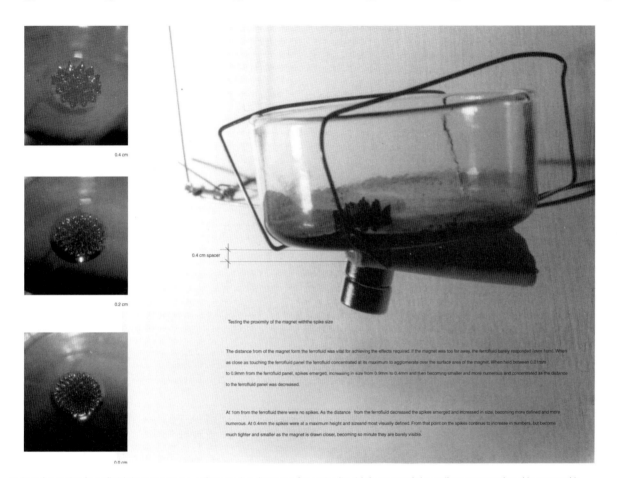

0.4 cm

0.2 cm

0.0 cm

0.4 cm spacer

Testing the proximity of the magnet with the spike size

The distance from of the magnet form the ferrofluid was vital for achieving the effects required. If the magnet was too far away, the ferrofluid barely responded (over 1cm). When as close as touching the ferrofluid panel the ferrofluid concentrated at its maximum to agglomerate over the surface area of the magnet. When held between 0.01mm to 0.9mm from the ferrofluid panel, spikes emerged, increasing in size from 0.9mm to 0.4mm and then becoming smaller and more numerous and concentrated as the distance to the ferrofluid panel was decreased.

At 1cm from the ferrofluid there were no spikes. As the distance from the ferrofluid decreased the spikes emerged and increased in size, becoming more defined and more numerous. At 0.4mm the spikes were at a maximum height and sizeand most visually defined. From that point on the spikes continue to increase in numbers, but become much tighter and smaller as the magnet is drawn closer, becoming so minute they are barely visible.

At 1cm from the ferrofluid there were no spikes as the distance from the liquid decreased the spikes emerged and increased in size, becoming more defined and more numerous. At 0.4mm the spikes were at a maximum height and size and most visually defined. From that point on the spikes continue to increase in numbers, but become much tighter and smaller as the magnet is drawn closer, becoming so minute they are barely visible.

"For maximum visual quality of spikes, the magnet has to be 4mm away from the ferrofluid panel."

"For maximum attraction and compaction of the ferrofluid, the magnet must be as close as possible.

The figure shows a close up of the largest spikes at 4mm from the ferrofluid

190

peter cook _vicente vidal _j.maria lozano _unit text salvador perez arroyo and marco
Architecture _James Foster//The Humanpower Architectural Transformation_exhib

Testing the projection of the ferrofluid
The ferrofluid canopy proposed, will be high up above the
main foyer space. The motion and response of the ferrofluid to the magnetic pulse is to be projected using the sun
onto the spaces below which rest on a thin film of black oil,
therefore acting as a screen to the ferrofluid patterns visual
projection of the ferrofluid.
It was therefore important to test the projections of this
changing fluid.
ferrofluid panel projections

An investigation using projectors, different lights, and then
recording the projection onto various surfaces aided me in my design of the location of the ferrofluid projected screen for my
design.
A light was used to project the ferrofluid shapes and patterns onto a white surface. The distance was tested form the ferrofluid to
the white surface with a fixed light at 1metre from the ferrofluid dish.

It was found that there was an optimal focal point where the
projection was clearest which varied with each container
due to the various shapes and sizes.

Application of former experiments: The design of a canopy

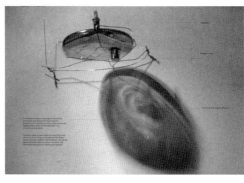

The research into ferrofluids was developed to be applied
to a conference center for oil in Texas City. In this the ferrofluidic panel becomes a major informative medium and
indication of the global oil market fluctuations.

The effect is that at a stable and absolutely static market,
the ferrofluid too is still. Visually it is a very thin film, lying flat and covering the ETFE panel. Gentle rays of light may penetrate and
diffuse through the panel dependant on the thickness and opacity of the ferrofluid.

Ferrofluid canopy

As soon as a figure changes in the oil price, a current is induced through each electromagnet and causes the ferrofluid to agglomerate at this point. It becomes dense at this point leaving the rest of the panel free and translucent. This then allows sunlight to
penetrate.

rens holm _briefs _fieldtrips _technical dissertations _Natalia Traverso//FerroFluidic
ritics_bartfolio_lecture series _thanks Ul201's _students _cirriculum viteas _index

191

After 2 seconds of attraction, the current through the electromagnet is switched off and the ferrofluid returns to becoming a film over the ETFE panel and obscuring the sunlight again.

This process of magnetization and demagnetization is continuous; totally dependant on the market fluctuations. As soon as a figure changes by 0.1 points, a current is induced and the attraction of the ferrofluid occurs, creating a pulse: 'current on', 'current off' With 2 seconds interval; magnetic field, no magnetic field. Simultaneously a tapping sound is created by the repulsion of the button magnets. If the jump is high enough it will smack the solid ETFE panel and create a sound (tap!) which when multiplied by hundreds of panels, will create a distinctive and desirable sound.

Section of panels

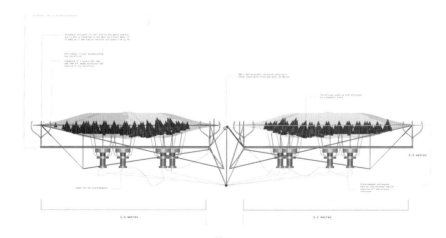

fig 3.11

192

peter cook _vicente vidal _j.maria lozano _unit text salvador perez arroyo and marco
Architecture _James Foster//The Humanpower Architectural Transformation_exhil

The canopy is constructed in 2 sections. These are a primary curved beam structure and a panel structure which laterally braces the canopy and holds the ferrofluid canopy together.
The ferrofluid containers are made from ETFE pneumatic panels. They are very light and versatile in terms of potential shape and form. A minimal structure is required and allowed by this lightweight material.
The panel is designed in 4 layers in section.

A lightweight ETFE sack seals the ferrofluid and then reinforces the strength and rigidity of the overall panel. A tube will be attached to the internal sack to enable site analysis of the ferrofluid, allowing for easy insertion and removal of liquid. The ETFE panel is bolted in position and connected by ms fixings to the panel structure. This allows for the ferrofluid panel to be removed at any point for panel maintenance or repair.

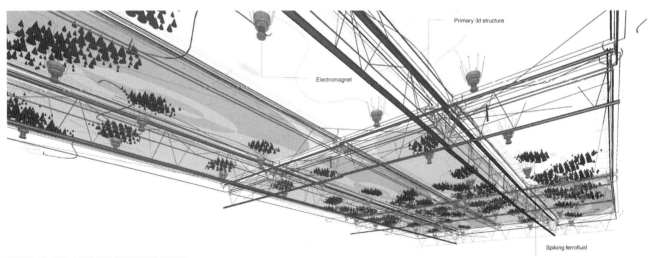

Image showing canopy view from below

The magnificent forms and effects of ferrofluids are proposed to become exposed and appreciated in their visual aesthetics. A unique flow against gravity is spectacular and the spiking result is unparalleled in any other material.

Ferrofluid panel or electrochromic panel

The panel designed primarily investigated the pulsating effect required for this design project. However, stemming from the investigations carried out was the opportunity to propose a shading device, using similar responsive principles to the 'electrochromic panel designs', which are currently 'revolutionary' in the glass manufacturing industry.

rens holm _briefs _fieldtrips _technical dissertations_Natalia Traverso//FerroFluidic
itics_bartfolio_lecture series _thanks Ul[20]'s _students _cirriculum viteas _index

193

The ability to control ferrofluids, their immediate response to electromagnetism, and spectacular visual performance renders ferrofluids as a fascinating material for this usage and application. An immediate area for investigation involves the use of ferrofluid panels as a possible variation for electrochromic glass panels. These are panels that change in colour for solar purposes becoming less translucent and more opaque for reduction of sunlight penetration.

Electrochromic panels have 2 major flaws. These are their slow response once activated, which an take up to 6 minutes to reach their maximum solar protection, and its limitation in opacity change, which only becomes partially tinted and not at all opaque.

Ferrofluids for solar protection

Ferrofluids could be used in the same way, and possibly improve on the electrochromic design.
The great advantages of ferrofluid panels over electrochromic panels are the dramatic opacity change (totally opaque to clear) and the instant response.
Ferrofluids respond immediately to a magnetic field, and so could have an immediate opacity if required. The opacity change could be great or could be slower, depending on the strength of the magnetic field. A slow response of the ferrofluid could be dramatic as the liquid slides against gravity, leaving an amber trace as it moves and creating magnificent visual effects.
The blackout possibility of ferrofluids is also an additional option not offered in electrochromic panels, and therefore far more advantageous as a solar panel.
Ferrofluids will not replace these panels in every occasion but can definitely be researched as an interesting substitute.

The fluid motion

Another great advantage is the liquidity of the ferrofluid panel and physical motion of the fluid. Architecture is usually static, and a visual liquidity is a relief and stimulating material option among the usual stillness of buildings.

image glass ferro from above

Controlling the colour

An interesting investigation to be carried out is an attempt to control the colour of the panel. This would lead to the possibility of controlling the hues, reflections and investigate deeper into the aesthetics of the panel providing wider markets and interest to the product.

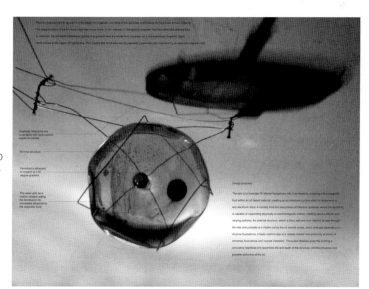

Stephen Clements Hydroponic Farm

Granja Hidropónica Bilbao, Spain 1999 - 2000

"The skin serves as a protective and sensory buffer between the organism and the environment... The dermis is richly endowed with sensory nerves and its blood vessels are exquisitely sensitive to temperature. The dermal appendages – hair, sebaceous and sweat glands – contain and dissipate heat and protect the body from physical injury."

Stenn, Kurt S, "The Skin" (Chapter 18), in Weiss, Leon (ed.) Cell end Tissue Biology: A Textbook of Histology (6 ed), (Munich: Urban and Schwarzenberg, 1988), P541

The site for this project is the industrial wastelands of Bilbao. Vast tracts of unused wasteland lie along the river side, too polluted for normal use. This proposal suggests the regeneration of these brown-field sites into a new, green industry - the industry of hydroponics. Hydroponics is the growth of normal farm produce, from flowers to tomatoes, without the use of soil. This proposal is for a greenhouse system that covers and utilizes these wastelands. It is a vast complex of soft membrane punctuated by rigid structures that provide the mechanics of the farm.

This study concerns itself primarily with the epidermal greenhouse membrane, the skin. It uses the biological principles of the human skin as a design precedent and seeks to further this concept by suggesting a technology that serves the requirements of the farm. Micro sensory nerve networks exist across the membrane surface to monitor and control the local environment. This is a direct interpretation of our own nervous system whereby local stimuli provoke an immediate response. Electrical conduits service the various locales of the farm and power an array of inflated bubbles that illuminate the greenhouse at night (similar to a neon bulb.) These membrane bubbles also form the structural solution with the use of hydrogen or a similar gas lighter than air to provide uplift to the membrane. This allows large areas of the farm to be covered without the need for ground supports - furthermore the functional requirements of the farm is dealt with by ceiling borne robots that are suspended from the underside of the membrane – pickers, sprayers, etc. This is intended to maximize the growth potential of the site by eliminating the need for access at ground level.

The results of this proposal suggest a utopian / dystopian view for urban regeneration. The Farm is potentially vast with no apparent boundaries; it can grow or shrink to suit the farming requirements. It is proposed that the membrane acts like a urban skin graft to cover areas of scarred land and to utilize the land's potential. It is a utilitarian architecture and a thing of beauty - a farm of the future.

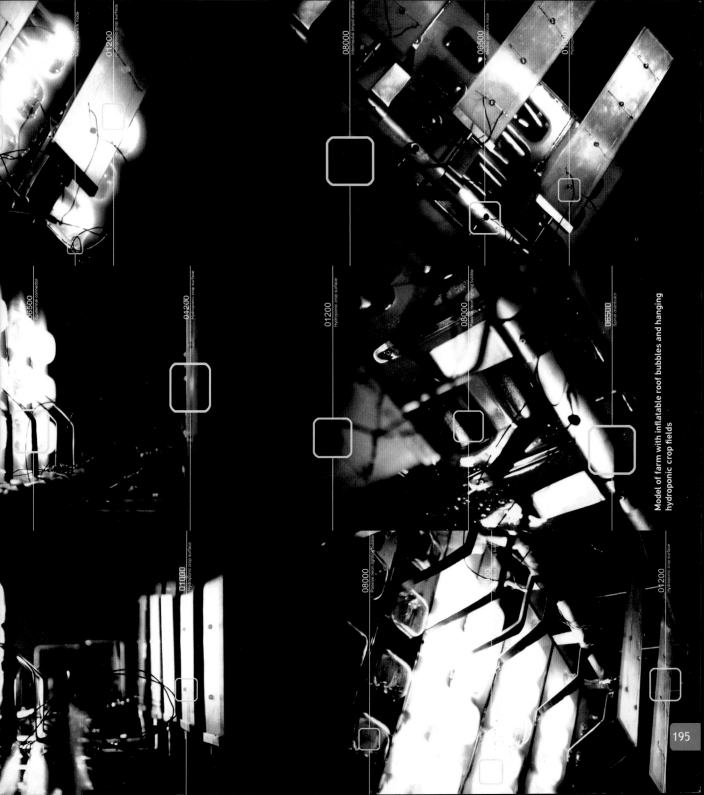

Model of farm with inflatable roof bubbles and hanging hydroponic crop fields

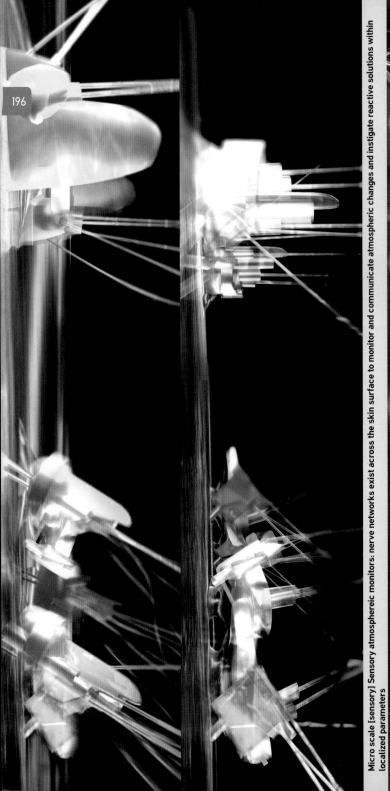

Micro scale [sensory] Sensory atmosphereic monitors: nerve networks exist across the skin surface to monitor and communicate atmospheric changes and instigate reactive solutions within localized parameters

Subcutaneous stratum [3]Localized structural elements form links to rigid non-edipermal construction and maintain tension across membrane while helium filled sacks provide uplift at centralized structural nodes

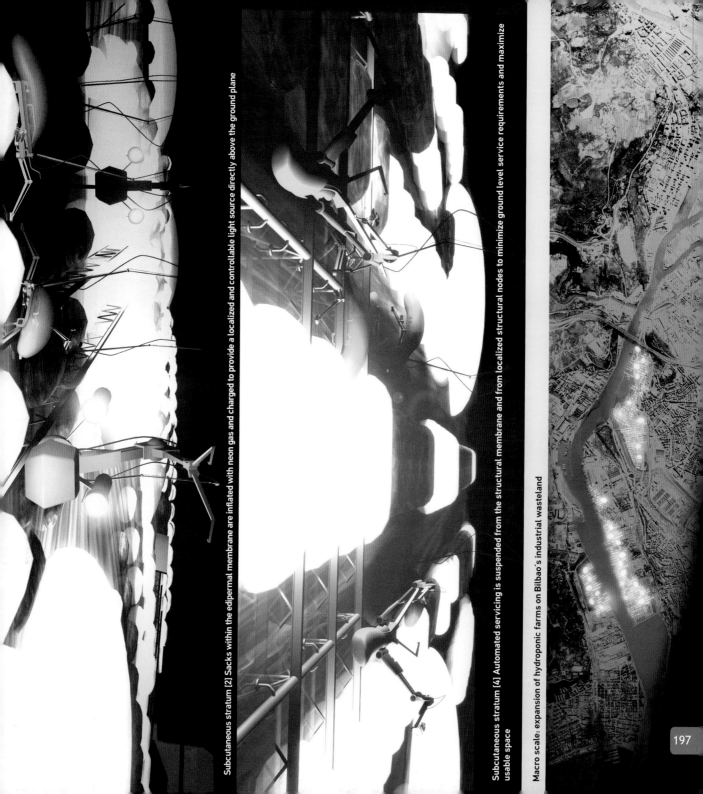

Subcutaneous stratum [2] Sacks within the edipermal membrane are inflated with neon gas and charged to provide a localized and controllable light source directly above the ground plane

Subcutaneous stratum [4] Automated servicing is suspended from the structural membrane and from localized structural nodes to minimize ground level service requirements and maximize usable space

Macro scale: expansion of hydroponic farms on Bilbao's industrial wasteland

197

anopheles

subterranus

Steve Pike U20 – a short tale of the underground.

Anopheles Subterranus.

Deep in the bowels of The London Underground lies a pool of water. Rain wanders downward through fissures, picking up the discharge of leaking pipes and the condensation of the breath of thousands of passengers along its way. Eventually it gathers below the platforms of Oxford Circus. The climate of The Tube is not like that of the city above; in places its temperature and humidity are far greater. At the surface of the pool, the micro-climate is just right for the breeding of mosquitoes. At some previous critical moment, an egg laden female has found its way to this water and a colony has begun. As the population became apparent, attempts at control through insecticide became more frequent and less successful. The colony adapted to these attacks, the almost total darkness and the specific conditions of its environment. A new resilient mutation, Anopheles Subterranus (The Underground Mosquito), was created. This unique subterranean population is largely anonymous to commuters, save for the occasional mysterious bite collected as they wait for the next train.

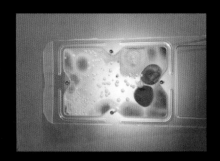
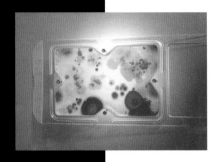

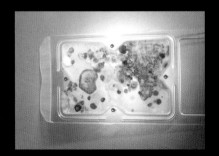
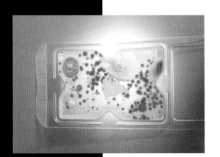

Activity Specific Monitors

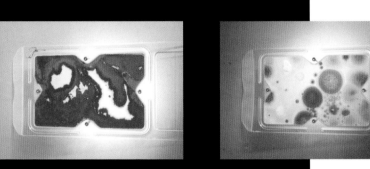

Bakery   Fruit Stall

Cairo, Tourism   Single Dwelling

Flower Market   Building Site

Steve Pike Contaminant
Holbron Tube Station, London, Uk 2001 - 2002
Contaminante

NON STERILE ENVIRONMENT

Direct encounters between humans and microorganisms are generally experienced in a negative context. We are surrounded by such organisms, populating the air and surface of our environment. Bacteria and viruses are responsible for numerous diseases and infections, many of which are potentially fatal. Cyanobacteria are only occasionally brought to our attention; usually in the form of 'algal blooms', where massive colonies affect lakes, streams and coastal waters. In these cases water purity is hindered and toxins are often released. Accumulating in the food chain, contaminating marine stocks. It is through the air that we breathe that we interact most frequently with microorganisms. Airborne particles are a major source of ailments, particularly respiratory illness, in humans. Viruses, such as influenza, are commonly transmitted from person to person by particle inhalation, along with severe bacterial diseases, such as Tuberculosis (Mycobacterium tuberculosis) (see appendix 1). The full extent of airborne infection is by no means understood. Fungal spores, long known agents of plant disease, are relatively recently being recognised as problematic for humans as well. Our skin plays host to many fungal colonies, but occasionally, certain inhaled fungal spores give rise to serious infections such as Aspirgillosis.

The link between the concentration of particles in ambient air and the health of its occupying population has been accepted by the scientific establishment. High particle concentrations have been linked to increases in mortality rates and greater incidences of heart and lung disease. For this reason, air sampling has become an important means of monitoring airborne particle populations, deducing the consequence of individual and accumulative microorganism presence. The provision of a canopy for the platforms of Helsinki Railway Station presents an opportunity to sample and monitor the air at a source relative to the population. As the main transport hub of the city, a large proportion of it's residents pass through daily, each breathing air and acting as hosts to numerous microbes. Their warmth and movement stirs the air which, in the confined 'cul de sac' of the station buildings, rises upward. In addition, the trains sporadically pull into the station, acting as huge pistons, driving the air against the buildings and turbulently upward. The careful placement of the canopy, relative to the airflow, will provide surfaces for potential capture of particles and organisms present in the passing air. A plane of growth medium in such a location would provide a means of sampling environmental microbes. According to the composition of the media and the conditions of incubation, particular organisms could be targeted, allowing for a degree of control over the type of monitoring conducted. Some sections of the canopy could incorporate devices specifically relevant to the inhalation of air. Of the various methods available, the 'Anderson Sampler' encompasses many benefits as it draws parallels to the human respiratory tract. Therefore, it is of particular value for detecting spore counts, allergenic particles, disease prediction and general air quality relative to localised human populations. To summarise the process; air is drawn through a cylinder consisting of several sections each containing agar plates:

Cross section through London Underground monitor vessel chamber rotation / sample recovery in Holborn Station.

The Vascular Channels Of The London Underground.

Longitudinal section through London Underground monitor vessel intermittent airflow / particle capture.

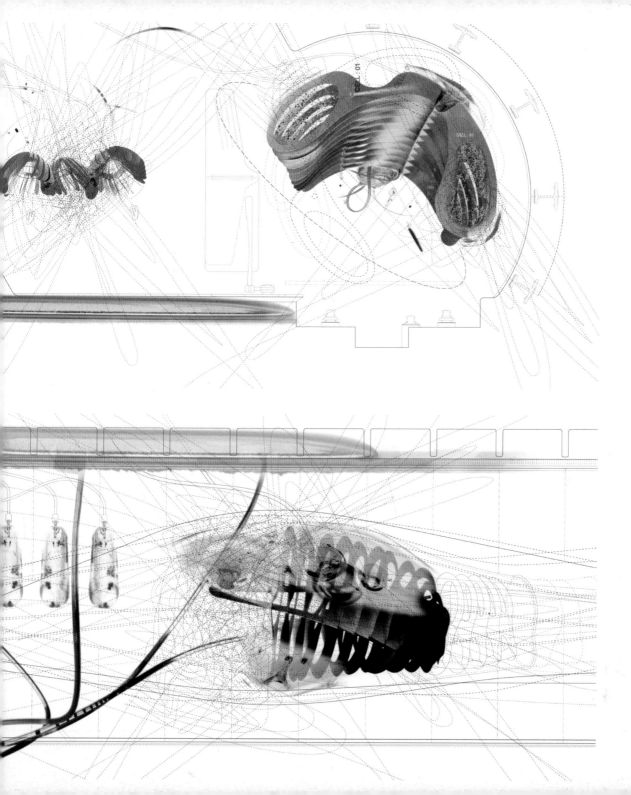

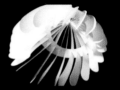

Proximity progression – monitor vessel MK3 – suspended canop

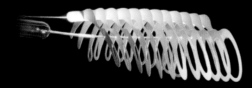
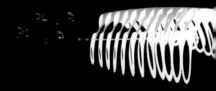

Rotational progression – monitor vessel MK6 – vascular channels / airflow compressio

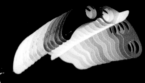
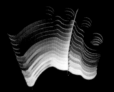

Rotational progression – monitor vessel MK5 – airflow directive captu

Rotational progression – monitor vessel MK2 – suspended raft / propagation caviti

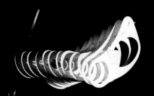

Proximity progression – monitor vessel MK4 – ambient particle mass / speed captu

"Air impinging onto the top agar plate is travelling at relatively low speed, and is deflected around the agar plate. Only the larger (heavier) airborne particles will have sufficient momentum to break free from this air current and impact onto the top agar surface. But then the same volume of air is sucked through a series of small holes, so its velocity is increased and this enables the smaller particles to impact onto the second agar plate. And so on, down the series of plates with increasingly smaller holes, so that the momentum of the airborne particles is increased at each stage."

(http://www.helios.bto.ed.ac.uk/bto/microbes/airborne.html)

The result is a separation of the particles by mass, similar to that which happens during human respiration. After a few hours exposure, the agar plates are removed and incubated, revealing the captured microorganisms for identification. Once again, the composition of the agar growth medium and the specific conditions of incubation can be varied in order to target specific organisms, facilitating different ranges of data accumulation.

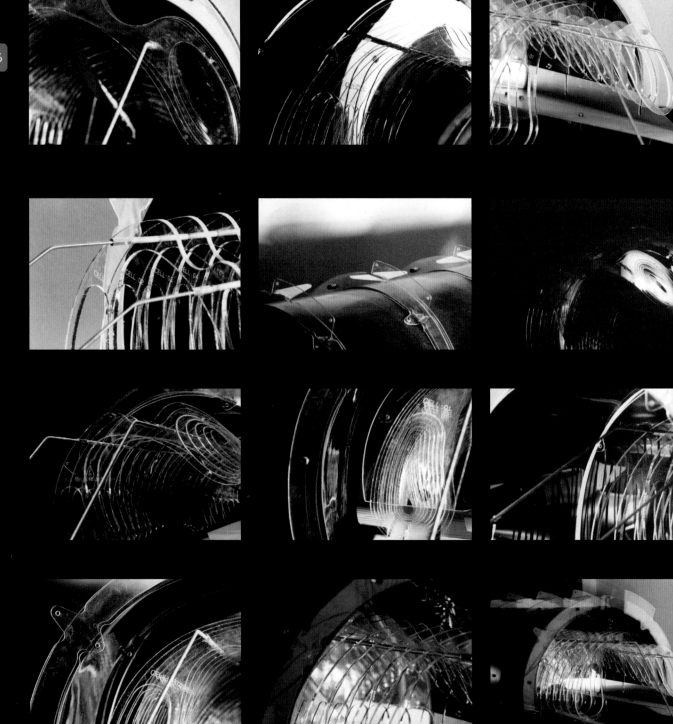

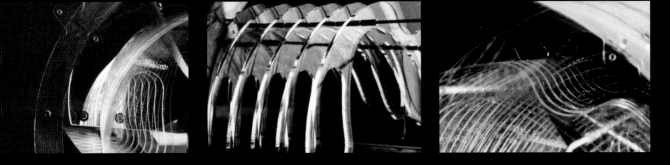

Holborn Station Particle Monitor Pre-exposure Component Assembly Tunnel Specific Sequential Chambers

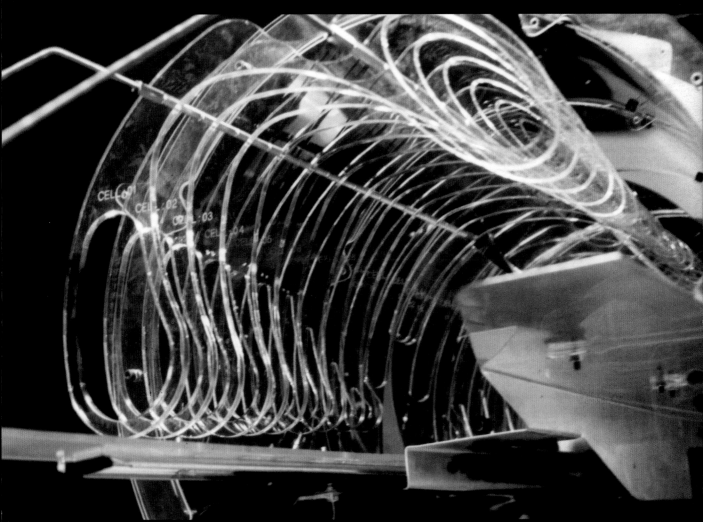

View of inflatable particle monitor from station platform

Onix Cave, Missouri USA

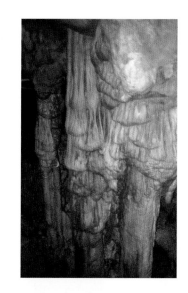

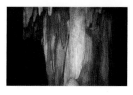

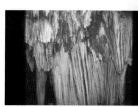

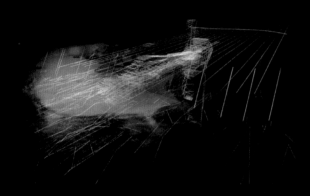

view from above expressing the extrusion of the building from the land ointo the sea

A **fish farm** develops from the interest in **fish locomotion**. The obsessive weaving and dynamics of shoals as they move in mass, create a unified structure with undefined boundaries.

The building stretches out into the ocean **stitching** land and sea together, merging the boundaries of the two, and expanding downwards into the deep, defining a **rhythm** maintained by the nets. Land becomes building, building becomes nets and nets become fish. **Boundaries become obscured and all forms are unified in a single shimmering surface of luminosity.**

The site plan illustrated is key for the design as it represents the transparent and luminous materiality of the project, creating a new landscape type: a seascape, which will now be associated with the fishfarming industry.

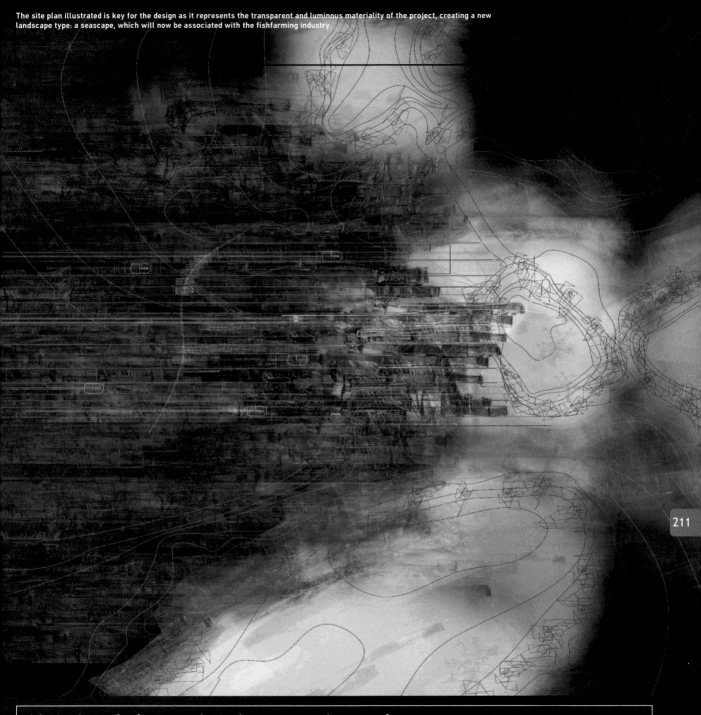

Undefined boundaries Limite Indefinido
Helsinki, Finland 2000-2001
Natalia Traverso Caruana

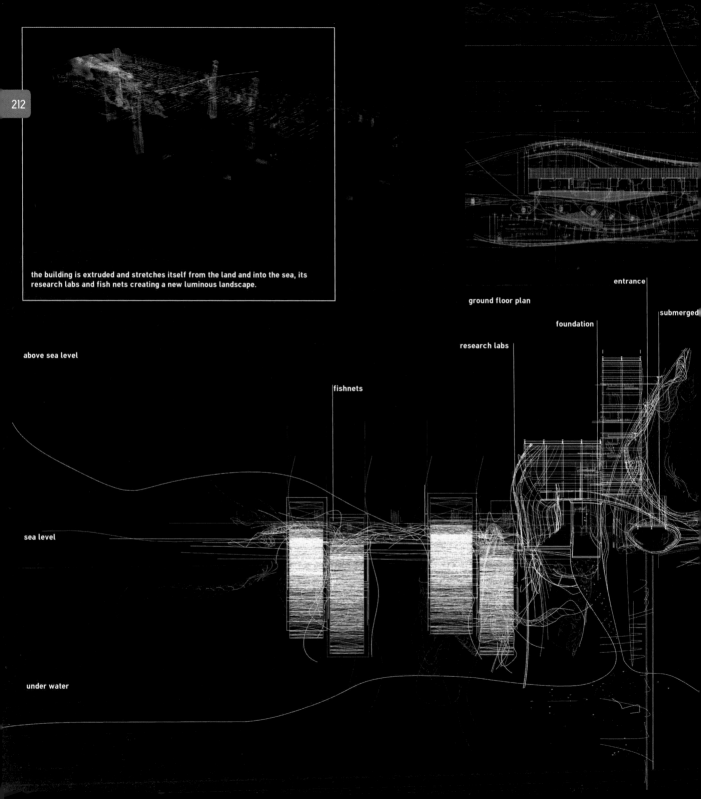

the building is extruded and stretches itself from the land and into the sea, its research labs and fish nets creating a new luminous landscape.

ground floor plan

entrance

foundation

submerged

research labs

above sea level

fishnets

sea level

under water

the sea seeps into the building and the fish tanks float inside. These are maintained, monitored by research scientists who operate within the central core.

sea bed

213

ames Foster

Helsinki
Finland

Crecimiento sobre paisaje
INHABitable
GROWTHSCAPE

A small boatyard, 200 metres off the coast of Helsinki requires a roofed area for the winter storage of boats. In order to justify the financial expenditure, the boatyard owners are planning to lease space within an **inhabitable roof** to an industry appointed to produce medicinal cannabis.

Under strictly controlled conditions, tissue culture will provide massive quantities of disease free cloned plants, and aeroponic systems. These allow growth to occur at twice the rate of a conventional system by spraying the suspended roots of each plant within a nutrient compound vessel, which will sustain plants until harvesting. A structural element forms an **aeroponic capsule**, a bank of three capsules forms a roof piece, and a network of roofpieces forms a protective canopy over the boatyard. The responsive capsule reacts to the growing plant within, descending with increasing weight, until a level is reached where the circulating harvester captures the plant. The **roofscape**, itself an extension of the landscape, becomes a representation of the growth it contains.

View from boatyard level looking up towards roof plantation

View from adjacent island showing boat launchers and roof structure

Roofpieces descend according to the weight of the plant inside

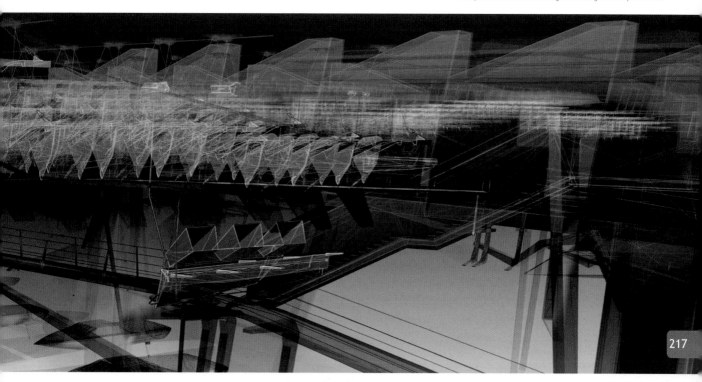

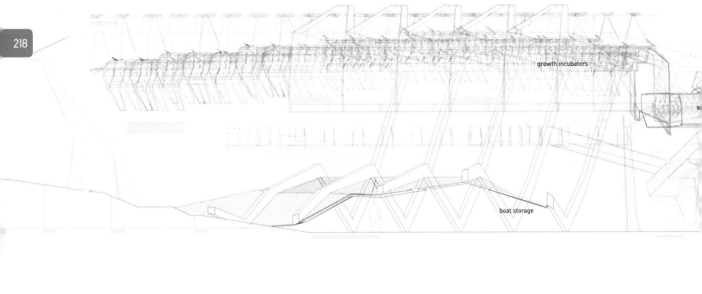

growth incubators

boat storage

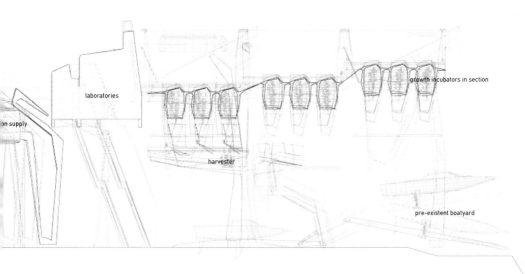

on supply

laboratories

growth incubators in section

harvester

pre-existent boatyard

Baltic Sea

Section through roof structure showing capsules at different levels according to plant size, and boat launchers below

Perspective while walking through roof structure

I search out the work of

rtists, and use art as a means

f inspiration. I

ry to rid myself and the other

embers of the firm, of the

urden of

ulture and look for new ways to

pproach the work. I want to be

pen-ended. There are no rules,

o right or wrong. I'm confused

s to what's ugly and what's

retty. "

et Nairn, Frank Gehry:

search for a 'No Rules' Architecture, Architectural Record, June 1976 (p. 95)

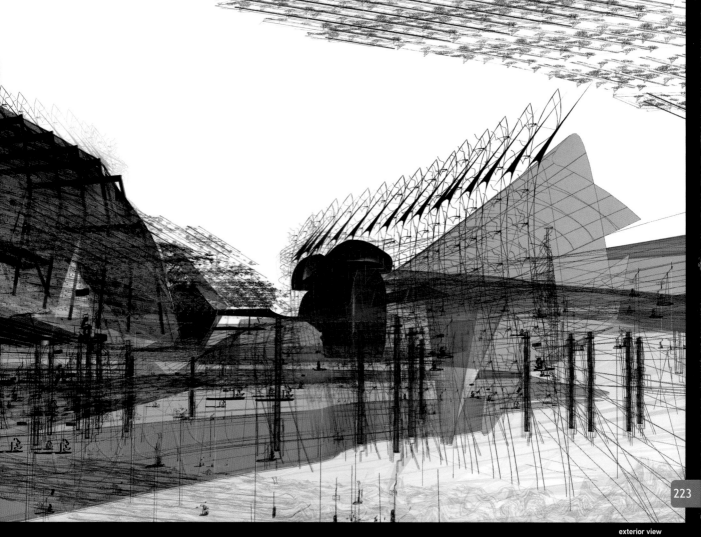

exterior view

Natalia Traverso Caruana

a viscous pulse
Un ritmo viscoso

Working Model

A silicone skin was developed as a representation of the hydrocarbon material (plastic/rubber like) requiredfor the skin of the building

A model is delicately hung in space, representative of the delicate and almost unstable nature of oil.

A VISCOUS PULSE
Cultural Branch for the Texaco Headquarter Building

Oil affects the world economically, politically, and socially. This proposal is a building celebrating oil and its multitudinous uses and functions. Oil and oil products are used throughout as building materials and also to operate various mechanisms.

The building is a tap for the oil extracted on the outskirts of Texas City, bordering the gulf of Mexico. The site on a collapsed oil well creates a large grove and slice in the ground with the building hovering over this area. A ferrofluid canopy is designed to pulsate dramatically in tune with the rhythm of the fluctuating stocks, changing and transforming dependant on the state of oil affairs and creating a visual representation of this process. Ferrofluid is part of a whole network of systems, which are physically affected by oil and its instabilities. The building becomes mortal and dependant on the availability of oil; a notion uncertain to all and defined by none.

A prototype was made and then reproduced following the 3 generalrules maintained by flocking animals:

1 move in same speed and direction

2 always keep a determined distance appart and never collide

3 motion is carried out with a supposed magnet in the centre which maintains the flock together

An investigation into flocking behavior led to the development of a responsive model which became affected and aggitated by the proximating predator...humans!

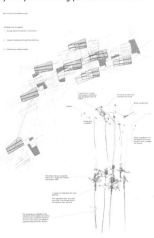
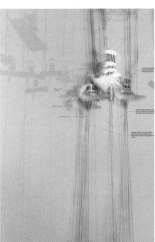

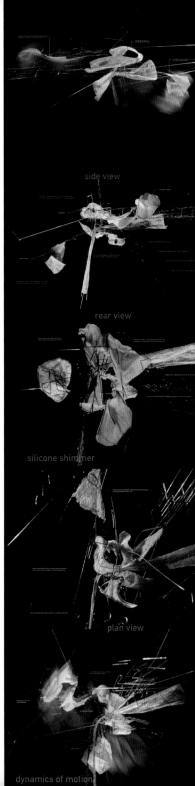

side view

rear view

silicone shimmer

plan view

dynamics of motion

Final model is responsive to human proximation_Sensors activate circuits within the model, vibrating moving and aggitating the model_Muscle wire causes the rod to swing gently all the boids in syncronised motion_When a human approaches sensors detect this and the motor is activated and spins the rod_If a person draws closer the boids rotate and incline and the spinning and swinging of the rod becomes a combined action of aggitation.

working computer
models

explorarion of building
forms
amalgamating the varios
volumes required for the
building

rear view expressing
how
forms pierce the ground
and extrude beneath

perspective view taken
from underground and
focussing on the pump-
ing sysyem of oil in the
foreground

frontal perspective view

rear perspective view-
from below

A computer model is developed to describe the spacial qualities
of the volumes and spaces designed.

A fluid impression and liquid finish isessential and simultani-
ously describes the effects below.

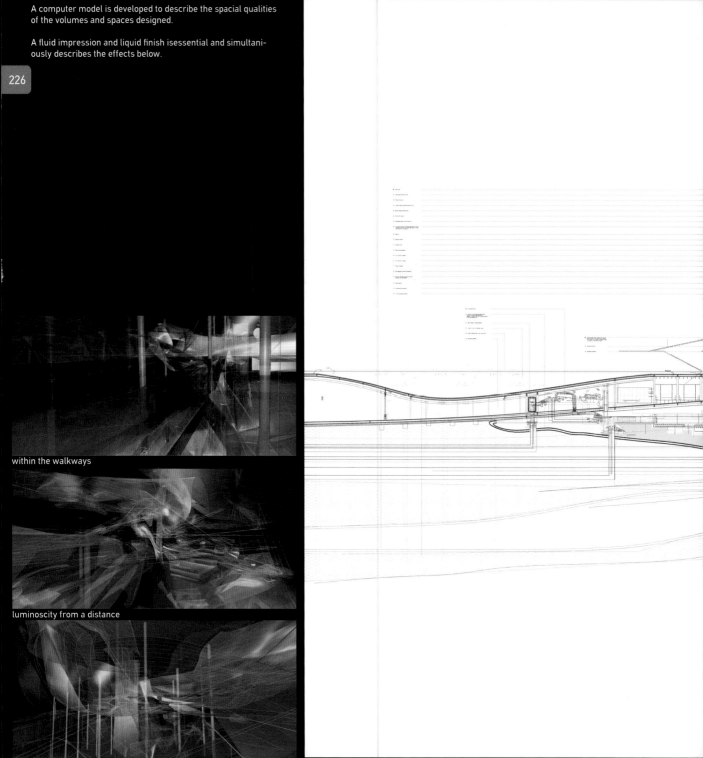

within the walkways

luminoscity from a distance

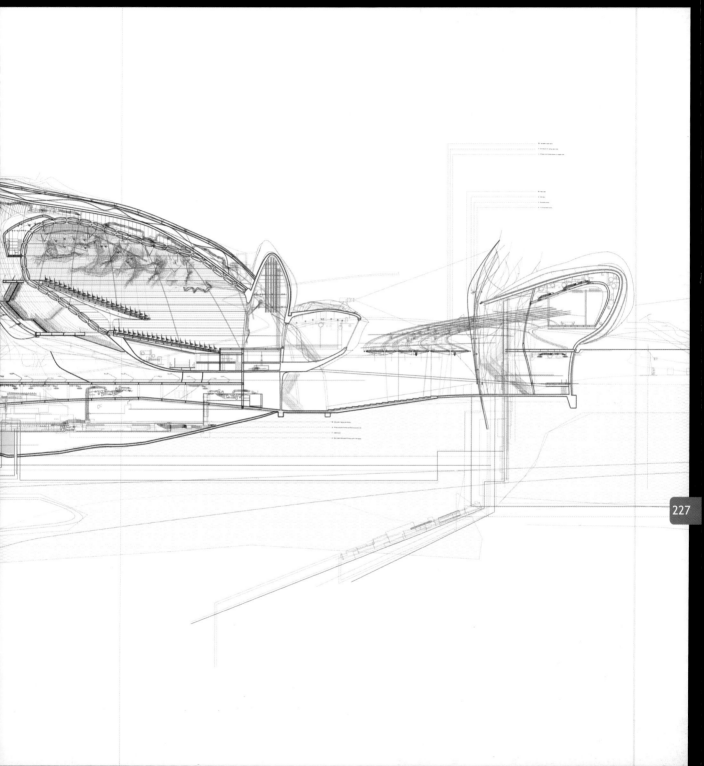

Close up of oil bag

view down the side of the conference hall

Approach under theatre belly

Approach to conference
hall entrance alongside the
acoustic oil bags

229

Interior view of
conference hall

c h i

a g o

BUILDING DETAILS

exposure

the light game and the abstract reflections in detail

close up image of the projection connection with the structure detail

view of the light shadow play as a reflection of the structure

view up from the ground into the void where the camera is positioned

Karen Willcox Vertigo Exposure in Chicago

The photographic and visual experimental laboratory

"…The cityscape at night as pure pulsating light sculpture. Car headlights could be frozen into paths of luminous tracery and illuminated advertisements would in time become the basis for an environmental art of darkness"

(Moholy Nagy)

The experimental laboratory for photographic and media studies is sited over a street junction in Chicago's downtown. It presents itself as a gigantic structure with an open core, which holds on its top a large photographic camera that captures both the movement within the building and traffic below. It integrates itself with the headquarters of a multinational printing press that uses the production of the photo lab for its own publishing purposes. The skin of the building contains **embedded spaces** of various technical functions, simultaneously working as light filters when their moveable lightweight floor plates cantilever over the empty spaces.

Enlarging the photographic process from the traditional dark room-based laboratory to the size of a skyscraper became the challenge of the project. This scale jump deals with major changes within the method of both picture taking and image developing. *The building becomes the camera and the images the elevation.*

View from the loop station 'Clark' viewing the building positioned in between the downtown skyscrapers of chicago

view from the camera which is positioned in the top of the building

the walkways and other pedestrian route making a labyrinth of interaction

paper process

view of the camera in the top from street level
view of the lightweight and moveable spaces which function as filters

view down into the void and heart of the building

view of the range of the camera seen from below

view of the vans in the top of the building

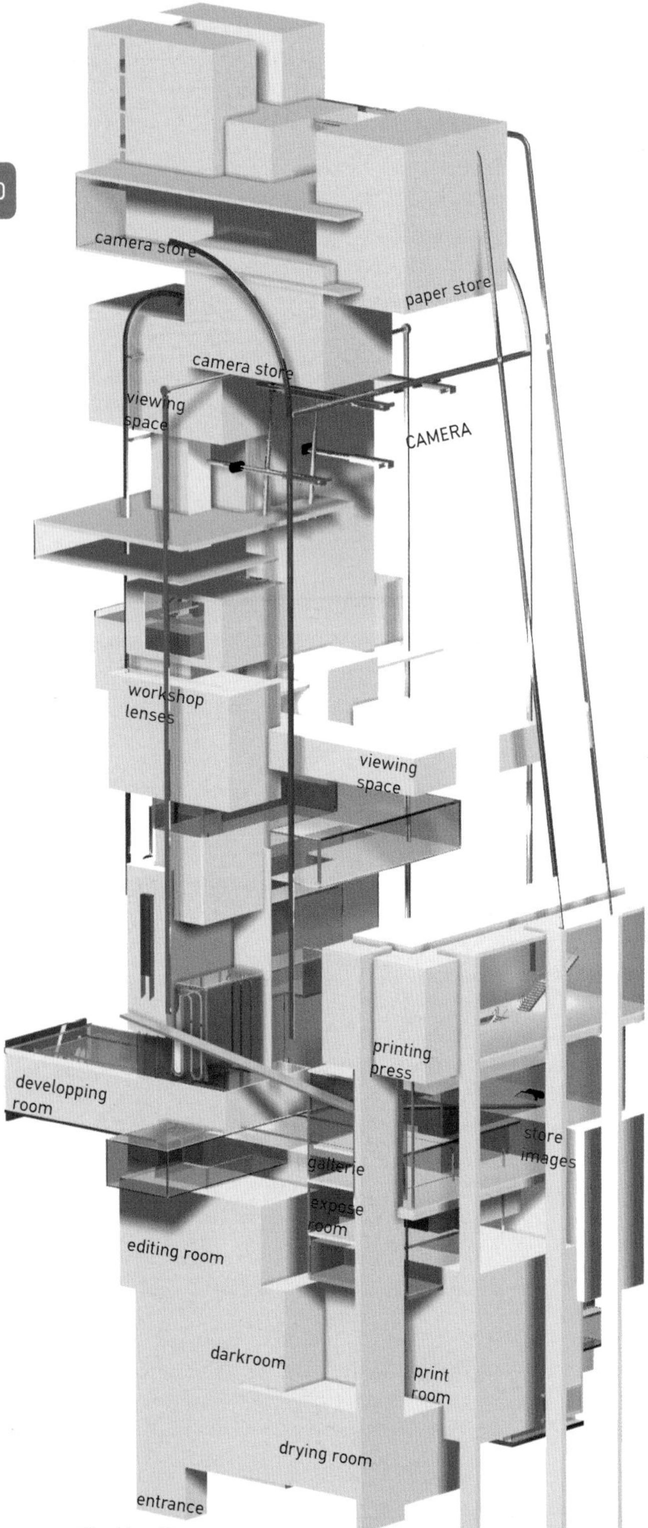

camera store

paper store

camera store

viewing
space

CAMERA

workshop
lenses

viewing
space

printing
press

developping
room

store
images

gallerie

expose
room

editing room

darkroom

print
room

drying room

entrance

axonometric of functions

perspective view from the south when a photograph is been taken

from the drying area after the developpartment

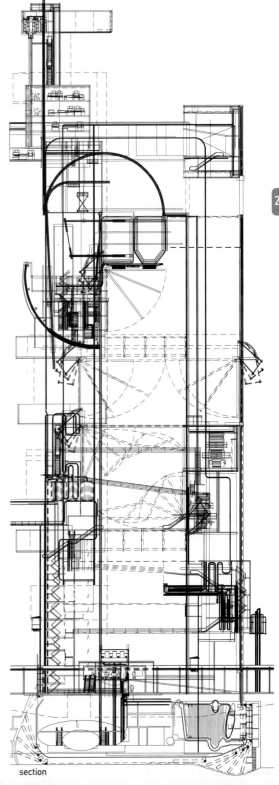

section

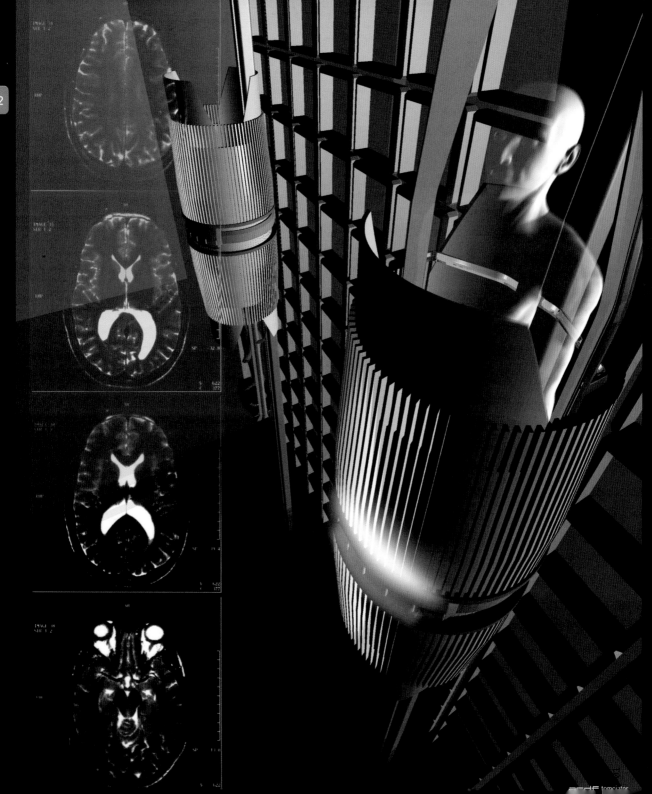

Daniel Schwaag

human resources center
Centro de recursos humanos
Helsinki, Finland

It is arguable that recent advances in biochemistry and forensics are causing a redefinition of spaces and their boundaries. They facilitate the use of minute samples of **human detritus** such as blood, urine, hair, skin, etc. as a means of gaining an almost comprehensive insight into a person's physiological makeup and identity for medical, political and forensic purposes. A short innocent contact might have lasting significance.

The border between the **body's in- and exterior**, demarcated by the skin, is thereby increasingly blurred, in order to delineate a significant barrier to physiological analysis or vision, which was initially only penetrated by conversation, touch, **stethoscope** and **X-rays**. In the not too distant future, a single **DNA sample** will potentially reveal much more, without any physical or temporal contact between examiner and examinee. Recent consideration to record the DNA of every person arrested in large **DNA banks**, outline a potential forensic application of such technologies.

Selected References
Foucault, Michael, Heterotopia and Other Spaces in Rethinking Architecture, ed. Nick Leach (London, Routeledge 1997

Graff, Laurine, Handbook of routine urinalysis (Piladelphia: Lippincott 1983)

Kimbrell, Andrew, The Human Body Shop – The Engineering and Marketing of Life (London: Harper Collins Religius: 1983)

tomolator
the device secretively performs computerized x-rays (tomography) on subjects using vertical building transportation (elevators).

urinalyzer

first generation: the first object of study was the design of a device in reaction to frequent urination in a specific doorway in North London. The janus faced device performs instant urinalysis and health consultation, repeat offenders are repelled by a smoke agent reacting with the urine to create a pungent smoke cloud.

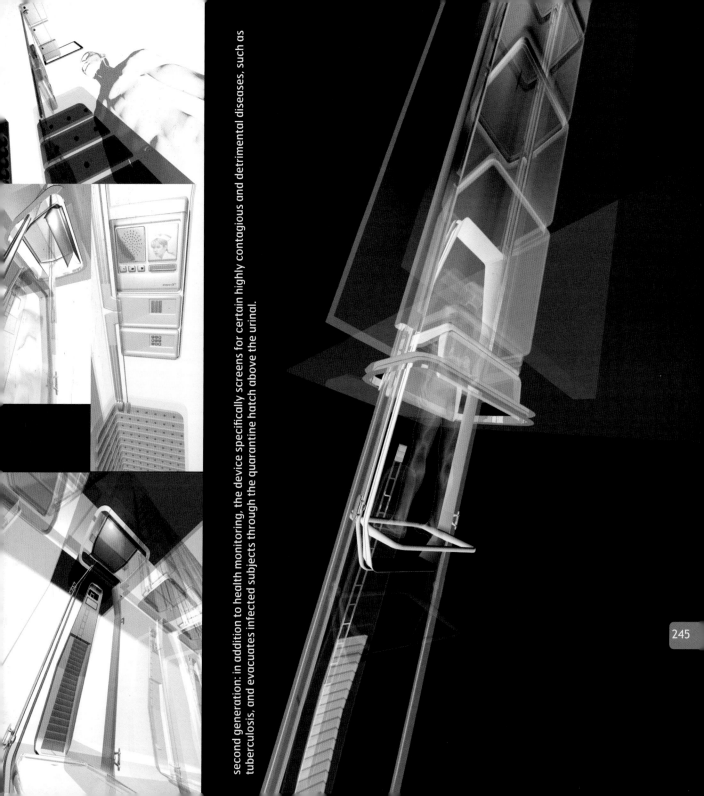

second generation: in addition to health monitoring, the device specifically screens for certain highly contagious and detrimental diseases, such as tuberculosis, and evacuates infected subjects through the quarantine hatch above the urinal.

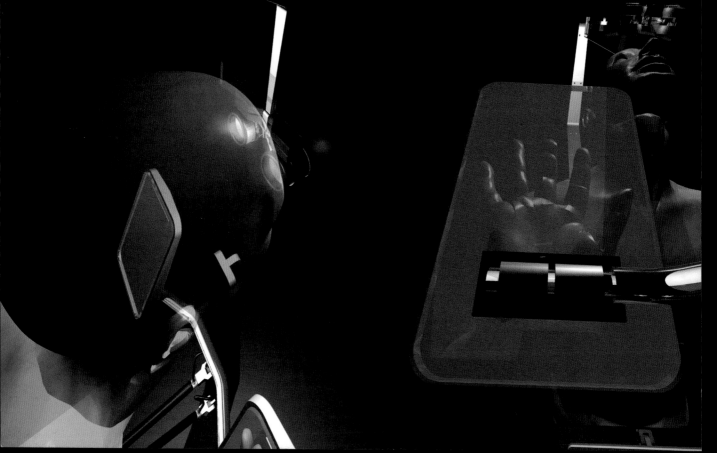

intellibule

consists of a series of devices form an intelligent vestibule which establishes a comprehensive health profile of visitors and passer-bys. Depending on the profile, people may be admitted or repelled.

retinascan

while a peeping subject satisfies its curiosity by looking though the aperture into the mystery box, the retina is scanned and analyzed according to twenty tests, subjects are forced to rest their hands on support pads which then obtain fingerprint scans.

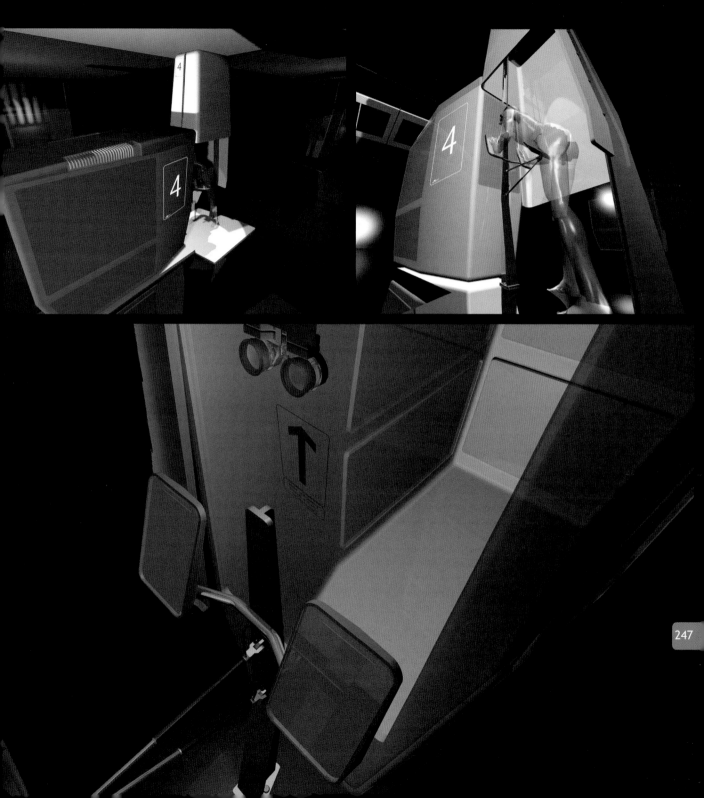

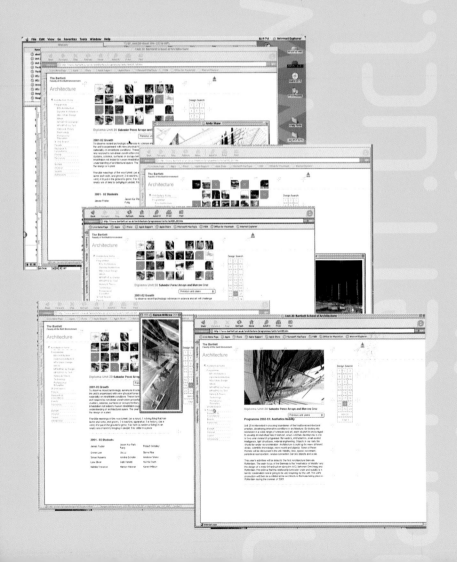

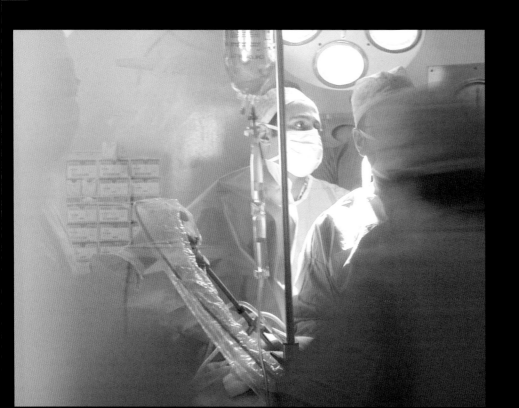

interdisciplinary work

Jai Lu research on plastic surgery supported by the Royel Free Hospital

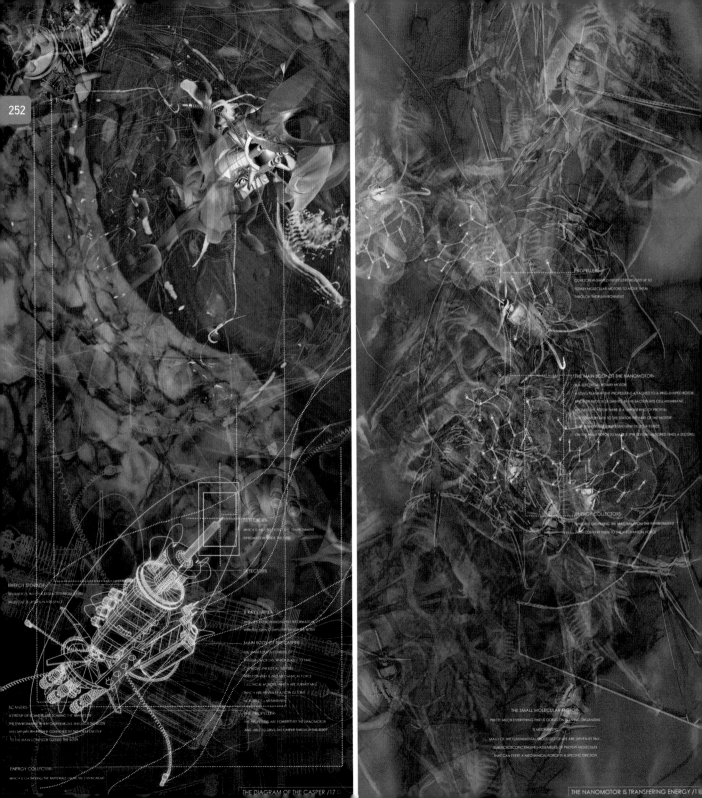

THE DIAGRAM OF THE CASPER /17

THE NANOMOTOR IS TRANSFERING ENERGY /11

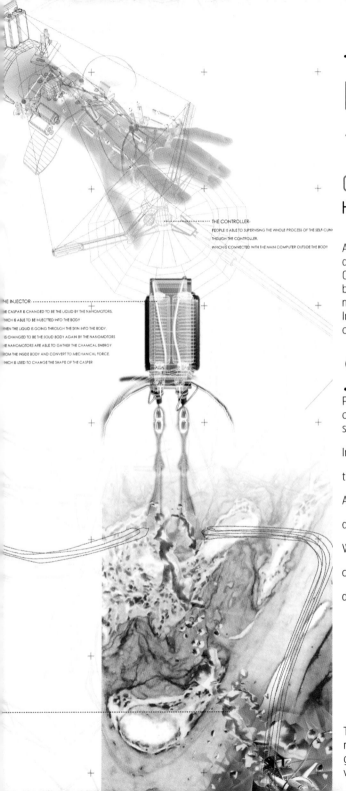

THE CONTROLLER-
PEOPLE IS ABLE TO SUPERVISING THE WHOLE PROCESS OF THE SELF-CLINIC
THOUGH THE CONTROLLER.
WHICH IS CONNECTED WITH THE MAIN COMPUTER OUTSIDE THE BODY

ME INJECTOR-
E CASPAR IS CHANGED TO BE THE LIQUID BY THE NANOMOTORS.
HICH IS ABLE TO BE INJECTED INTO THE BODY
HEN THE LIQUID IS GOING THROUGH THE SKIN INTO THE BODY.
IS CHANGED TO BE THE SOLID BODY AGAIN BY THE NANOMOTORS
E NANOMOTORS ARE ABLE TO GATHER THE CHAMICAL ENERGY
ROM THE INSIDE BODY AND CONVERT TO MECHANICAL FORCE.
HICH IS USED TO CHANGE THE SHAPE OF THE CASPER

Jia Lu
Reconstruction lounge
Centro de reconstrucción
Heathrow Airport, London, UK 2001 - 2002

Aesthetic surgery is being increasingly used to improve appearances. However, surgery continues to be a frightening term. Giving away the control of our body to someone else, opening the body's natural seal, and the memories of digusting bloody imagery, makes patients nervous, uncomfortable and fearful.
In order to change this condition patients need a higher degree of control and ease in the process of body transformation.

Self becomes the key for self-transformation.
Patients take the active role in determining the outcome of surgery, controlling the pace and results of the operation, without pain and suffering.

In the future, this might be the next step in creating an individualism

that goes beyond one's adornments or clothing.

A site at Heathrow is chosen for the reason that the client's (patient's)

anonymity will be respected in a 'a politically and morally territory'.

With the advancement in nano-technology, the majority of the jobs

can be done painless and with machine. The individual surgery spaces

dictate the layout of the proposed Body Transformation lounge.

The idea of altering the body is inspired by the growth and manipulation of bone tissue in side the human body. The logic of growth, is conducted the graduate transformation process from very 'soft' issue to the hard 'tissue structures.

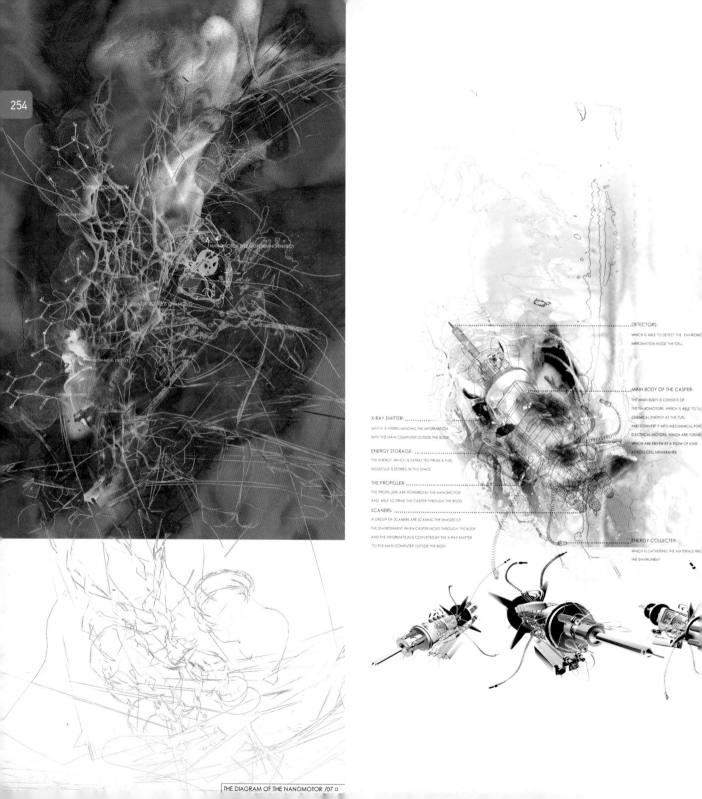

ENERGY CONVERSION

CHEMICAL ENERGY

MECHANICAL ENERGY

NANOMOTOR IS TRANSFORMING ENERGY

CONSTRUCT IS CHANGING

MECHANICAL ENERGY

CHEMICAL ENERGY

DETECTORS-
WHICH IS ABLE TO DETECT THE ENVIRON(
INFROMATION INSIDE THE CELL

MAIN BODY OF THE CASPER-
THE MAIN BODY IS CONSISTS OF
THE NANOMOTORS, WHICH IS ABLE TO Te
CHEMICAL ENERGY AS THE FUEL
AND CONVERT IT INTO MECHANICAL FOR
ELECTRICAL MOTORS, WHICH IS TOPA
WHICH ARE FRIVEN BY A FLOW OF IONS
ACROSS CELL MEMBRANES

X-RAY EMITTER-
WHICH IS INTERCHANGING THE INFORMATION
WITH THE MAIN COMPUTER OUTSIDE THE BODY

ENERGY STORAGE-
THE ENERGY, WHICH IS EXTRACTED FROM A FUEL
MOLECULE IS STORED IN THIS SPACE

THE PROPELLER-
THE PROPELLERS ARE POWERED BY THE NANOMOTOR
AND ABLE TO DRIVE THE CASPER THROUGH THE BODY

SCANERS-
A GROUP OF SCANERS ARE SCANING THE IMAGES OF
THE ENVIRONMENT WHEN CASPER MOVE THROUGH THE BODY
AND THE INFORMATION IS CONVEYED BY THE X-RAY EMITTER
TO THE MAIN COMPUTER OUTSIDE THE BODY

ENERGY COLLECTER-
WHICH IS GATHERING THE MATERIALS FR(
THE ENVIRONEMT

THE DIAGRAM OF THE NANOMOTOR /07

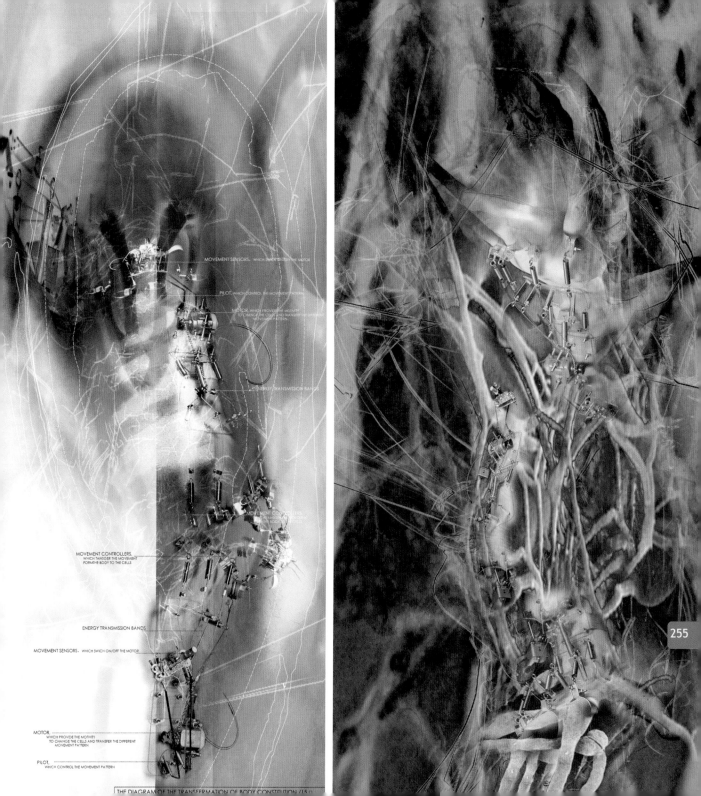

MOVEMENT SENSORS, WHICH SWITCH ON/OFF THE MOTOR

PILOT, WHICH CONTROL THE MOVEMENT PATTERN

MOTOR, WHICH PROVIDE THE MOTIVITY TO CHANGE THE CELLS AND TRANSFER THE DIFFERENT MOVEMENT PATTERN

ENERGY TRANSMISSION BANDS

MOVEMENT CONTROLLERS, WHICH TRANSFER THE MOVEMENT FORM THE BODY TO THE CELLS

MOVEMENT CONTROLLERS, WHICH TRANSFER THE MOVEMENT FORM THE BODY TO THE CELLS

ENERGY TRANSMISSION BANDS

MOVEMENT SENSORS, WHICH SWICH ON/OFF THE MOTOR

MOTOR, WHICH PROVIDE THE MOTIVITY TO CHANGE THE CELLS AND TRANSFER THE DIFFERENT MOVEMENT PATTERN

PILOT, WHICH CONTROL THE MOVEMENT PATTERN

255

THE DIAGRAM OF THE TRANSFERMATION OF BODY CONSTITUTION /1.5 r1

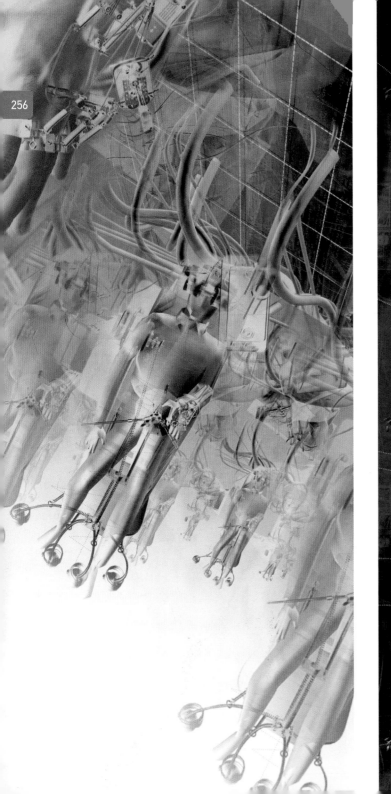
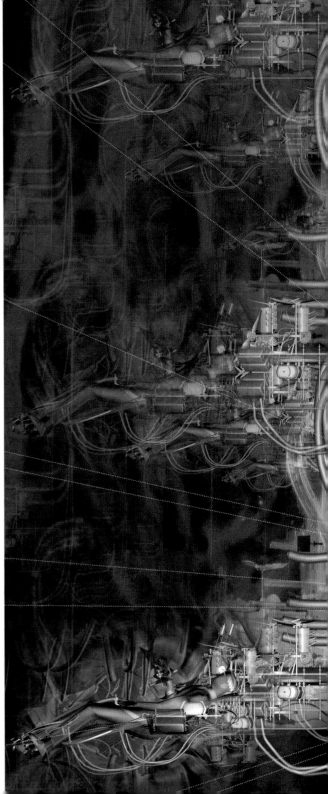

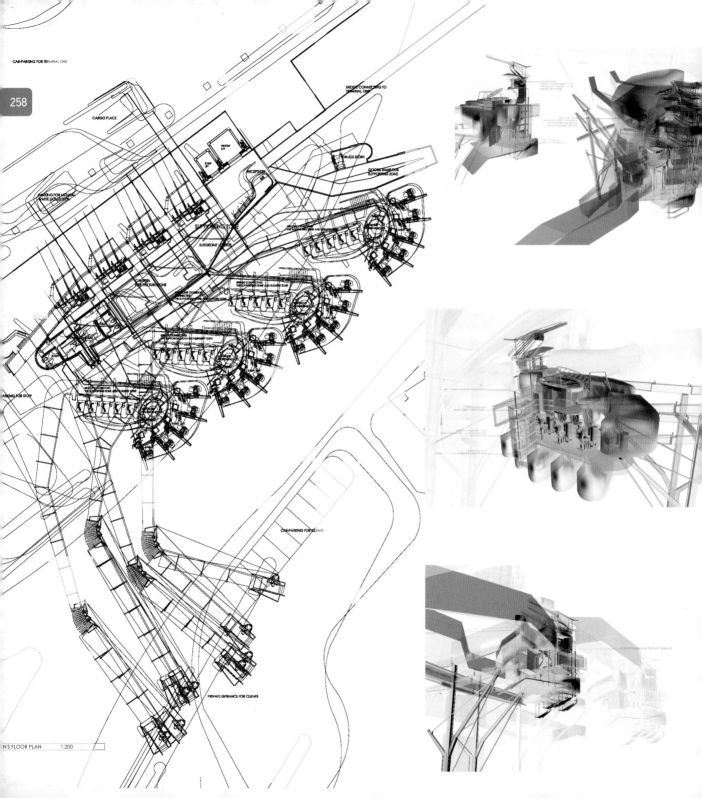

CAR-PARKING FOR TERMINAL ONE

CARGO PLACE

BRIDGE CONNECTING TO
TERMINAL ONE

FRIGHT LIFT

DRUGS STORE

RECEPTION

GOODS RAMP FOR
SUPPORTING ZONE

PARKING FOR MEDICAL
WASTE COLLECTION

SUPPORTING ZONE

SURGEONS ZONE

CHAPEL
ONLY FOR SURGEONS

CAR-PARKING FOR CLIENTS

PARKING FOR STUFF

PRIVATE ENTRANCE FOR CLIENTS

N'S FLOOR PLAN   1:200

HEATHROW AS THE LAND OF FREEDOM

259

THE PROCEDURE OF THE SELF-BODY TRANSFORM

RECOVERY SPACE

SURGERY PROCEDURE

CHECK UP

BODY SCAN

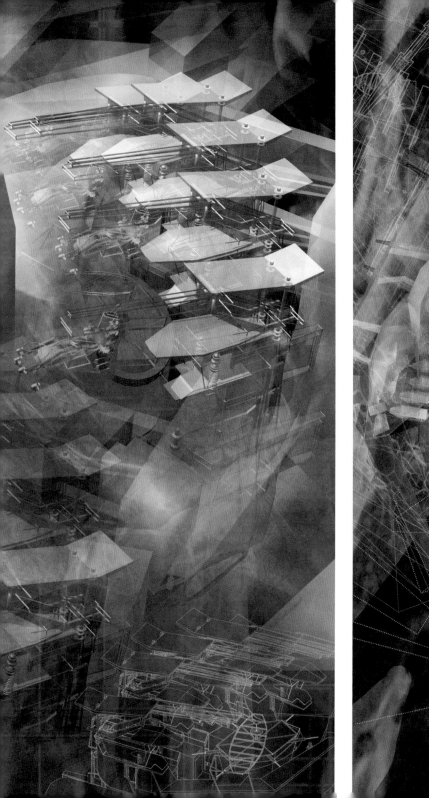

261

XTRAS

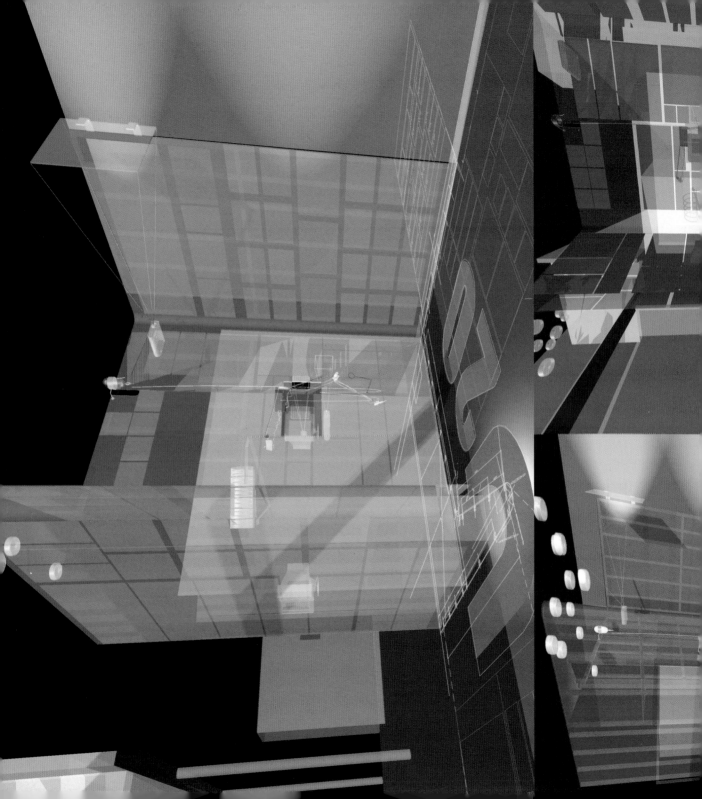

This year, for the first time, the

BARTFEST multimedia exhibition

was held in the galleries of the

Slade School of Fine Art at UCL with

over **400** students showing

innovative drawings, models,

devices, animations and

installations.

01/02

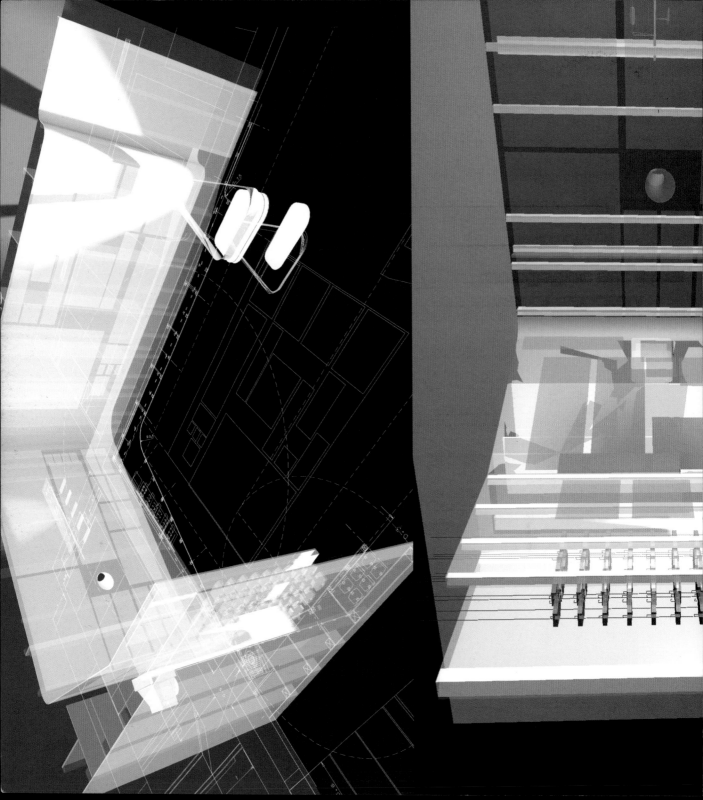

Bartlett school of Architecture

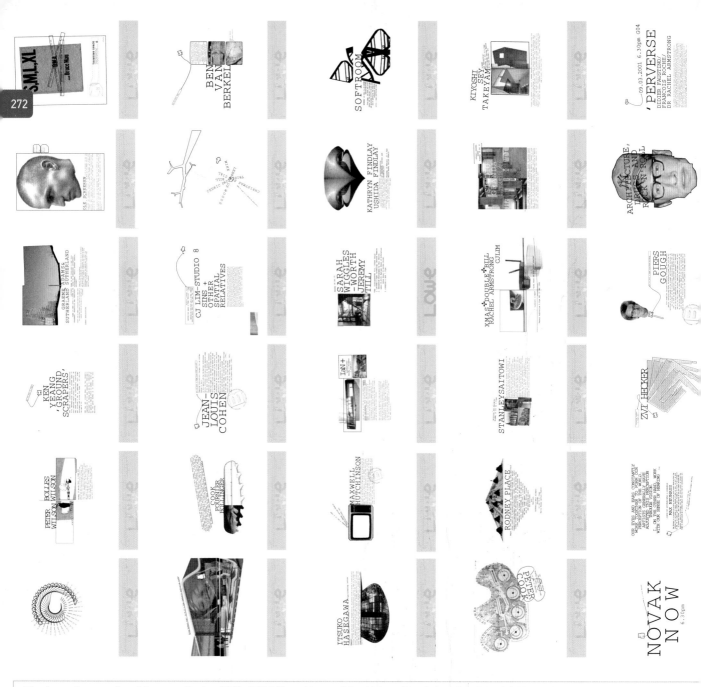

The Lowe International Lecture Series 2001 -2002 Thom Mayne -Winy Maas - Greg Lynn - Kyong Park [Urban Adventures and Political Fictions in Detroit] - sixteen*(makers) ['A Year in the Making']- Andy Bow - Dominique Perrault - Mark Wigley ['How Old is Young: The Concept of the Young Architect'] - Kathryn Findlay ['Transformation of Sequence, Aikido + Materiality']-Tarla MacGabhann ['Fields of View']- Tom de Paor ['ARTERIAL- Some Strategies or Margins + Edges']- Rick Mather [Recent Work and Great Expectations'] - Graeme Williamson Zoe Smith ['Block City']- Lars Spuybroek [NOX Architects]- Maxwell Hutchinson [Architecture and Television']- Kengo Kuma ['Architecture as Anti-object']- Mark Goulthorpe deCOi - Ben Nicholson [The World-who wants it and who gets it']- Nat Chard ['Drawing indeterminate architecture, indeterminate drawings of architecture']- Ian+ ['Earthscapes'] [ianplus.it] - Tetsou Furuichi ['Critical Inconsistency']- Itsuko Hasegawa['Landscape Architecture']- Stanley Saitowitz['Buildings and Projects']- Studio Granda - Rodney

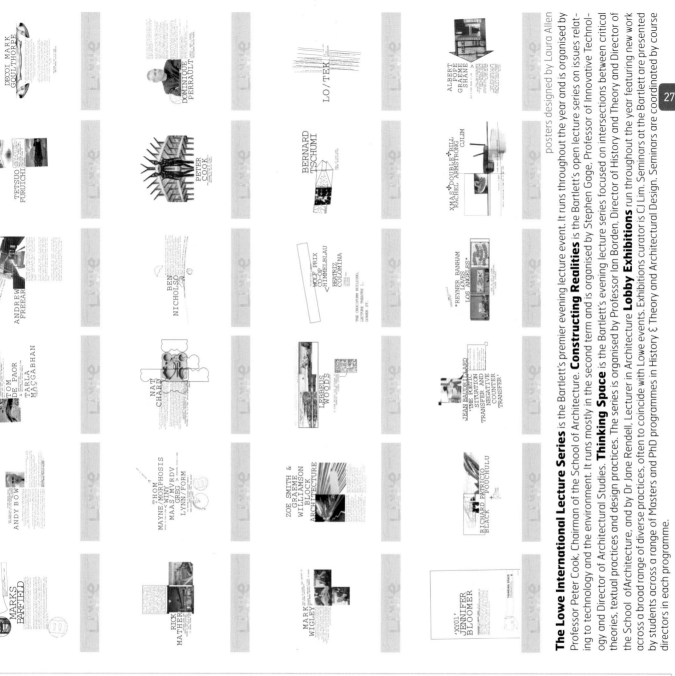

posters designed by Laura Allen

The Lowe International Lecture Series is the Bartlett's premier evening lecture event. It runs throughout the year and is organised by Professor Peter Cook, Chairman of the School of Architecture. **Constructing Realities** is the Bartlett's open lecture series on issues relating to technology and the environment. It runs mostly in the second term and is organised by Stephen Gage, Professor of Innovative Technology and Director of Architectural Studies. **Thinking Space** is the Bartlett's evening lecture series focused on intersections between critical theories, textual practices and design practices. The series is organised by Professor Ian Borden, Director of History and Theory and Director of the School ofArchitecture, and by Dr Jane Rendell, Lecturer in Architecture **Lobby Exhibitions** run throughout the year featuring new work across a broad range of diverse practices, often to coincide with Lowe events. Exhibitions curator is CJ Lim. Seminars at the Bartlett are presented by students across a range of Masters and PhD programmes in History & Theory and Architectural Design. Seminars are coordinated by course directors in each programme.

Poster labels (within image):

DECOI MARK GOULTHORPE · TETSUO FURUICHI · ANDREW FREEAR · TOM DE PAOR / TARLA MACGABHAN · ANDY BOW · MARKS BARFIELD · DOMINIQUE PERRAULT · PETER COOK · BEN NICHOLSON · NAT CHARD · THOM MAYNE/MORPHOSIS / WINY MAAS MVRDV / GREG LYNN/FORM · ZOE SMITH & GRAEME WILLIAMSON BLOCK ARCHITECTURE · RICK MATHER · MARK WIGLEY · LO/TEK · BERNARD TSCHUMI · WOLF PRIX CO-OP HIMMELBLAU / BEATRIZ COLOMINA · THE CRUCIFORM BUILDING, LECTURE THEATRE 1, GOWER ST. · LEBBEUS WOODS · JEAN BAUDRILLARD 'THE POETIC SITUATION TRANSFER AND NEGATIVE COUNTER TRANSFER' · RICHARD PATRICIO POUCHULU · 'XY01' JENNIFER BLOOMER · ALBERT POPE / GRAEME SHANE · XMAS DOUBLE BILL RACHEL ARMSTRONG CJ LIM · *REYNER BANHAM LOVES LOS ANGELES*

Place['RETREKS–a metro allegory']–Kiyoshi Sey Takayama['Screen and Reflection']– Wigglesworth and Till ['9/10 Stock Orchard Street']– Peter Cook ['The Architecture Of Optimism'] 2000-2001 General Lighting and Power – Peter Cook – Colin Fournier – Graeme Sutherland – Ole Scheeren – Bruce Mau – Richard Gregory – Marcos Novak – Lars Spruybroek/NOX – Cedric Price – Mike Webb – Max Neuhaus – Marks Barfield – Zvi Hecker – Ken Yeang – Cj Lim – Dr Rachel Armstrong – Francois Roche – Didier Faustino – Peter Wilson – Piers Gough – Neil Denari – Ben van Berkel – Jean Louis Cohen – Norman Foster 1999-2000 Lebbeus Woods – Paul Finch – Peter Cook – Philip Steadman – Bernard Tschumi – Edouard Francois & Associates – Mary Banham – AHMM – Urban Salon – Kas Oosterhaus – STELARC – Softroom – Sumet Jumsai – Joel Sanders – Marcos Novak – LOT/EK – Cj Lim – Rachel Armstrong – Roche, DSV&SIE –

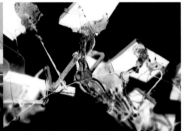

STEPHEN Clements // [Hydroponic Farm] 1999-2000
A model built with vacuum formed Perspex, aluminium structure and electric circuits demonstrates the spatial and technical complexity of hydroponic farms on the polluted waste land of former industrial areas along the Bilbao river.

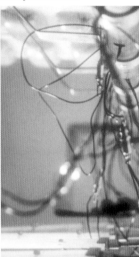

TOM Foster // [Bilbao Healthculture Matrix] 1999-2000
A bio-technological chassie is employed as the underlying food, medical and energy supplier to a series of floating wards for a floating hospital.

NATALIA Traverso Caruana // [Rodograph / Flocking Boids] 2000-2001
Installation of nine mechanical rods as an alternative fishing system off the coast of Tenerife, Canary Islands. movement and agitated their character.

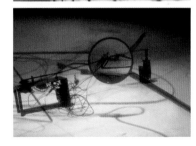

KEVIN Chu // [Incentrix – Cluster City] 2000-2001
A device to record the movement of living locusts in an enclosed vessel. Surface mounted sensors translate movement into sound and laser projection.

ANNIKA Schollin // [Decycle – Dirty Rotten Architecture] 2001-2002
Decay-machine installation on an existing wall. Surface decomposes chemically, physically and biologically.

STRAVOULA-FRYNI Yannopoulou // [Reinvented Dehumidifier] 2000-2001
A dehumidifier was decomposed and rebuilt to create a cycle of water for domestic tea consumption.

CARMEN Jimenez // [Ferry Terminal] 1999-2000
Model in fabric,, latex and metal thread.

LORI Avakian // [Water Purification Station] 1999-2000
An inflatable creature was constructed to study expandable movements of a rubber membrane.

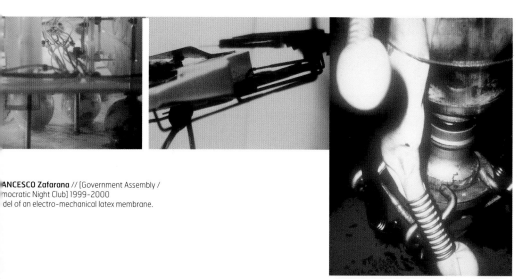

ANCESCO Zafarana // [Government Assembly / mocratic Night Club] 1999-2000
del of an electro-mechanical latex membrane.

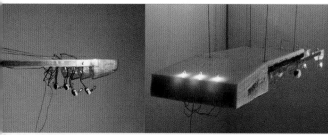

ARTEMIS Theodoridi // [Sismograph] 2000-2001
Several water containers were designed as precision tanks to measure the earth vibrations on the Teide Vulcano in Tenerife, Canary Islands.

NATALIA Traverso Caruana // [Rodograph / Flocking Boids] 2000-2001
Studies with responsive architecture: an architecture which can learn, sense and act from its surroundings. A stimulus triggers a reaction which may then become affected according to other external or environmental factors.

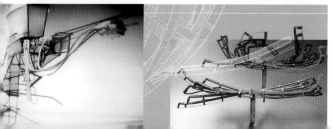

ZORAN Orescanin // [Spider expansion] 1999-2000
Studies of contraction and expansion of arm-like mechanisms.

critic's list

Constantin Kaskanis

David Portman [Nicholas Grimshaw & Partners]

Prof. Christine Hawley **U21**

CJ Lim **U21** [Studio 8 //Bartlett Architecture Lab]

Prof. Stephen Gage **U14** [Electric Clinic + Bartlett interactive workshop]

Goncalo Furtado [Mute]

Niel Spiller **U19**

Prof. Peter Cook **MArch** [Spacelab]

Yael Reisner **MArch**

Mathis Osterhage

Laura Allen **U8** [Allen and Smout]

Dr. Jonathan Hill **U12**

Marjan Colletti **U5** [marcosandmarjan]

Penelope Haralabidou **U2** [Tessera]

Yeoryia Manolopoulo **U17** [Tessera]

Lesley Lokko North London University

Barbara-Ann Campbell-Lange **MArch**

Lorens Holm

Prof. Shimon Shapiro Cambridge University

Nick Callicott **U6** [Sixteen*[makers]

bartfolio list

ex Bartlett Diploma students
presen their work the the unit
[in 1 or 2 hours]

Kristina Ehlert
John Puttick
Mathias Osterhage
Jens Ritter
Stephen Clements
Nicola Haines
Jochum Ledgister
Bernd Felsinger

rens holm _briefs _field trips_ technical studies_natalia traverso caruana//ferrofluidic
re series _ critics_bartholin _students _curriculum vitae_acknowledgements _index

277

Kristina Emert

Ana Betancour U24 East London University,

Stockholm University [p.h.a.b.architects]

Sonia Arbaci

Alejandro Romanutti

Eva Hurtado[Perez Arroyo Hurtado]

Barnaby Gunning | CRITS: PUBLIC PRESENTATIONS

Gwenola Kergall | OF STUDENT WORK WITH INVITED

Marko Jobst Kingston University | CRITICS EVERY SECOND MONTH

Bob Sheil U6 [Sixteen*[makers] | OF THE YEAR

Karin Damrau [Damrau + Pasing]

Prof. Phil Tabor U17

Tom Foster ex U20

Emmanuel Pringer

Niels Jonkhans

D. Conrad Mollinaux Microbiology Department,UCL

Tea lim

Aaron Udvardy

Kenneth Fraser [Arup Associates]

Marcos Cruz U20 [marcosandmarjan]

Salvador Perez Arroyo Hurtado, [Perez Arroyo Hurtado,

University of Madrid]

Laura Petruso

1999–2002

1999-2000 Kevin Chu - Tom Foster - James Henman - Zoran Orescanin – Jeremy Marsden – Steven Pike - Jens Ritter - James Sweet - Francesco Zafarana – Lori Ava-

kian – Carmen Jimenez – Timothy Wray - Oliver Lee – Stephen Clements – Yasmin Kaygusuz – James Reed 2000-01 Kevin Chu - James Foster - Tom Foster - James

Henman - Mark Mueckenheim - Zoran Orescanin - Jens Ritter - Daniel Schwaag - Lisa Silver - James Sweet - Gabriel Tang - Artemis Theodoridi - Natalia Traverso

- Stavroula-Fryni Yannopoulou - Karen Willcox - Annette Yan Yah Yeung - Steven Pike – Ingrid Hora 2001-02 Lisa Silver - Andy Shaw - Karen Willcox - James Foster-

Hui Hui Teoh - Jia Lu- Annika Schollin - Galit Tandet - Gwen Shao Jun Lee -Martyn Weaver - Jason Park Fung - Natalia Traverso- Robert Grindley - Simon Roberts

Commendation in theoretical dissertation

1999–00

Tom Foster

Kevin Chu - James Henman - Zoran Orescanin –
Jeremy Marsden – Steven Pike - Jens Ritter - James Sweet -
Francesco Zafarana – Lori Avakian – Carmen Jimenez – Timothy Wray
Oliver Lee – Stephen Clements – Yasmin Kaygusuz – James Reed

1999–2000

Commendation in architectural design

2000-01

Commendation in architectural design
Archigram prize for cheerfulness

Commendation in theoretical dissertation

Kevin Chu

James Foster – Tom Foster – James Herman –
Mark Mueckenheim – Zoran Oresconin – Jens Ritter
Daniel Schwaag – Lisa Silver –
Natalia Traverso – Stavrola Fry Yannopoulou –
Steven Pike – Ingrid Hora

Artemis Theodoridi –
Karen Wilcox – Annette Yan Yah Yeung

further development
into Masters Program

2001-02

Commendation in architectural design

further development into Masters Program

James Foster –
Annika Schollin – Galit Tandet
Hui Hui Teoh – Martyn Weaver – Jason Park Fung –
Robert Grindley – Simon Roberts

Lisa Silver:
Andy Shaw – Karen Wilcox
Jia Lu:
Gwen Shao Jun Lee:
Natalia Traverso:

Commendation in Technical Dissertation

Distinction in Architectural design
Sir banister Fletcher Prize for the highest marks in the Diploma in
Architecture final Examination
Nomination for RIBA Presidents Silver Medal

Liftschutz Davidson Award for Learning from Practice. (jointly awarded
to 5 outstanding students)

Distinction in Architectural design
Ambrose Poynter Prize for promising student in Architecture
Commendation in technical dissertation

Commendation in Technical Dissertation.

Opener's Prize awarded by Thom Mayne, sponsored by Lee Associates, awarded for best Exhibit or Best Unit in Show

Curriculum vitae

ANNIKA SCHOLLIN was born in Lund in Sweden in 1975. After gaining her degree in architecture at The Royal Danish Academy of Fine Arts, Copenhagen, she moved to London where she got her BSc(Hons) and diploma at the Bartlett. Annika worked in several offices in Sweden and Denmark including Henning Larsen Office and Samark in collaboration with Santiago Calatrava, also collaborated with AMP Arquitectos in Tenerife, and with David Chipperfield in London. She is currently working for Wilkinson Ayre Architects in London, while working on the design and organisation of the U20 publication. Technical tutor: Brendan Woods and external examiner: Ben Menkin

DANIEL SCHWAAG was born in Detroit, USA in 1972 He gained his bachelor of science in architecture at the University of Virginia, School of Architecture, USA. He worked in Vienna, Austria with Bus before moving to London, where he gainedmasters degree in science andurban design at the Bartlett. This work was awarded a distinction. After graduating he started working as Senoir Illustrator for a multimedia office Three dI ltd Design in London. Currently he is working as a freelance architect in London.Technical tutor: Rachel Amstrong.

JAMES FOSTER was born in Middlesbrough, UK, in 1978. He obtained a BA honours degree in Architecture at the University of Nottingham. After working for Edward Cullinan Architects he completed his diploma at the Bartlett with a Commendation in sedign. He has since worked for MacCormac Jamieson Prichard Architects. Theory tutor: Peg Rawes, Technical tutor:Charles Walker and external examiner: Ian Ritchie

JENS RITTER was born near Kassel, Germany in 1974 . He studied Architectural Design at the University of Applied Science in Regensburg where he graduated in 1998. During this time he studied as an affiliate student at the Ecole d'Architecture de Lille–Régions Nord. After working as an architectural designer in Regensburg he came to the Bartlett, where he graduated in 2001 with a Commendation in Design. Jens worked for Eger Architects in London and is currently practicing at Steidle + Partner, BDA in Munich. His work is part of the exhibition and publication 'Actions re Form' for the Architekturgalerie München. external examiner: Svein Toensager

KEVIN CHU was born in Hong Kong in 1975. After starting his architectural studies at the Architectural Association in London, he transferred to the Bartlett School of Architecture, UCL, where he got his diploma in 2001. His diploma was awarded a Commendation in design and also the Archigram Annual Design Prize. Kevin worked in architectural practices in Bangkok and Hong Kong. Currently, he is working at Sheppard Robson Architects in London. His work is part of the exhibition and publication 'Actions re Form' for the Architekturgalerie München. external examiner: Svein Toensager

JIA LU was born in Kunming, China in 1975 She studied architecture at the Tsinghua University, School of Architecture in Beijing, from which she graduated in Architecture and Urbanism in 1997. While teaching as an architectu'al assistant, she obtained a masters degree in architectural history and historic preservation at Tsinghua University. After working as a freelance architect in Beijing, she moved to London, where she studied at the Bartlett. Currently, Jia is developing her diploma project further in an MArch research programme at the Bartlett. Technical tutor: Rachel Amstrong and external examiner: Ben Nicholson

LISA SILVER was born in London, UK in 1978. She studied for a BA in Architecture at the University of Nottingham. She completed the Diploma at the Bartlett School of Architecture with distinction and Sir Banister Fletcher Prize for the highest marks in the Diploma in Architecture final Examination. Her work was considered by the RIBA as Presidents Silver Medal Runner-up 2002. Lisa has worked for TP Bennett Architects and Sheppard Robson Architects, and is currently working for Ian Ritchie Architects in London. Theory tutor: Ana Betancour, technical tutor: Brendan Woods and external examiner: Ian Ritchie.

KAREN WILLCOX was born in Harrogate, UK in 1976 with dual nationality Dutch/Britsh. Having grown up in the Netherlands she returned to the Uk to study a Btec in art and design, which was followed by Ba(hons) Architecture at the University of Plymouth. Having both worked in the Netherlands and the Uk she graduated from the Bartlett in 2000. She is in charge for the design and organisation of both the publication and exhibition of U20. Theory tutor: Ana Betancour, technical tutor: Peter Fink and external examiner: Cathryn Findley

MARK MUECKENHEIM was born 1970 in Aachen, Germany. He studied architecture at the FHS Düsseldorf and from 1997 in New York, where he gained a masters degree at the Parsons School of Design. He worked in Los Angeles before moving to London for his further studies at the Bartlett. Mark is a founding member of the Office Urban Environments in Düsseldorf and is currently teaching at the University of Wuppertal. He received a Fulbright Fellowship in 1996 and a DAAD (German Academic Exchange Service) post graduate scholarship in 2000.

NATALIA TRAVERSO was born in Gibraltar in 1978. She started her architectural education at the University of Sheffield School of Architecture after working in London for various offices including Ian Ritchie Architects. She graduated from the Bartlett, her work being awarded a distinction in design and the Ambrose Poynter Prize for a promising student in architecture. Her technical studies were also awarded a commendation. Natalia collaborated in competition projects at Volker Giencke Architekt in Austria. Theory tutor: Neil Spiller, technical tutor: Jason Slocombe and Tom Holdom and external examiner: Volker Giencke

ROBERT GRINDLEY was born in Leeds in 1977. He gained a first class BA honours degree from Newcastle Upon Tyne, School of Architecture. After working in the Netherlands for Koen van Velsen Architectenburo he moved to London to gain his Diploma in architecture at the Bartlett. His technical dissertation was awarded a commendation. He is currently working at Denton Grindley Architects in Milton Keynes. Technical tutor: Andrew Walley and external examiner: Ian Ritchie

STEPHEN CLEMENTS was born in Newport, UK in 1976 with a dual nationality British/Australian. Stephen gained his degree in Architecture from the University of Brighton, School of Architecture. Having worked at various architectural offices in London he obtained his diploma in architecture at the Bartlett in 2001. Upon graduating he began working for General Lighting and Power before co founding MVOR a multimedia design agency based in London, working in print video and digital media.

STEVE PIKE was born in London, UK in 1966. He remained in the city until university education took him to Manchester, where he studied interior design. Returning to London in 1988, he was employed by Purcell, Miller and Tritton. He began his architectural studies in 1996, first at Westminster University and then at the Bartlett. Currently, he is working for Alan Ward Architects, whilst completing his MArch research. His work is part of the exhibition and publication 'Actions re Form' for the Architekturgalerie München. In 2002 Steve became founder of Studio Colony in London. Technical support: Dr. Conrad Mullineaux technical tutor: Dr. Ben Croxford and external examiner: Elsa Prochazka

TOM FOSTER was born in London, UK in 1976. After briefly studying art he began his architectural training at the University of Nottingham, graduating with a BA (hons) in 1998. He studied for his Diploma in architecture at the Bartlett. He received a commendation for his theoretical work on 'virtual playgrounds, the videogame and the development of spatial reality' - exerts of which have been published in The Architects Journal (2000). He is currently employed at Richard Hywell Evans Architecture & Design. His work is part of the exhibition and publication 'Actions re Form' for the Architekturgalerie München. external examiner: Elsa Prochazka

ZORAN ORESCANIN was born in Novi Sad in 1972 in Yugoslavia. He studied architecture and architectural engineering at the University of Budapest before coming to London where he gained an MSc in Environmental Design and Engineering. In 1997 he studied as an affiliate student at the Bartlett School of Architecture, which was followed by the diploma in architecture. Zoran has worked both in Yugoslavia and the UK. Technical tutor: Jason Slocombe and Tom Holdom; external examiner: Svein Toensager

SALVADOR PEREZ ARROYO was born in Madrid, Spain in 1945. He is a practicing architect and a Professor of Building Technology at the Madrid School of Architecture, ETSAM. Awarded the Extraordinary Prize for the best Doctoral Thesis in Architecture presented by the "Universidad Politécnica de Madrid", (UPM). He has been a Visiting Professor at the Instituto Universitario di Architettura di Venezia, the Kongelige Danske Kunst Akademi de Copenague and at Cracow's School of Architecture, among others. He is the editor of the architecture journal RC/ Building Files and is a regular contributor to the architecture page in the newspaper ABC. Since 1995 he is a Visiting Professor at the Bartlett School of Architecture, UCL in London. He participates in the redaction and signed of the new Carta Internacional de la Restauración, signed the 26 October 2000 in Cracow, Poland. This "Carta" will substitute the one of Venice 1964 and it has been supported by all the international organisms: UNESCO, Icomos, etc. He has done. monographic publications on his own works: Architecture Projects, 1984-1998 by Rueda Editions, Madrid).

MARCOS CRUZ was born in Porto, Portugal in 1970. He studied architecture at the School for Higher Education in Arts of Porto (ESAP), from where he received his professional degree with distinction in 1997. During these years he worked in practices in Portugal, Spain and Germany and attended in 1993 the International Viennese Architecture Seminar in Austria. In 1993/94 and 1995/96 he also studied in Barcelona where he followed courses at the Polytechnic University of Catalunya (ETSAB). Back in Porto he worked as a freelance architect and as an invited tutor for the International Architecture Seminar 'PubliCity' in Kassel, Germany. In 1998 he moved to London with a scholarship from the Foundation of Science and Technology of Portugal, receiving his master degree in Architectural Design with distinction from the Bartlett School of Architecture, UCL, which he continued by researching in a PhD about 'Artificial Skin Growth in Architecture', under the tuition of Prof. Peter Cook and Dr. Jonathan Hill. In 2000 he was co-founder of 'marcosandmarjan'.

Stephen Clements [1999-2000]

James Foster [2000-2002]

Mark Mueckenheim [2000-2001]

unit meal [2001-2002]

Jia Lu [2001-2002]

Fieldtrip Helsinki [2000-2001]

Steve Pike [1999-2002]

Kevin Chu [1999-2001]

Natalia Traverso [2000-2002]

Robert Marinus Grindley [2001-2002]

fieldtrip US [2001-2002]

Fieldtrip US [2001-2002]

Zoran Orescanin [1999-2001]

Fieldtrip Tenerife [2000-2002]

Fieldtrip Tenerife [2000-2002]»

Lisa Silver [2000-2002]

Annika Schollin [2001-2002]

Jens Ritter [1999-2001]

Tom Foster [1999-2001]

Salvador Perez-Arroyo

Marcos Cruz

Karen Willcox [2000-2002]

Bartfest exhibition [2002]
Thom Mayne, Peter Cook, Karen
Wilcox and Natalia Traverso Caruana

‹Fieldtrip Tenerife [2000-2002]

MARTYN Weaver // [Urban Light Dance] 2001-2002
Animations projected on planimetric drawings.

MARK Mueckenheim // [Urban Farming] 2000-2001
Animation of cyclical movements on a 'smart surface'

ANDY Shaw // [Chicago Urban Farm] 2001-2002
Conceptual studies of technical appliances based on the work of Eduardo Paolozzi

ZORAN Orescanin // [Media Centre, Bilbao] 1999-2000

JAMES Sweet // [Cinematographic Archive, Bilbao/ Mire Ecology Forum] 1999-2000

JIA Lu // [Bone-tissue Transformation] 2001-
Installation, which tests a physical transform from liquid to solid states, suggesting the pro calcification in human bone growth.

JAMES Henman // [Fluvial Sports Association, Bilbao /
Seasonal Affective Disorder Clinic, Helsinki] 1999-2000

GWEN Shao Jun Lee //
[AlgaEnergy] 2001-2002

JASON Park Fung // [Hydroscopic Regeneration]
2001-2002

LISA Silver // [Transient News – Information
Manipulation] 2000-2001

ACKNOWLEDGEMENTS

This book would have never possible without the support of Prof. José María Lozano at the Polytechnic University of Valencia. We have to thank them for their interest in the Unit 20 work and for making viable to exhibit and publish the work in this manner. Their generosity and openness towards new ideas is unlimited.

It was thanks to Karen Willcox, who completely gave up her personal private life for 3 months in order to dedicate all her talent and passion to the book that this project became a reality. She assisted us in every aspect of the work, especially being able to manage so much scattered information and taking in account wishes of all people involved. This book is also very much hers.

Annika Schollin had a crucial contribution in collaborating with Karen and being an important team member all along this time.

The work was often supported by Anja Tränkel and Leandre Linares at ACTAR who in Karen's words became her 'technical gurus' for the layout. We would also like to thank Ciro M. Vidal Climent for all time and patience while helping Karen in Valencia.

We are particularly indebted with Prof. Peter Cook, Prof. Vicente Vidal, Prof. Jose Maria Lozano and Lorens Holm for their written contributions. Without these, the book would certainly be much poorer in substance.

We are grateful to the Bartlett School of Architecture, University College London for the permission to use all students material and for allowing us to develop all these thoughts and ideas. In particular the continuously inspiring and powerful influence of Prof. Peter Cook who has been decisive for this unit to be what it is. This book is also very much his.

Inside the Bartlett Laura Allen was very generous in giving us all necessary information about the school. In the voice of all students we would like to thank Abi Abdolwahabi and Bim Burton in the Bartlett workshop, Nicholas Callicott in the CAD/CAM laboratory, Prof. Conrad Mullineaux at the Micro-biology Department, UCL and Dr. Richard Strange at the Micology Department, UCL, who supported technically the work of Steve Pike. Also many thanks to the Royal Free Hospital for their help with Jia Lu's technical research. The help of Dr. R. R. Simons at the Laboratory of Fluid Mechanics at UCL was crucial for the work of Jens Ritter.

Many thanks to all critics that have so decisively contributed to the developement of each project. Also the influence of previous Bartlett students who kindly showed their portfolios to U20 students was of great importance.

Our work has benefitted from the assistance of numerous friends and students. We are particularly thankful to Wanda Yu-Ying Hu, Hui Hui Teoh, Jason Park Kur, and Zoran Orescanin for their precious help in the last weeks of work; Miklos Deri also gave hands in the last minutes.

Several individuals have assisted us on editing and revising texts: Gwen Shao Jun Lee, Chadi Chamoum, and in particular Tom Foster whose contribution was so amasing.

In our field trips to Bilbao in 1999, Canary Islands, Helsinki and Tampere in 2000, and the American Mid-West in 2001 we were supported by several people and institutions in these places: Javier Cenicacelaya in Bibao; Alejandra Vera, Juan Palop, J.Luis Armas and AMP office in Tenerife. The Colegios de Arquitectos of Tenerife and Bilbao. Rainer Mahlamäki and Ilmari Lahdelma who enabled us to see one of their latest works in Helsinki, Valvomo, which studio we visited also in Helsinki; and special thanks to Mack Caldwell, professor at the University of Oklahoma who so generously and efficiently organised the visits to many Bruce Goff and Herbert Greene houses in Norman and Oklahoma City. Without him we would never have seen these spectacular pieces of architecture. Sydney Robinson was also memorable in the way he showed us around in his Bruce Goff house in Aurora.

Apart from our own, we included photographs of buildings and landscapes taken by Karen Willcox, Wanda Yu-Ying Hu, Steve Pike and Marjan Colletti.

At last we would like to take this opportunity to thank all students of Unit 20 under our supervision for their interest, devotion and patience in working with us. The time spend together will always stay in our memories. We understand this book as the reward for their achievements and hope it may stimulate them in further development of their careers. We hope that all students will continue to show the imaginative and experimental approach they developed during their journey through the Bartlett. All the best for their futures!

Marcos Cruz and Salvador Perez Arroyo